Essential Statistics for Social Research

Second Edition, Revised and Updated

Essential Statistics for Social Research

Michael A. Malec

BOSTON COLLEGE

RAWAT PUBLICATIONS

Jaipur • New Delhi • Bangalore • Hyderabad • Guwahati

ISBN 978-81-316-0550-9

Indian Reprint, 2012

Published in 1993 in the United States of America by Westview Press, Inc.
A member of Perseus Books Inc.

First published in 1977 by J.B. Lippincott & Co.

Published by
Prem Rawat for **Rawat Publications**
Satyam Apts., Sector 3, Jawahar Nagar, Jaipur - 302 004 (India)
Phone: 0141 265 1748 / 7006 Fax: 0141 265 1748
E-mail : info@rawatbooks.com
Website: rawatbooks.com

New Delhi Office
4858/24, Ansari Road, Daryaganj, New Delhi 110 002
Phone: 011-23263290

Also at *Bangalore, Hyderabad* and *Guwahati*

Printed at Chaman Enterprises, New Delhi.

To my parents
with love and appreciation

Contents

List of Tables xi
List of Figures xv
Preface to the First Edition xvii
Preface to the Second Edition xix

1 Introduction 1

A Fear of Statistics? 2
A Small Example 3
An Overview of the Chapters 5
Measurement and Levels of Measurement 7
Computers and Statistics 11
Important Terms 15
Suggested Readings 15

2 Organization and Presentation of Data 17

Rates 17
Frequency Distribution 19
Pictorial Presentation 24
An SPSS Example: FREQUENCIES 26
Important Terms 31
Suggested Readings 31

3 Descriptive Measures: Centrality 33

The Mode 34
The Median 36
Quartiles, Deciles, and Percentiles 37
The Mean 39
Grouped Data 43
Coded Data 49

Notes on the Measures of Centrality 51
An SPSS Example 56
Important Terms 59
Suggested Readings 59
Quick Quiz Answers 59
Important Symbols Introduced in This Chapter 60

4 **Measures of Dispersion** 61

Ranges 62
Deviation Measures 65
The Standard Deviation and the Normal Distribution 71
An SPSS Example: z-Scores 76
Important Terms 78
Suggested Readings 78
Quick Quiz Answers 78

5 **Bases of Statistical Inference, I: Probability and the Logic of Hypothesis Testing** 81

Probability: A Way of Viewing the World 82
Basic Rules of Probability 85
Probability and Social Science 87
The Binomial Distribution and the Normal Curve 90
Probability and the Logic of Hypothesis Testing 93
One-Tail and Two-Tail Tests 95
Important Terms 98
Suggested Readings 98
Quick Quiz Answers 98

6 **Bases of Statistical Inference, II: Sampling and Estimation** 99

Populations and Samples 100
The Sampling Distribution of a Statistic 103
How Big Must a Sample Be? 105
An Adjustment for Small Populations 106
Estimation 107
The Standard Error 108
Sample Size and the Standard Error 113
Estimation from Finite Populations 114
Important Terms 116

Suggested Readings 116
Quick Quiz Answers 116

7 Testing for the Difference Between Means 117

The t-Test 117
An SPSS Example of the t-Test 127
Important Terms 129
Suggested Readings 129
Quick Quiz Answers 130

8 Analysis of Variance 131

An SPSS Example: ANOVA 143
Important Terms 145
Suggested Readings 145

9 Measuring the Association Between Two Nominal Variables 147

The Concept of Statistical Association 147
Percentage Difference 150
Chi-Square: A Test of Statistical Independence 151
Additional Notes on Chi-Square 160
Other Measures of Association Based on Chi-Square 163
Lambda: A "Proportional Reduction in Error" Measure for Nominal-Level Data 166
The General Logic of PRE: Prediction Rules and Error Rules 172
Goodman and Kruskal's Tau 175
An SPSS Example 179
Important Terms 181
Suggested Readings 181
Quick Quiz Answers 182

10 Measuring the Association Between Two Ordinal Variables 185

Gamma: A Symmetric Measure of One-Way Association 185
Kendall's Tau Statistics: Symmetric Measures of Mutual Association 197
Which Measure to Use? 200
Somers's d: An Asymmetric Measure of Association 200

Testing for the Significance of Gamma, Tau, and d 202
Spearman's Rank-Order Correlation Coefficient, Rho 206
An SPSS Example 212
Important Terms 214
Suggested Readings 214
Quick Quiz Answers 214

11 Measuring the Association Between Two Interval Variables 217

The Pearson r^2 as a PRE Measure 218
The Pearson r 226
Computing Formulas 228
Testing for the Significance of r 230
Additional Notes 232
Measuring Curvilinear Correlation: Eta-Square 236
An SPSS Example: The Pearson r 238
Important Terms 239
Suggested Readings 239
Quick Quiz Answers 239

12 Multivariate Analysis: Three or More Variables 241

Elaboration: Tabular Analysis of Percentage Differences 241
Partial Correlation 247
Multiple Correlation 252
Three or More Independent Variables 255
Correction for Sampling Error 256
An SPSS Example: Partial Correlation 257
Important Terms 258
Suggested Readings 258
Quick Quiz Answers 258

Appendix 261
References 281
Index 285
About the Book and Author 291

Tables

1.1 Levels of measurement 12

2.1 Murder rates for a sample of 145 urban areas 20
2.2 Frequency distributions of 145 murder rates 21

3.1 Family income in Doe City 34
3.2 Deviation scores 41
3.3 Frequency distribution (with cumulative frequencies) of 145 homicide rates 42
3.4 The mean and Formula 3.6 48
3.5 Guessed deviations 48
3.6 Coding 49
3.7 The guessed mean and Formula 3.7 50
3.8 Another application of the guessed mean 52
3.9 The weighted mean 53
3.10 Summary of characteristics of mode, median, and mean 56

4.1 Dispersion example 66
4.2 Computation of variance and standard deviation 70

5.1 A sampling distribution of the probability of obtaining a given number of heads when twenty coins are tossed 89
5.2 Type I and Type II errors 95

6.1 Random sample of thirty homicide rates 108
6.2 Partial list of 100 sample values 108

7.1 Homicide rates of thirty-six eastern and thirty western cities 118
7.2 Violent crime rate (rounded) for fifteen cities 126

8.1 Data for analysis of variance example: Three schools, nine students 132
8.2 Comparison of four samples 136
8.3 Data for analysis of variance: Four schools, twenty-four students 140

9.1 Sex and preference for Brand X (percentage distribution) 148
9.2 Sex and preference for Brand Y (percentage distribution) 148
9.3 Hypothetical coin-tossing results 152
9.4 Religious and political preferences (hypothetical data) 152
9.5 Expected cell frequencies based on data from Table 9.4 154
9.6 Schematic representation of a 2 × 2 table 155
9.7 Expected frequencies for Table 9.6 155
9.8 Work table for computing Chi-square using data from Table 9.4 156
9.9 Critical values of Chi-square for various levels of Alpha (α) and for varying degrees of freedom 157
9.10 Coin-toss example 158
9.11 Illustration of empty cells 159
9.12 Illustration of one fixed cell 159
9.13 Religious and political preferences (hypothetical data) 163
9.14 Coin toss (N = 120) 165
9.15 Club membership and delinquency (hypothetical data), example 1 168
9.16 Club membership and delinquency (hypothetical data), example 2 170
9.17 Parent's and child's religious preferences (hypothetical data) 170
9.18 Husbands' and wives' religious preferences (hypothetical data) 171
9.19 Parent-child political preferences, example 1 173
9.20 Parent-child political preferences, example 2 173

10.1 An example of three subjects ranked on two variables 187
10.2 Ranking of five occupations by two students (three hypothetical examples) 188
10.3 List of pairs from Table 10.2 189
10.4 Computation of Gamma with tied ranks (ungrouped data) 191

10.5 Income and education (hypothetical data) 192
10.6 Summary of characteristics of measures of ordinal association 203
10.7 Values needed for testing the significance of S from Table 10.5 206
10.8 Computing ρ with tied ranks 208

11.1 Hours studied and quiz scores 219
11.2 Calculation of E_1 220
11.3 Calculation of a_{YX} and b_{YX} 222
11.4 Calculation of $\hat{Y}$ and E_2 224
11.5 Deviation scores 226
11.6 Standard scores as a basis for calculating the Pearson r 227
11.7 Calculation of $\hat{z}_Y$ 228
11.8 Hypothetical homicide and suicide rates 231

12.1 Number of storks and human birthrate 243
12.2 Storks and babies by type of area 244
12.3 Party and voting 245
12.4 Party and voting by social class 245
12.5 Social class and attitude toward abortion (hypothetical data) 246
12.6 Social class and attitude toward abortion by religious liberalism (hypothetical data) 246

A Proportions of the area under the normal curve 264
B Critical values of Student's t 267
C Critical values of F 269
D Critical values of Chi-square 274
E Probability that S attains or exceeds a specific value 276
F Critical values of Rho 277
G Critical values of the Pearson r 278

Figures

2.1	Class boundaries	22
2.2	Histogram of the distribution of 145 murder rates	23
2.3	Frequency polygon of 145 murder rates	24
2.4	Frequency curve superimposed over frequency polygon	25
2.5	Pie charts	25
2.6	Pictograph (bar chart, using figures) of U.S. population data, 1790–1990	26
3.1	Illustration of the median as a position average	38
3.2	Location of quartiles in a symmetric distribution	39
3.3	The mean as center of gravity	42
3.4	Another example of the mean as center of gravity	42
3.5	Central locations for differently shaped distributions	55
4.1	Identical ranges, different patterns of dispersion	64
4.2	The standard deviation and the normal distribution	72
4.3	Raw scores and z-scores, an example	73
4.4	The area between two scores	75
5.1	The probability of observing a given number of heads when twenty coins are tossed	92
5.2	One-tail test and two-tail test	96
6.1	A stratified sample	102
6.2	A population value and three possible sample values	105
6.3	The sample mean and sampling error	110
6.4	Probability and confidence intervals	112
6.5	Sample size and standard error	114
7.1	Point and interval estimates from Table 7.1	120
7.2	Point and interval estimates, another example	122

8.1 Schematic representation of Table 8.2 136

9.1 Approximate shape of the Chi-square distribution when df = 1 and when df = 10 158

10.1 Calculation of similar and dissimilar pairs for Table 10.5 193
10.2 Yule's Q as a special case of Gamma 196
10.3 Illustration of complete mutual association 198

11.1 Prediction error as deviation from the mean 220
11.2 Prediction error as deviation from the regression line 221
11.3 Using deviation scores 225
11.4 Using z-scores 229
11.5 Homicide and suicide rates 232
11.6 Types of relationships 233
11.7 Homo- and heteroscedasticity 234
11.8 Within-category means as a prediction rule for Eta-square 237

12.1 Storks and babies 247
12.2 Perfect and zero association 248
12.3 Storks, babies, and rural-urban areas 248
12.4 Simple relationships among three variables 253
12.5 Relationships among three variables 254

Preface to the First Edition

In the past few years there have been many texts written on statistics in the social sciences. Other than contributing to the author's publication record, recognition by peers, or wallet, is there any justification for yet another statistics text? Obviously, I think there is; in fact, there are two reasons that justify this book: practicality and purpose.

It is my contention that many of today's texts contain much material that is impractical or useless for the beginning student and omit much material that the beginning student could well use. This contention is based on an unpublished study of mine in which I examined the use of statistics in four major sociology journals (*American Sociological Review, American Journal of Sociology, Social Forces,* and *Sociometry)* between 1966 and 1973. This study confirmed what I have long suspected—that sociologists actually use a very small number of statistics in their published work, that some statistics are not covered at all or are given only superficial mention in many texts (e.g., simple descriptive statistics or analysis of variance) and that many of the statistics that appear in texts rarely or never appear in sociology journals (e.g., the Mann-Whitney U). This disjunction between what sociologists emphasize in their textbooks and what sociologists actually use as statistical tools has come about for a variety of reasons, not all of which, I suspect, are good. However, this situation is easily remedied by first determining what statistics are used and then by teaching these to students.

The question of purpose is related to that of practicality. Why do we write statistics texts? What do we hope that students will learn? Why do we want the student to learn a particular subject? I suggest that our goal is to help students gain some appreciation of how sociologists do their work. From the beginning course, we tell students about the importance of *method* in sociology (and statistics is a method), but we rarely encourage them to grapple with the statistical method. Consequently, students do not read the current literature, or if they do, they are not able to appreciate it fully, because the literature today is so heavily dependent on statistics. In other words, we allow students to be literate but not numerate; they may understand words but not numbers. Thus, my purpose in writing this book is to encourage students to become numerate, to give them the knowledge and understanding of statistics that will enable them to more intelligently read the current sociological literature.

To the Student

This book is written for you, a student just beginning to study statistics. The greater bulk of the text has been used in my classes for four years. My students have pointed out to me the weak spots in earlier drafts, and if this text is an improvement, it is they who have helped to make it so. I now hope that you will continue this helpful process. If, as you use this text, you find sections that are not clear or if you think a better example or illustration could be developed, please let me know. You may contact me directly or through the publisher.

Acknowledgments

I wish to give special thanks to three men who introduced me to the art and science of statistics and statistical thinking. They are N. M. Downie, B. J. Winer, and especially Richard J. Hill, a gifted teacher who made exhilarating the study of statistics. Thanks are also due to President J. Donald Monan, S.J., and Dean Charles F. Donovan, S.J., of Boston College, who have wisely maintained the leave policy that gave me the time and support to finish this work. Jeanne Fleming and Kichiro K. Iwamoto carefully corrected the final manuscript, though whatever errors may remain are my sole responsibility. My best friend, my wife, Myrna, deserves my deepest thanks for always being there whenever I needed support and a smile. Finally, as the dedication attests, I wish to pay special tribute to my parents, who have given me a lifetime of love.

Michael A. Malec
Boston College

Preface to the Second Edition

Sixteen years have passed since the first edition of this book was published. In that time, this book has been used by more than ten thousand students at colleges and universities around the globe.

In that time, not much has changed in the world of introductory-level statistics. Former readers of this book will therefore find comfort in the fact that the changes have been kept to a minimum—it is not my intention to reissue this book every three or four years for the sake of new sales. "If it ain't broke, don't fix it." And many of you have let me know that the first edition needed only minor fixing. For that, I thank you.

In that time, however, there has been one important change. We have entered the age of computers, and the revised version of this book pays attention to our new age. At the end of nearly every chapter you will find a short section that shows how one computer software package, the Statistical Package for the Social Sciences (SPSS), can be used to make easier our computational work. The computer examples are not essential to the understanding of statistics; rather, they are there to give some small indication of how computers might be used. If, at your institution, some statistical package other than SPSS is used, these examples will still be of some utility. In any case, you and your instructor will have to work out the details of using a computer at your local facility.

Acknowledgments

I again want to thank some special people who have made the revised edition of this text possible. Dean Birkenkamp of Westview Press was the man who believed that it was time to reissue the book; I thank him for his faith. Deborah Lynes did a wonderful job of transforming a sometimes garbled manuscript into clear English. My colleagues at Boston College gave me the encouragement to finish this work. The Faculty Microcomputer Research Center staff at Boston College, especially Professors Michael J. Connolly and Richard Jenson, were always patient and helpful in guiding me through the arcane details of word processing. Eunice Doherty typed most of the text—even though she still insists that she distrusts statistics! The students in my courses at Boston College provided the initial impetus for this book; during the revision, they helped me find numerous errors and weak points. I especially thank two eagle-eyed readers, Brian Melket and Idaliz Santos. Jeffrey W. Lynch prepared most of the figures and tables, and I am most grateful for his patience and creativity. Many of the equations were prepared using *Expressionist*™ software, from Prescience. Professor Kichiro K. Iwamoto of the University of Santa Clara carefully corrected an early draft. Despite all of this help, it should be clear that whatever errors may remain are my sole responsibility.

Again, as the dedication attests, I wish to pay special tribute to my parents, who have given me a lifetime of love.

My best friend, my wife, Myrna, deserves my deepest thanks for doing without a summer vacation and for always being there whenever I needed a hug and a smile.

Michael A. Malec
Boston College

1

Introduction

We need only scan a newspaper or magazine, turn on a news broadcast, or open a sociology text or journal to see that we live in an age that is heavily dependent on statistical information. The extent of this dependency is such that it is rather difficult to be an educated person without having at least a passing acquaintance with basic statistics. More to the point, it is virtually impossible to be a capable social scientist without having a definite, if elementary, understanding of some basic statistics and statistical methods of analysis. But a casual acquaintance with a few simple statistics will not serve the social scientist who attempts to read competently the literature of the field. And if one wishes to do quantitative social research—and most research published today is quantitative—a more thorough knowledge of statistics is imperative. The aspiring sociologist need only examine the books and articles that are being published today for evidence of this claim. A very large portion of the articles published in the major sociology journals use some form of statistical analysis. Some of these articles and other works published by sociologists are incomprehensible without a statistics background; others will simply be read less intelligently or with a lessened sense of appreciation or criticism.

Of course, not all of the subfields of sociology require the same degree of familiarity with statistics. Certain areas of sociology, for example sociological theory, require little statistical knowledge. However, in other fields such as demography, a strong competence in quantitative techniques is essential.

In this book, we hope to provide you, the student, with an understanding and appreciation of some of the basic statistics used in sociological work. We will not focus exclusively on how to compute a certain statistic, but we will indicate how such computing can be done. We will also present general ideas about the purpose and nature of statistics and the uses and abuses of statistics, so that you will have a fuller understanding of what you do and what you read. Stated differently, our goal will be to give you a fuller appreciation of the way in which many sociologists do their work. Because much of today's sociology depends on the use and understanding of statistical methods, you must understand not only the words of the English language but also the numbers of statistical "language." To understand much of contemporary social research, you must be "numerate" as well as literate.

A Fear of Statistics?

This book was written for the undergraduate student of sociology who presumably has little or no background in statistics and who, judging from past classroom experience, does not approach this subject with any interest or enthusiasm. Indeed, many students approach statistics with considerable fear and anxiety and, if the course is required, with a great deal of resentment and antipathy. We will try to persuade you that such feelings are misplaced.

If you are intelligent enough to have graduated from high school, you are fully capable of handling the mathematics and logical reasoning demanded of you in the following pages. The most complicated thing you will have to do mathematically is to find the square root of a number, which you can do with a small electronic calculator. Other than that, if you can add, subtract, multiply, and divide, you can certainly handle all of the mathematics you will encounter here. As you progress, some of this basic arithmetic will get quite cumbersome; for example, the numbers may become very large or very small. In these instances, a calculator will be a great time-saver and will probably ensure greater accuracy. But always remember that you still will be performing the simple arithmetic operations of addition, subtraction, multiplication, and division. No calculus, advanced algebra, or the like is required. You *can* do the work in this book. It will be easier if you put away any fears and anxieties about mathematics.

Another point should be emphasized. At first, do not try to understand what you are doing in a mathematical sense. Rather, *think* about what is happening in a *logical* sense. Do not obey statistical formulas in a rote, unthinking fashion. As you approach each problem, ask yourself, What am I doing? Why am I doing this? What does this problem ask me to do? What does my solution mean? Does it make sense? If you can answer these questions, your understanding of the mathematics involved will be greatly increased. You will be an intelligent consumer of statistical information, not a robot regurgitating gibberish that you do not understand and will immediately forget.

A Small Example

As noted previously, statistics is like a language. It has a vocabulary and a grammar. For our purposes you already know enough of the grammar (the rules for addition, subtraction, multiplication, and division) to enable you to hold a simple conversation. You are probably not as familiar with the vocabulary of statistics, the special symbols and terms used by specialists in the field. This lack of familiarity may contribute to whatever uneasiness you may have brought to this course. But be assured that the vocabulary you will have to acquire is used for very good reasons. It enables us to communicate with each other in a precise fashion, and more important to you now, it saves a great deal of time and work. The statistical vocabulary in this book is simple and will be introduced slowly and clearly.

Part of this vocabulary is already familiar to you, for example, the arithmetic *mean*. This is the "average" that you learned to compute in the fourth grade: To compute the mean of a series of numbers, we add all of the numbers in the series, then divide that total by the number of figures in the series. Thus, if we have five numbers, 2, 4, 7, 8, and 11, the mean is found by adding, or summing:

$$2 + 4 + 7 + 8 + 11 = 32$$

then dividing this sum by the number of items in the series:

$$\frac{32}{5} = 6.4$$

We can also use the mean to calculate a baseball player's batting average. This "average," technically, is the *mean* number of hits per time at bat. A player who is batting .300 has made, on the average, three-tenths of a hit for each official time at bat. (Of course, there is no such things as three-tenths of a hit. Such a hit is only a mathematical construct, or idea or image in our minds. More commonly, we might think of the .300 hitter as one who hits safely three times out of ten, or thirty times per hundred at bats, or *three hundred* per thousand.) We will give a much fuller discussion of the mean and other averages in Chapter 2. Here, we simply wish to illustrate that the ground you are on is not totally unfamiliar.

In general, the kinds of statistics used by sociologists fall into one of two classifications: *descriptive statistics* and *inferential statistics.* The distinction between the two is not always precise, but it does have practical utility. Descriptive statistics, as the term implies, give us at a glance a picture of the data with which we are dealing. These statistics are generally intended to give a reasonably accurate representation of a large mass of data, a representation that is based directly on the raw data. Often, these statistics are used to summarize a body of information. For example, the decennial census of the United States can tell us such things as whether there are more televisions than bathtubs in this country or how many families own more than two cars. Inferential statistics take us beyond the raw data to generalizations about even larger units of study. For example, public opinion polls such as the Harris or Gallup polls might tell us that 52 percent of the voters prefer Senator Phogghorn, and this might be a reasonably accurate description of the preferences of the 1,500 people who were interviewed. But the pollster, the senator, and the public are not interested in just these 1,500 people; they want to know how *all* of the prospective voters feel. Consequently, the statistician is called upon to draw certain inferences from the responses of the 1,500 and to predict how *all* of the voters will behave. Inferential statistics are extremely useful when we are confronted with situations in which it is impossible to assemble all of the data we might need. For example, if you manufacture light bulbs, you might want to tell your customers about the life expectancy of the bulbs. You could determine this by taking each bulb as it came off the production line and burning it until it gave out. You could then compute some very accurate descriptive information about light bulb life expectancy. Unfortunately, you would have no bulbs to sell because you destroyed each one in the process of measurement. An alternative procedure would involve *sampling* your supply of bulbs, say, 1 bulb of every 200 produced, taking your measurements of life expectancy on this sample, and making an inference about all the bulbs on the basis of your measurements on the sample. Indeed, this is how much industrial quality control is done, and it is how Harris and Gallup make their estimates of voter behavior.

An Overview of the Chapters

We will now briefly discuss a few of the specific types of descriptive and inferential statistics. In so doing we will also summarize the remaining chapters in this book.

Most generally, the purpose of statistics is to help us interpret information, or data. There are many ways to do this. You are probably already familiar with at least one of the several averages that are used to calculate a *typical* measure, or measure of *central tendency* (Chapter 3). We will discuss three of these averages: the mean, the median, and the mode. For example, we might note from a census report that the median family income in the (imaginary) town of Jonesville in a given year was $8,400. It is certainly far easier to work with this single, simple figure than it would be to handle the hundreds or thousands of particular family income figures for each family in Jonesville. This ease of handling is one of the great advantages of descriptive statistics. (However, by reducing the many particular family income figures to a single average figure, we necessarily lose some of the finer points of information that are contained in the large mass of data. This illustrates a never-ending dilemma for the user of statistics: At what point does the convenience of a summary measure outweigh the utility of having many measures? Or to state it differently, when does the luxury of having information on each individual unit of measurement—in this case, the family—become too cumbersome to handle? Such questions must be answered according to the purposes of the research and the available resources.)

Taken by itself, a measure of central tendency is, therefore, quite limited. Fortunately, the statistician has additional statistical tools with which to work. Thus, although we may know that the median family income in Jonesville is $8,400, we are also likely to want information about how the total income in the community was distributed among the many families: How many families had incomes of less than $3,500? What proportion earned over $50,000? Answers to these questions come from statistical measures of *dispersion*, variability, or spread (Chapter 4).

Properly chosen, measures of centrality and dispersion tell us much about a set of data. The measure of centrality gives us a central, focal point, and the measure of dispersion tells us how the various scores in the data set, or distribution, are spread about this focal point.

A *variable* is some aspect, characteristic, or quality of an individual or object that can change or take on different values. For example, "religion" is a variable: An individual might be Protestant or Muslim or Hindu. (The term *variable* refers to any characteristic or trait of an individual that can be described by two or more qualities. These qualities are called *categories*. For example, we might study the variable of social class and we might define social class as having four possible categories: lower, working, middle, and upper.) A common use of statistics involves the creation and application of measures that enable us to compare different variables and to relate them to one another. For example, a question such as "How much is two apples plus three oranges minus one banana?" cannot be answered on its own terms (apples, oranges, bananas). It is either a fool's question or the wise person can find some common element and answer, "Four pieces of fruit." A statistical analog comes in the form of *standard scores* (Chapter 4). Standard scores enable the sociologist to look at very different social measures such as income (measured in dollars) and suicide rate (measured in suicides per 100,000 population) and create the common ground for a meaningful discussion of how the two are related. As with the average, you are already familiar with such standard scores as those you received on the College Board exams. Your performance on various tests (verbal, quantitative, and others) were "standardized" so that, for example, your verbal score could be compared with your quantitative score, or with the average verbal score obtained by all high school seniors the previous year.

Statistics that indicate how different variables are related to each other are called measures of *association*, or correlation (Chapters 9-11). We might use such measures to describe, for example, the relationship between family income levels and academic performance of children in elementary school.

Because sociologists are often interested in questions that relate to large numbers of people and because of the high costs (including costs of time, personnel, and other resources) of obtaining measures on such large numbers, they often take measures on only a small portion, or *sample* (Chapter 6), of the people in whom they are interested. Then, using their knowledge of *probability* (Chapter 5), they can make certain *estimates* (Chapter 6) of the larger population. These estimates are based on the data gathered from the small sample. From these estimates, certain predictions are often made. Public opinion polls use many techniques of statistics. Some of these are related to the more general topic of *hypothesis testing* (Chapters 5-8).

In conclusion, we simply note that a variety of other statistics techniques and procedures which will enable us to analyze three or more variables simultaneously will also be discussed (Chapter 12).

Measurement and Levels of Measurement

All statistical work in sociology rests on the fundamental assumption that we can, within reasonable limits, *measure* whatever it is that we are studying, whether it be suicide, crime, religiosity, alienation, or any other variable. The problem of measurement is particularly acute for us because many of our variables cannot be measured precisely. We have no agreed-upon yardstick with which to measure alienation. There is no measuring cup to tell us how much religiosity is in a person. Part of our problem as social scientists is to create our own measuring devices and to get others to agree that these devices are reasonable, accurate, reliable, and valid. The general problem of creating such devices is not a statistical one; it is a problem dealt with in books on research methods or, better yet, in courses dealing with the particular substantive area in which the research is being framed. Yet the statistician cannot be oblivious to the problems of measurement. Indeed, basic decisions about when to use which statistics as opposed to others rest upon our knowledge of the type of measurement being used.

Following Stevens (1946: 3) we shall define *measurement* as "the assignment of numerals to objects or events according to rules." Stated differently, this definition tells us that we shall take an object or event (or thing or circumstance or quality or quantity) and assign to that entity one or more symbols, 1, 2, 3, . . . n, which are called numerals. [NOTE: A *numeral* is distinguished from a *number* by the fact that the numeral does not necessarily have any quantitative value attached to it. Numerals may be numbers, but they are not necessarily numbers.] According to the definition, we must assign numerals according to rules. In the social sciences, we generally have three or four different sets of rules we can use in our assignment of numerals. These different rules lead us to different *levels of measurement.*

Nominal Measurement

Think for a moment of a basketball team. The five players wear jerseys, and each jersey has an identifying numeral, let us say 3, 5, 12, 20, and 24. What do these "numbers" mean? Is player 24 twice as good as player 12? Is player 5 taller than player 3? Because 3 + 5 + 12 = 20, does it follow that player 20 is the equal of the other three combined? Whatever the answers to these questions, they cannot be known from the numbers on the players' jerseys. The numbers are merely identifying signs, which are technically known as numerals. These numerals have no mathematical meaning. So it is with the assignment of numerals to certain types of sociological data.

Many of the variables that the sociologist works with have no real arithmetic qualities: Religion, sex, political party, and ethnicity are but a few examples. A person is Protestant, Catholic, Jewish, or "other"; male or female; Democrat, Republican, or Independent, and so on. Thus we "measure" political affiliation by determining the party to which a person belongs. We might, however, have reason to change the symbols used to identify people's party preference. For example, we might say that Democrats will be labeled with numeral 1, Republicans with the numeral 2, and Independents with the numeral 3. Now instead of naming these people Democrat, Republican, and Independent, we have named them 1, 2, and 3. *But we should not fool ourselves into thinking that these numeral-names are numbers.* We have simply given a new name (the Latin word for "name" is *nomine,* hence the nominal-level of measurement) to the objects of our observation. Having made our nominal classification, we cannot now say that 1 + 2 = 3 (that is, that Democrat plus Republican equals Independent). At this nominal level we must remember that 1, 2, and 3 are not numbers, they are numerals.

When we have a nominal-level variable, we should be certain that the categories of the variable adhere to the following characteristics (Reynolds 1984: 10). First, the categories should be *homogeneous.* If the variable was body size, it would not make sense to have the categories be tall, medium, short, and heavy—the first three suggest that size is defined in terms of height and the fourth, heavy, suggests that size is a matter of weight. Second, the categories should be *mutually exclusive*. That is, every respondent should be assigned to one, and only one, category. In the previous example, some people might be considered as both tall and heavy—in which category should they be placed? Finally, the categories should be *exhaustive*. That is, every respondent must fit into one of the categories. For example, if the variable was religion and the only defined categories were Protestant and Catholic, we would have no category in which to place people who claimed some other religion or none.

The nominal level of measurement is sometimes called the *qualitative* level. This term emphasizes the fact that at this level we are simply concerned with determining whether various objects are equal in the sense that they possess the same quality. Nothing is implied about the relationships that might exist among different qualities. In our example of political preference, our task is to find all the people who share a certain quality, such as being a Democrat, and to distinguish these people from others who do not possess that quality. Whether we do this by labeling our people as D, R, or I or as 1, 2, or 3 is unimportant. R and 2 are both merely naming devices for the quality of being a Republican.

The only thing we can say about objects that are measured at the nominal level is that they are either equal to each other or not equal to each other. This level of measurement is thus very simple. We cannot perform even elementary arithmetic operations on such data. But because such measurement is simple does not mean it is of little use. In many instances, nominal-level statistics are the only appropriate measures to use. We shall see evidence of this in the following chapters.

Ordinal Measurement

My acquaintances who have been to the racetrack tell me that they are quite uninterested in the time of the winning horse or in the distance between the first and second horses, the second and third horses, and so on. The only important thing to them is the *order* in which the horses finished. In other words, these latent statisticians are interested in ordinal measurement.

Ordinal measurement is concerned with the ranking of objects or events. Ordinal measurement is thus more sophisticated than nominal measurement. At the nominal level, we are only concerned whether two objects, A and B, are equal or unequal in their possession of a certain quality. In ordinal measurement, we are additionally interested in whether A is greater than (larger than, weaker than, and so on) B or in whether B is greater than A. (Of course, A and B may be equal.) Ordinal measurement allows us to *rank* objects or events according to some quality. This frequently happens when we lump data together into categories such as low, medium, and high. If these terms refer to education, we can then know that all the people in the high category have more education than the people in the other two categories and that the people in the medium category have more education than the people in the low category but less education than the people in the high category. We have simply ranked our subjects into three categories. Consequently, we know that there is a "distance" between categories, but *we do not know what the distance is.* We cannot add these categories to each other or perform other mathematical operations on them. But having our categories rank ordered gives us a higher level of measurement than does simply naming the categories.

At this point we introduce some mathematical symbols or notations. These symbols are a kind of shorthand. Suppose we want to express an inequality between two objects, A and B. We might say that A is greater than B or A is less than B. Using mathematical notations, we can say the same thing with $A > B$ and $A < B$. The symbols $>$ and $<$ are inequality signs, just as $=$ is the sign of equality. In the usual sentence that reads from left to right, $<$ means is less than (or smaller than, weaker than, and so on). (Occasionally you might also see these symbols: $\leq$ and $\geq$. These mean, respectively, is less than or equal to and is greater than or equal to.) Note also that if $A < B$ and $B < C$, it *must* also be true that $A < C$.

Sociologists make frequent use of ordinal-level data. Socioeconomic status, birth order, and the many attitude scales that range from strongly agree or agree to disagree or strongly disagree are examples of ordinal measurement.

As with nominal measures, we cannot perform the familiar mathematical operations of addition, subtraction, multiplication, or division on ordinal numbers. Ordinal measurement does permit a *ranking* that cannot be done with nominal-level data, but neither of these levels is quantitative or arithmetical in the usual and familiar sense.

Interval and Ratio Measurement

We can begin to perform arithmetic operations on data that are at the interval level of measurement. Interval numbers have magnitudes because they are based on a common unit of measurement; so the distance from one number to its adjacent number is equal to the distance from any other number in the system to its adjacent number. Thus, such numbers are marked by equal intervals. For example, if we consider a simple series of numbers, 1, 2, 3, 4, and 5, the distance between 2 and 3 is the same as the distance between 4 and 5 and is the same as the distance between 1 and 2. You might also have noticed that the distance between 1 and 3 is the same as the distance between 2 and 4 and between 3 and 5. Because the existence of equal intervals on such a measurement scale gives rise to magnitudes, we can perform arithmetic operations at this level.

The ratio level is distinguished from the interval level in that the ratio scales of measurement have a point of absolute zero. A frequently cited example of the difference between an interval and ratio scale is found in the various systems we have for measuring heat. The Fahrenheit and Celsius thermometers have equal intervals, but their zero points are arbitrarily fixed. The Kelvin thermometer also has equal intervals, but its zero point is set at absolute zero, the point at which there is a complete absence of heat.

In sociological research, the distinction between the interval and ratio levels is usually not important; the same statistics are often used for both levels. Examples of sociological variables used at these levels are income (ratio), IQ (interval), and family size (ratio).

Table 1.1 summarizes the key points about the various levels of measurement.

Computers and Statistics

[NOTE: In this text, the sections on computers are optional. Whether you use the computer sections of the text will depend on how your particular instructor has organized your course.]

We live in a time when some degree of familiarity with computers is essential. In the field of statistical analysis, computers are more than essential—they are tremendous savers of time and energy; they enable us to look at much larger masses of information and to do so in a

Table 1.1. *Levels of Measurement*

	Nominal	Ordinal	Interval	Ratio
Can two objects be determined to be equal or unequal?	Yes	Yes	Yes	Yes
Can two objects be rank ordered?	No	Yes	Yes	Yes
Can distances between objects be determined?	No	No	Yes	Yes
Does the scale have an absolute zero point?	No	No	No	Yes

much shorter period of time and with a greatly reduced number of simple computational errors.

A computer is a complex machine that manipulates information according to the commands we give it. When we speak of computers, reference is often made to two different components. Hardware refers generally to the physical machine and its physical peripherals such as disks and keyboards. Software refers generally to the commands, or programs, that tell the computer what to do. In this text, we are going to focus only on the latter, and only on one form of software. We will do so because there are too many different types of machines (such as those manufactured by Apple, IBM, Digital, and others) and software for us to give adequate consideration to more than one.

To illustrate the use of computers in analyzing statistical data, I have chosen to use a software package known as SPSS (Statistical Package for the Social Sciences), which is perhaps the most widely used statistical software in the social sciences. In this text, we will be able to give only a very basic introduction to the use of computers and SPSS. The emphasis will be placed on understanding the output that is given to us by a computer.

An Example

Each year, the National Opinion Research Center (NORC) conducts a scientific survey, known as the General Social Survey (GSS), of the characteristics, behaviors, attitudes, and beliefs of the American population. Using rigorous sampling procedures (see Chapter 6), NORC interviews a representative sample of about 1,400 adult Americans. (In 1990, usable interviews were obtained from exactly 1,372 persons.) From this information we can infer, with a measurable amount of error, a great deal about the characteristics, behaviors, attitudes, and beliefs of not only these 1,372 people, but the entire adult population of the United States.

Following are some of the actual questions asked, along with the possible responses, in the 1990 General Social Survey. (The bracketed terms in caps, e.g., [SEX], are the "names" of the various items used in the survey.)

1. [SEX] Sex of respondent
   1: Male
   2: Female
2. [RACE] What race do you consider yourself?
   1: White
   2: Black
   3: Other

[NOTE: Respondents were not actually asked if they were male or female. The interviewer simply observed a respondent's sex and entered the appropriate code, 1 or 2. In the case of race, observation was also used unless there was any doubt in the interviewer's mind, in which case the interviewee was asked. For "other," further specification was sought.]

3. [EDUC] What is the highest grade in elementary school or high school [or college] that you finished and got credit for? [NOTE: Exact number of years, from 0 to 20, is entered.]
4. [DRUNK] Do you sometimes drink more than you should?
   1: Yes
   2: No

5. [ABANY] Please tell me whether or not you think it should be possible for a pregnant woman to obtain a legal abortion if the woman wants it for any reason?
   1: Yes
   2: No
6. [HELPSICK] In general, some people think that it is the responsibility of the government in Washington to see to it that people have help in paying for doctors and hospital bills. Others think that these matters are not the responsibility of the federal government and that people should take care of these things themselves. Where would you place yourself . . . ?
   1: I strongly agree it is the responsibility of government to help.
   2: I somewhat agree it is the responsibility of the government.
   3: I agree with both answers.
   4: I somewhat agree people should take care of themselves.
   5: I strongly agree people should take care of themselves.
7. [WHYPOOR] Now I will list reasons some people give to explain why there are poor people in this country. Please tell me whether you feel each of these is very important, somewhat important, or not important in explaining why there are poor people in this country.
   A. Failure of society to provide good schools for many Americans
      1: Very Important
      2: Somewhat Important
      3: Not Important
   B. [List of reasons continues.]
8. [POLVIEWS] We hear a lot of talk these days about liberals and conservatives. [O]n a seven-point scale . . . from extremely liberal . . . to extremely conservative, [w]here would you place yourself?
   1: Extremely liberal
   2: Liberal
   3: Slightly liberal
   4: Moderate, middle of the road
   5: Slightly conservative
   6: Conservative
   7: Extremely conservative

The first GSS was conducted in 1972. It has been repeated every year since, except in 1979 and 1981. There are several hundred questions in the survey, many of which are asked in each and every year and some of which are asked on a rotating basis. A typical interview lasts about one and one-half hours (Davis and Smith 1990).

It is not our purpose here to detail how this information is transferred from the actual interview to the computer's memory. For our purposes, we will assume that the GSS data are already stored in a computer. I also assume, if you are using this section of the text, that your instructor has taught you how to use the computer located at your school. Our purpose here will be to take the NORC data, manipulate them statistically, generate output (results), and interpret the output. We will look at some of this output at the end of the chapters that follow.

Important Terms

Descriptive statistics
Inferential statistics
Variable
Category

Level of measurement:
- Nominal
- Ordinal
- Interval
- Ratio

Suggested Readings

Every student beginning the study of statistics should read Darrel Huff's (1954) little book, *How to Lie with Statistics.* An excellent but highly detailed and somewhat technical description of the NORC surveys is Davis and Smith's (1990) *General Social Surveys, 1972-1990: Cumulative Codebook.* A thorough introduction to SPSS is Norusis's (1990) *SPSS Introductory Statistics Student Guide.* See also Dometrius (1992).

[NOTE: A list of the complete references for the suggested readings is found at the end of the text.]

2

Organization and Presentation of Data

Before statistical analysis of data can begin, we must organize our data in a meaningful, coherent fashion. After statistical analysis is complete, we must present our information to readers in a meaningful, coherent fashion. In this chapter, working with very simple data, we shall examine some of the basic techniques for organizing and presenting data. If there is a single theme in this chapter it is this: Any use of data, especially for purposes of comparison, must be *meaningful.* All of the statistical "facts" in the world are useless if they are not meaningfully organized and presented. Let us begin our examination of this theme with a simple example.

Rates

In a hypothetical year, there were 550 cases of murder or nonnegligent manslaughter in the greater Gotham City area; in that same year, there were 375 such cases in the greater Metropolis area. Examination of these two facts might initially lead us to conclude that, in terms of meeting a violent death, Metropolis is safer than Gotham City. But is this comparison meaningful? For example, what would we conclude if we also considered the fact that these two areas differ in population? Suppose that greater Gotham City's population was about 4,800,000 and the population of greater Metropolis was about 1,600,000. If we divide the number of murders in each area by the corresponding population and multiply by 100,000, we obtain the following murder *rates:* for Gotham City, 11.5 per 100,000 population and for Metropolis, 23.4 per 100,000 population. These new statistical facts have been made more meaningful than our original facts because the rates take into consideration the different populations of the two cities. Furthermore, the rates point to a conclusion that is directly opposite to our original conclusion. Our new conclusion is not that Metropolis is safer than Gotham City but that it is about twice as dangerous. Perhaps fans of Superman can find a flaw in this argument.

A *rate* is a statistical measure that makes meaningful, direct comparison between two or more unequal data sets. Statistical rates usually consist of three elements. In our example, these elements are (1) the number of murders in the area, (2) the population of the area, and (3) the arbitrary value of 100,000. (The value 100,000 is merely a convenient *numerical base*. It is simpler to refer to a murder rate of 21.8 per 100,000 people than to a ratio of 0.000218 murders per person.) The number of murders can be called a *criterion variable* (CV) and the population a *norming variable* (NV). (Here, the population is the norm, or standard, against which we measure the number of murders.) We can define any rate as

(Formula 2.1)
(Mueller, Schuessler, and Costner 1970: 183)

$$\text{Rate} = \frac{\text{Frequency of CV}}{\text{Frequency of NV}} \times \text{Numerical Base}$$

We can show how we computed the murder rate for Metropolis by using Formula 2.1. The criterion variable, number of murders, had a frequency of 367; the norming variable, population, was 1,684,000, and the numerical base was 100,000. The murder rate was thus calculated as

$$\frac{367}{1{,}684{,}000} \times (100{,}000) = 21.8$$

Other examples of commonly used rates in sociology are the birth rate, death rate, marriage rate, and divorce rate. Rates can be viewed as percentages or proportions that have been numerically adjusted to facilitate meaningful comprehension.

In addition to rates, data are frequently reported as *percentages, proportions, or ratios.* A ratio is simply a rate whose numerical base is 1. Some rates are popularly referred to as ratios; for example, the sex ratio is defined as the number of males per one hundred females.

Frequency Distribution

A second device that facilitates comprehension and thereby makes data more meaningful is the *frequency distribution*. A frequency distribution is a count of the total number of cases within well-defined categories of a variable. As an example, Table 2.1 lists murder rates for a sample of 145 urban areas. Even a careful examination of this table will leave most readers with an unclear idea of the frequency of murder in American metropolitan areas: There is too much detail and the data are not well organized. But we can present these data in a clearer and more meaningful fashion if we *group* the 145 murder rates and simply list the frequency for each group. Table 2.2 presents three possible ways of grouping the data into a frequency distribution. Which of these three shall we work with? How shall we decide which distribution is most useful? Let us briefly explore some principles to be observed in the construction of any frequency distribution.

In constructing any frequency distribution we perform two basic operations. First, we decide the appropriate number of categories (or classes or intervals) into which we shall group the data; second, we sort and count all of the data into appropriate groups. The second task is purely clerical, so let us devote our attention to the criteria for determining the categories. Freund (1988: 17) has listed three such guidelines. *Rule 1: Use at least six and not more than fifteen classes.* Too few classes, as in Table 2.2(c), will result in a homogenization of the data, and distinctions between classes will be blurred. Too many classes, as in 2.2(a), will be almost as confusing as the original mass of ungrouped data. *Rule 2: Each case should fit into only one class.* Simply put, classes should not overlap. For example, if two classes are 5-10 and 10-15, it is unclear where a score of 10 should be recorded. *Rule 3: Whenever possible, the class intervals should be of equal size.* In other words, each class should cover the same range of scores as every other class. The reason for this is that if the width of the class interval changes, comparisons become difficult and, as mentioned, further statistical manipulation of the data becomes awkward or impossible. To these three rules, we can add a fourth. *Rule 4: Define classes so that all cases will be included.* There are two points to consider here. First, care must be taken to see that extremely high scores or extremely low scores are included in some class. For example, if we added a 146th area, with a murder rate of thirty-seven, we would have to add fifteen classes to 2.2 (a), even though fourteen of them would have a frequency of zero;

Table 2.1. *Murder Rates for a Sample of 145 Urban Areas*

5	10	12	11	10	7	2	15
4	15	6	16	16	5	11	4
13	16	16	2	10	16	5	4
3	11	14	8	17	4	10	12
3	3	14		5	6	20	12
5	14	15	19	10	8	2	18
2	18	6	3	17	21	4	1
22	4	19	5	4	20	15	9
12	6	15	3	14	10	8	19
10	5	7	4	13	2	5	16
5	10	12	5	3	4	5	
4	15	8	6	7	12	5	
16	2	4	17	20	8	3	
15	7	5	13	5	8	6	
2	8	14	7	17	9	9	
5	13	3	4	7	7		
4	3	16	17	4	3		
2	9	8	6	3	6		
22	12	13	11	16	13		
18	3	4	4	2	18		

or we would have to add eight classes to 2.2(b); or we would have to add three classes to 2.2(c). (In certain limited circumstances, it might be permissible to define the last class as "22 or more" and thereby avoid the need to create extra classes. However, this makes it impossible to perform certain other statistical operations on the data.) Second, there should be no gaps between classes. For example, it would not be appropriate to have the classes 1-4, 5-9, and 12-16, because there would be no place to record scores of 10 or 11.

A word should be said about the importance of defining *class boundaries*. The murder rates presented in Table 2.1 were recorded as whole numbers. As such, they conceal the fact that these rates were originally reported as decimal figures. Metropolis's murder rate of 21.8 was rounded to 22 and Gotham City's rate of 11.5 was rounded to 12. As a result, the data became easier to read, but some of the precision of measurement was masked. Furthermore, we must now realize that a

Table 2.2. *Frequency Distributions of 145 Murder Rates*

(a) Class Interval = 1

Murder Rate	Frequency
1	1
2	9
3	12
4	16
5	16
6	8
7	7
8	8
9	4
10	8
11	4
12	7
13	6
14	5
15	7
16	10
17	5
18	4
19	2
20	3
21	1
22	2
	Total = 145

(b) Class Interval = 2

Murder Rate	Frequency
1-2	10
3-4	28
5-6	24
7-8	15
9-10	12
11-12	11
13-14	11
15-16	17
17-18	9
19-20	5
21-22	3
	Total = 145

(c) Class Interval = 6

Murder Rate	Frequency
1-6	62
7-12	38
13-18	37
19-24	8
	Total = 145

rate of 22 does not necessarily mean *exactly* 22, for scores such as 21.8, 21.6, 22.1, 22.256, 22.43, and the like are all represented by the single value of 22. In working with frequency distributions, we recognize this fact by utilizing class boundaries (or class limits or true limits). The class boundaries of 22 are, therefore, defined as 21.5 (lower boundary) and 22.5 (upper boundary). Similarly, the class interval of 5-6 has as its lower and upper limits the values 4.5 and 6.5; and the class 13-18 has its true limits defined as 12.5 and 18.5. Figure 2.1 illustrates other classes and their true limits. Note that when we work with decimal figures accurate to *one* place (for example, 9.5., 11.3, 6.6), we define our

(a) Data Expressed in Units

Class	True Lower Limit	True Upper Limit
0-5	-0.5	5.5
6-10	5.5	10.5
etc.	etc.	etc.

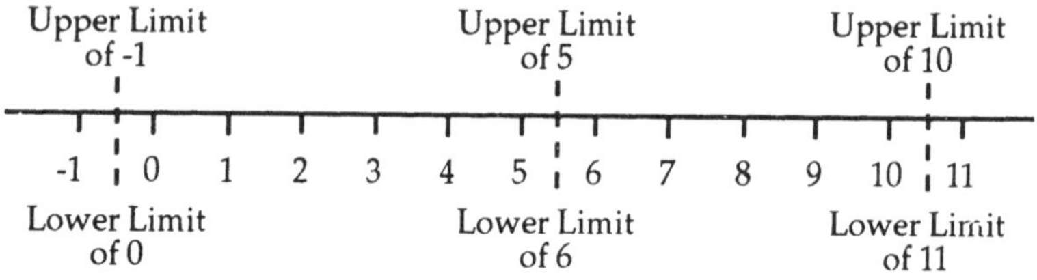

(b) Data Expressed in 1,000s

Class	True Lower Limit	True Upper Limit
40,000-49,000	39,500	49,500
50,000-59,000	49,500	59,500
etc.	etc.	etc.

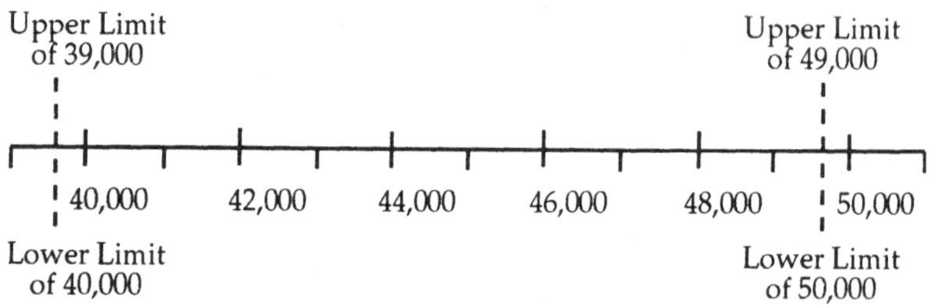

(c) Data Expressed in Decimals

Class	True Lower Limit	True Upper Limit
10.5-19.4	10.45	19.45
19.5-29.4	19.45	29.45
etc.	etc.	etc.

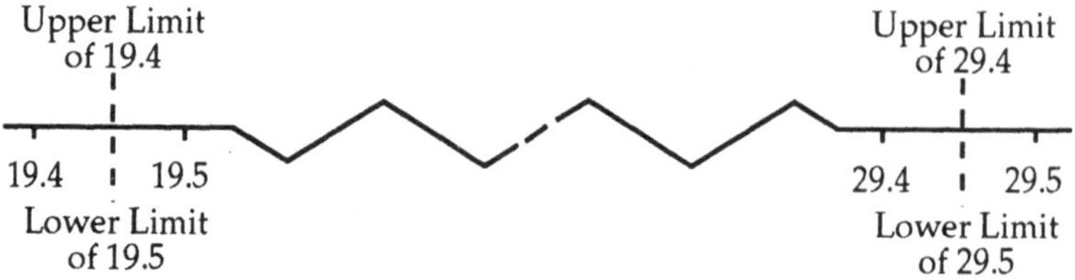

Figure 2.1. *Class Boundaries*

boundaries by using two decimal places. Thus the limits of 9.5 are 9.45 and 9.55; the limits of 6.6 are 6.55 and 6.65. (In general, if the set of values that are to be classed consists of k significant digits, the values that define the limits should have k + 1 significant digits.)

Even though frequency distributions do a remarkable job of condensing large masses of data, we can still further simplify our task by presenting the data in visual form. One of the most commonly used graphic devices is the *histogram*. A histogram is constructed by drawing rectangles whose widths correspond to class intervals and whose heights correspond to frequencies. For example, Figure 2.2 uses a histogram to present the data on murder rates found in Table 2.2(b). Note that the markings on the horizontal axis of the histogram represent the true class limits, while the markings on the vertical axis represent the class frequencies.

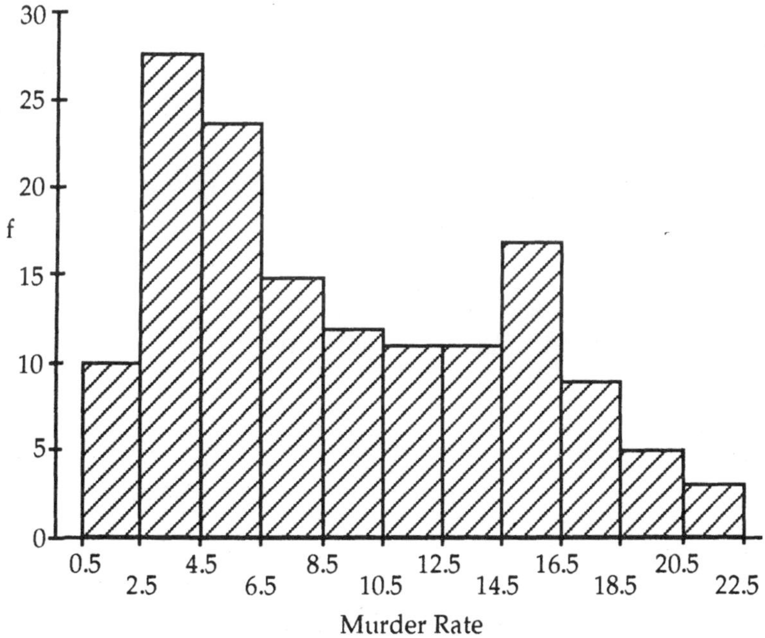

Figure 2.2. *Histogram of the Distribution of 145 Murder Rates*

Pictorial Presentation

In the previous section we gave four guidelines for the construction of frequency distributions. These same guidelines, especially numbers 2, 3, and 4, should be applied to the construction of histograms. Otherwise, distortion of data will most certainly be introduced. An alternative to the histogram is the *frequency polygon*. A frequency polygon is constructed by plotting the frequency of a class score at the midpoint of the class interval and connecting the points with straight lines. Figure 2.3 presents a frequency polygon for Table 2.2(b). We can also present these data as a *frequency curve,* which is simply a smoothed version of the frequency polygon (Figure 2.4). Many other graphic techniques can be used to organize and present data. Two of these are illustrated in Figures 2.5 and 2.6. For a further, more detailed discussion of graphic techniques and other forms of data organization and presentation, see most elementary texts.

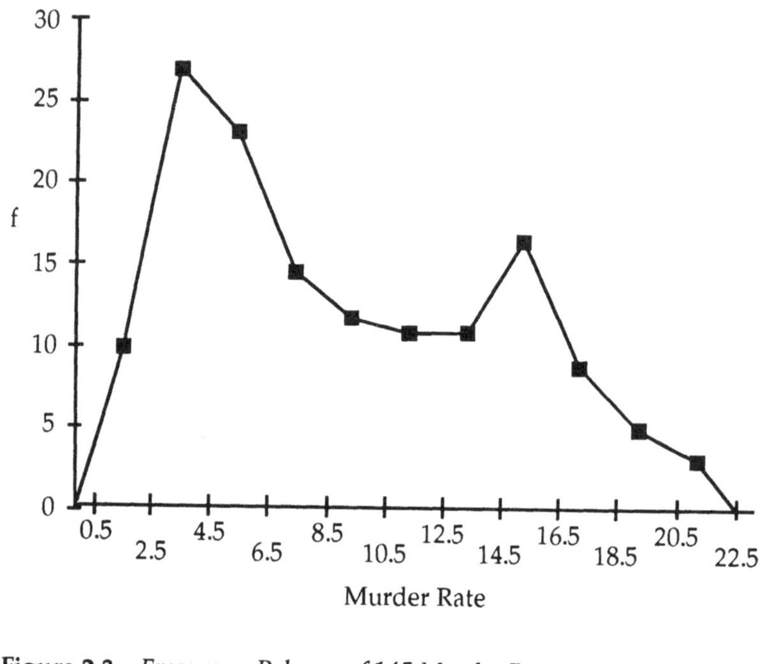

Figure 2.3. *Frequency Polygon of 145 Murder Rates*

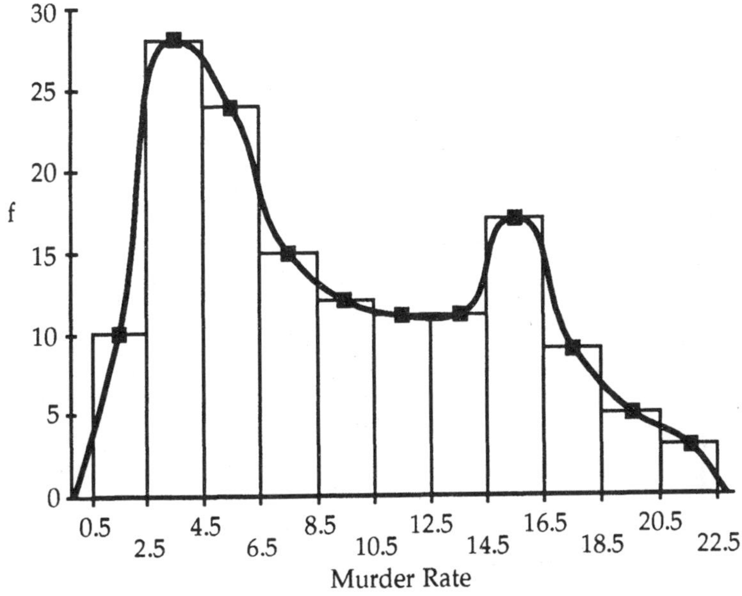

Figure 2.4. *Frequency Curve Superimposed over Frequency Polygon*

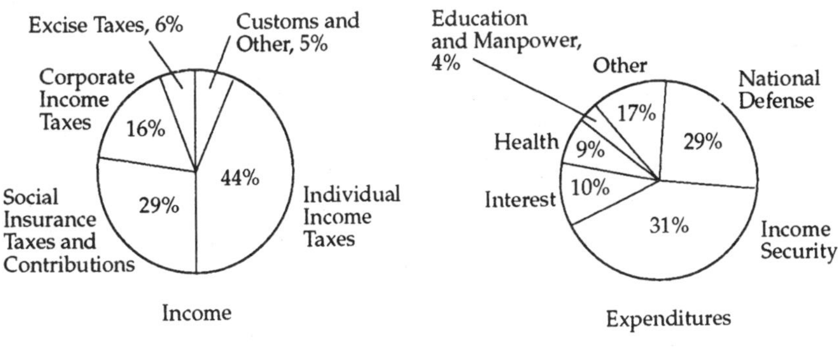

Figure 2.5. *Pie Charts*

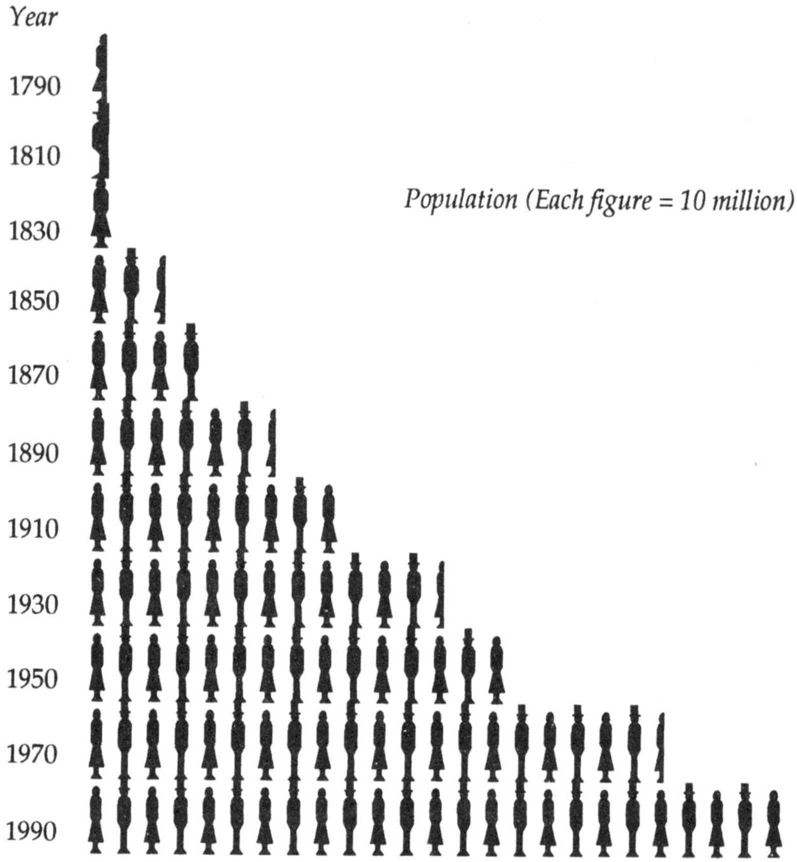

Figure 2.6. *Pictograph (Bar Chart, Using Figures) of U.S. Population Data, 1790-1990*

An SPSS Example: FREQUENCIES

The four lines that follow contain SPSS commands used to generate information about the frequency with which certain variables appear. (The numbers in brackets are not part of the actual commands—they are there simply to help us identify which command lines are being discussed.)

```
[1] SET WIDTH = 80
[2] GET FILE = 'SOC_DISK:[NORCLIB]MMNORC90.SPX'
[3] FREQUENCIES  VARIABLES = EDUC RACE
[4]       /HBAR
```

The first two lines are *system command* lines. These lines are *not* part of the SPSS commands. Rather, they are commands given to the computer. Such commands vary from computer system to computer system. Your instructor will give you the exact commands needed for your computer system.

Line 1 tells my computer to produce the final output in an eighty-column format; that is, in a format that can be printed on a standard-letter-size sheet of paper.

Line 2, the GET FILE command, tells the computer to get a certain set of data and where the data are stored. In this instance, the data are stored on a large disk that is named SOC_DISK. On SOC_DISK there is a portion of the computer's memory that is called NORCLIB. In NORCLIB there is a specific data set called MMNORC90.SPX. The latter contains the raw data that we will analyze.

Line 3 is the first actual SPSS command. The FREQUENCIES command, together with its associated subcommand (/HBAR), tells the computer to execute a certain sequence of commands that are invisible to us but that constitute the actual SPSS software. Line 3 also specifies which of the many variables that exist in the data set are going to be analyzed. In this exercise, I have chosen two variables, education and race (here named EDUC and RACE).

Line 4, sometimes referred to as a subcommand, tells the computer to produce a graphic representation of the frequency distributions of the specified variables. FREQUENCIES can produce either a histogram or a bar chart. If you prefer a histogram, you can specify /HISTOGRAM; if you prefer a bar chart, you can specify /BARCHART. In using /HBAR, I have chosen to let the computer decide.

The lines in the following EDUC example represent the actual printed output that is received as a result of the previous commands. The command FREQUENCIES produced the following example. Note the information that is provided—this information will be provided each and every time that you run FREQUENCIES. The *Value Label* does not appear for EDUC because the Value of EDUC would be the same as the Value Label. That is, for someone who has eight years of education, the Value Label would be the same as the Value, that is, eight. The column headed *Frequency* is just that—the actual count for each Value. In the example below, 1 person has received four years of EDUC, 18 people have had eight years, and 7 people have had twenty years of education. The *Percent* column tells us the percentage of our 353 respondents who have a given Value. In the above, 0.3 percent of the total have four years of EDUC, 4.8 percent have eight years, and 2.0 percent have twenty years of education. The next column, *Valid Percent*, is based on the proportion of the 353 respondents who actually answered this question. In this case, all 353 people did answer; so the Percent and Valid Percent columns are identical. *This will not always be the case.* The last column gives the *Cumulative Percent*, that is, the percent of people who have a given Value or less: 7.1 percent of our 353 respondents have eight or fewer years of education.

EDUC Example from an SPSS Run

```
[1]  SET WIDTH = 80
[2]  GET FILE = 'SOC_DISK:[NORCLIB]MMNORC90.SPX'
[3]  FREQUENCIES  VARIABLES = EDUC RACE
[4]           /HBAR
```

EDUC HIGHEST YEAR OF SCHOOL COMPLETED

Value Label	Value	Frequency	Valid Percent	Cum Percent	Percent
	4	1	.3	.3	.3
	5	1	.3	.3	.6
	6	2	.6	.6	1.1
	7	3	.8	8	2.0
	8	18	5.1	5.1	7.1
	9	15	4.2	4.2	11.3
	10	20	5.7	5.7	7.0
	11	20	5.7	5.7	22.7
	12	109	30.9	30.9	53.5
	13	28	7.9	7.9	61.5
	14	36	10.2	10.2	71.7
	15	18	5.1	5.1	76.8
	16	43	12.2	12.2	89.0
	17	12	3.4	3.4	92.4
	18	17	4.8	4.8	97.2
	19	3	.8	.8	98.0
	20	7	2.0	2.0	100.0
Totals		353	100.0	100.0	

After producing the frequency table, FREQUENCIES/HBAR will produce either a histogram or a bar chart. Following, we see the histogram for EDUC. In this histogram, *Count* is the same as Frequency in the preceding example, and *Value* is defined as Value in the preceding example. What follows Value in the histogram is a series of asterisks (***), which gives us a graphic representation of the frequency distribution. The note tells us that each asterisk represents about four cases; thus, the 20 people who have ten years of EDUC are represented by five asterisks. Each bar is followed by the actual frequency count of each Value. Immediately below the histogram there appears a graphic base line and numeric scale that help us to visualize the data.

Example of EDUC Histogram

```
Count   Value   One symbol equals approximately 4.00 occurrences

  1      4.00   |
  1      5.00   |
  2      6.00   |*
  3      7.00   |*
 18      8.00   |*****
 15      9.00   |****
 20     10.00   |*****
 20     11.00   |*****
109     12.00   |***************************
 28     13.00   |*******
 36     14.00   |*********
 18     15.00   |*****
 43     16.00   |***********
 12     17.00   |***
 17     18.00   |****
  3     19.00   |*
  7     20.00   |**
                +------+------+------+------+------+------+------+
                0      20     40     60     80     100
                          Histogram frequency

Valid cases   353    Missing cases    0
```

RACE: Example of a Bar Chart

RACE Race of Respondent

Value Label	Value	Fre- quency	Percent	Valid Percent	Cum Percent
WHITE	1	289	81.9	81.9	1.9
BLACK	2	52	14.7	14.7	96.6
OTHER	3	12	3.4	3.4	100.0
Total		353	100.0	100.0	

```
           |
WHITE      |*************************************  289
           |
BLACK      |*******  52
           |
OTHER      |**  12
           |
           +----------+----------+----------+----------+
           0         80        160        240        320
           Frequency
```

Valid cases 353 Missing cases 0

Following the histogram, you will find the results of our SPSS command for the variable RACE. The format of this part of the computer output is exactly as in the EDUC histogram, except for two things. First, there *is* a Value Label for RACE. The Value of 1 represents a white person; the Value of 2 represents a black person; and 3 represents any other person. Second, the computer has printed a bar chart rather than a histogram. Note that the bar chart does not provide any indication of the value of each asterisk, and it does provide the exact frequency corresponding to the asterisks.

Important Terms

Rate	Frequency distribution
Histogram	Frequency polygon
Class boundary	Frequency curve

Suggested Readings

Huff (1954: 60-73); Hamilton (1990, Chap. 2); Ott et al. (1992, Chap. 3).

3

Descriptive Measures: Centrality

As we saw in Chapter 2, frequency distributions of large masses of data are useful devices for condensing great quantities of information, and as such, they enable us to convey a large amount of information in a relatively small amount of space or time. However, even this condensation of data can be too detailed and cumbersome for certain purposes. In this chapter we shall examine some of the statistics that are generally known as *measures of location,* and we shall place particular emphasis on measures of central location, or *centrality.* These measures convey a great deal of information in a small amount of space and time, for they reduce a large quantity of data to a single value that, in certain respects, represents the entire mass of data. These measures of centrality are popularly known as averages, but this term is not sufficiently precise for our work, as the following example illustrates.

Suppose that a certain community was being described by three different commentators. (1) In describing the community's financial well-being, the representative of a national booster club states: "Doe City is a thriving, healthy financial community; why, its average family income is $24,500, far above the national average." (2) Describing the same town, a visiting Marxist comments: "Doe City epitomizes the decadence of capitalism; the average family income is only $13,500." (3) Finally, a beginning sociology student (who has not yet taken a statistics course) writes in a term paper: "Doe City has an average family income of $17,000." Remember that all three people are speaking about the same city in the same year and their

Table 3.1. *Family Income in Doe City*

$13,500	$20,000
$13,500	$35,000
$13,500	$40,000
$13,500	$40,000
$13,500	$40,000
$13,500	$50,000
$17,000	

calculations are based on the same factual information (Table 3.1) and are accurate. All are telling the truth—but not the whole truth. They are all telling the truth because the term *average* has multiple meanings. All are telling less than the whole truth because they do not specify *which* average they are using when they report their data. In sociological work, one or more of three common averages are used. These three averages are the mode, the median, and the mean. Each is a descriptive measure of central location. Each provides a way of reducing a large mass of data to a single representative value. Most important, each average has a unique meaning that is different from that of the other averages; each represents a different aspect of the data.

The Mode

The *mode* is perhaps the simplest of all averages, simple in both concept and computation. The mode is defined as the measure that occurs most *frequently* in a distribution. In Table 3.1, for example, the family income that occurs most frequently is $13,500. Therefore, we can state that the modal family income is $13,500. As another example, ten students received examination scores of 65, 70, 70, 75, 75, 75, 75, 80, 80, and 90. The mode, or the modal score, is 75 because 75 is the score that occurs most frequently.

Because the mode is concerned only with the *frequency* associated with a certain measure, it does not make any arithmetic assumptions about the measurement process. Therefore, it is an especially useful measure of qualitative data; indeed, *the mode is the only appropriate measure of centrality for nominal-level data.* (The other averages discussed further on are inappropriate for nominal measurement; the mode, however, can be used to describe ordinal-level or interval-level data.)

Suppose that twenty persons report their ethnic backgrounds as follows. The mode of the distribution is *European*. It is important to note that the mode is *not* 8, which is the *frequency* of the *modal category*. Here we see that the mode need not be expressed numerically. It can, and often does, refer to a qualitative variable.

Ethnicity	f
African-American	3
Asian	3
European	8
Hispanic	4
Native American	1
Other	1
Total	20 = N

The mode is sometimes called the probability average because, in any distribution of scores, the mode is the score one is most likely to encounter. If you were to randomly select one of the eleven incomes of Table 3.1, you would have five chances in eleven of selecting $13,500; the probability of selecting any other income would be less than 5/11. (Taken by itself, however, the mode does not tell us how probable its occurrence is.)

It is possible for a distribution to have more than one mode. For example, if in our first example, one of the exam scores of 75 was changed to 70, there would be three scores of 70 and three scores of 75. Such a distribution can be described as *bimodal* because there are two modes, 70 and 75.

One difficulty with the mode is that it is quite unstable because it is very sensitive to the grouping procedure used. If we had used part (a) of Table 2.2 to determine the modal homicide rate, our answer would have been not 3.5 but 4.5, because 4.5 is the midpoint of the categories 4 and 5, categories with the greatest frequency. You might also note in (a) that if only one of the scores of 4 is changed to 5, the mode changes from 4.5 to 5.0. (Before going on, review Table 2.2 to make certain that you understand what has just been said.) For similar reasons, the mode is usually not very useful for describing small samples or populations unless there is some overwhelming point of clustering that should not be ignored. Finally, it should be noted that the mode is a dead-end statistic in that it does not lend itself to any further arithmetic manipulation.

*Quick Quiz**
3.1

Calculate the mode of the following distributions:

(A) 16, 17, 21, 16, 18, 21, 16, 24, 25, 17, 16, 20

(B)

Eye Color	f
Blue	4
Brown	15
Gray	7
Green	3
Other	5

(C)

IQ Score	f
85-89	3
90-94	9
95-99	15
100-104	19
105-109	17
110-114	8
115-119	4

*Answers to quick quizzes are at the end of each chapter.

The Median

The *median* is defined as *that point in a distribution that divides an ordered set of scores into two equal parts,* so that one-half of the scores fall above and one-half below it. Calculation of a median requires that data be at least at the ordinal level of measurement, because it is absurd to talk of above and below (or greater and lesser, and so on) with regard to qualitative data. In Table 3.1, the median family income is $17,000 because that value, and only that value, has an equal number of scores above and below it. (Unlike with the mode, *there can be only one median for any set of data.*)

In the distribution of scores 1, 3, 4, 7, 8, the median is that point that has one-half, or N/2, scores above and below it. In general, the *position* of the median can be determined by (N + 1)/2. With five scores, (N + 1)/2 = 3. The median therefore, is located at the third case, which is the midpoint of the distribution. The score associated with that position is 4. Therefore, 4 is the median of the distribution. This point is graphically described in Figure 3.1 (a).

In another example, we have the following distribution: 1, 2, 4, 7, 8, 10. Here, N/2 = 3, so we want to find that point that has three cases above and three cases below. Actually, any value between 4 and 7 could satisfy this condition, but if we follow the convention of true limits, the median point must be 5.5, the midpoint of the distance that separates 4 from 7. Figure 3.1 (b) illustrates this.

Remember, if N, the number of cases, is odd, the median score is the middle score in a series of ordered scores. If N is even, the median is the midpoint of the distance between the two midmost scores. In this sense, you can see that the median is a *position* average: It identifies the middle position in a distribution. The actual value of the median is obtained from whatever score is associated with that position.

Like the mode, the median is a reasonably simple concept. It is the central, or middle, point in a distribution. Fifty percent of the cases are above it, and 50 percent are below it. Also like the mode, the median cannot be manipulated arithmetically. The median is unlike the mode in that it is relatively stable; that is, it is not greatly influenced by grouping procedures. As already mentioned, there is one and only one median for any set of data. Finally, the median cannot be calculated for nominal-level data but can be calculated for ordinal-level or interval-level data.

Quartiles, Deciles, and Percentiles

There are frequent occasions when we are interested not in the middle position of a distribution but in some other position. We might, for example, want to define the top 10 percent of family incomes, the lowest 25 percent of homicide rates, or the top 16 percent of IQ scores. The procedure for identifying these locations is similar to that of locating the median except that we are not interested in finding the N/2 case but the 9/10 of N case or the N/4 case or the .16N case.

Quartiles are measures of location that divide a distribution into four equal parts (just as the median divides a distribution into two

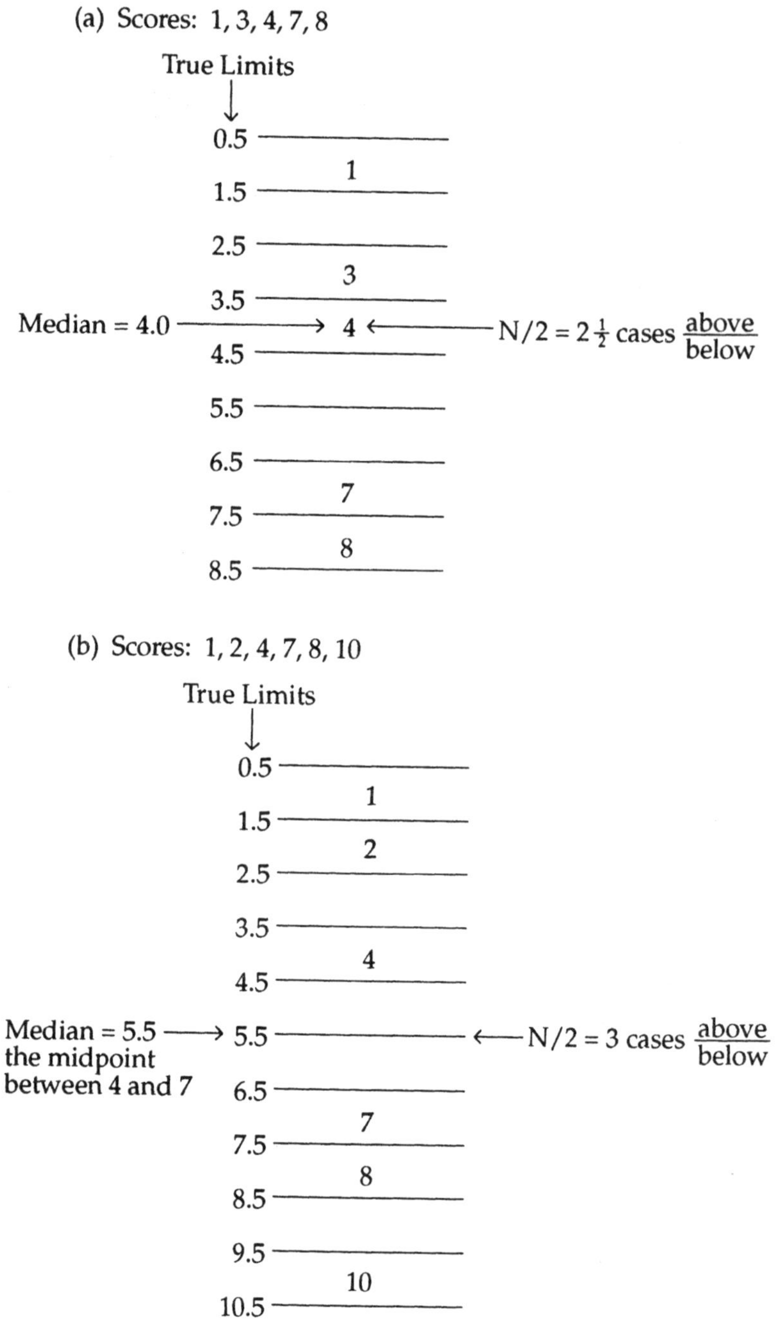

Figure 3.1. *Illustration of the Median as a Position Average*

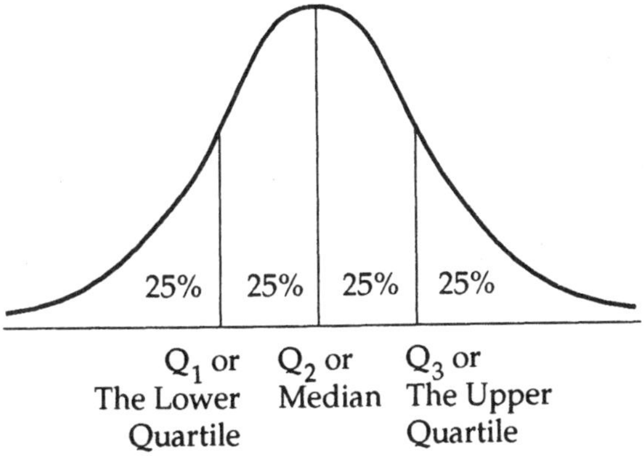

Figure 3.2. *Location of Quartiles in a Symmetric Distribution*

equal parts). The first quartile, Q_1, is that point in a distribution that has 25 percent of the cases below it and 75 percent above it. The third quartile, Q_3, has 75 percent of the cases below it and 25 percent above (see Figure 3.2). The second quartile is, of course, the median. *Deciles* are measures that divide a distribution into ten equal parts. The first decile, D_1, has 10 percent of the cases below it and 90 percent above. The third decile, D_3, has 30 percent of the cases below it. The fifth decile, D_5, is the median. The ninth decile, D_9, has 90 percent of the cases below it. *Percentiles* (or centiles) are measures that divide a distribution into one hundred equal parts. C_{37} is the thirty-seventh percentile (or thirty-seventh centile), and has 37 percent of the cases below it and 63 percent of the cases above it.

The Mean

The arithmetic mean is the average that most of us think of when we hear the word *average*. As we saw in Chapter 1, it is the average we use to determine batting averages in baseball, grade-point averages in college, and many other commonly used averages.

A mean can be determined only for data that are at least at the interval level of measurement, because the mean takes into account the value or magnitude of each score that enters into the computation. The mean for a set of ungrouped data is simply computed: Sum all scores in a data set and divide by the number of scores. Thus if we have five scores, 3, 8, 0, -5, and 9, we add (or sum) these five values, obtain a sum of 15, and divide this total by the number of scores, 5. The mean is therefore, 15/5 = 3.

Very often a data set will contain a score that appears more than once, for example, 3, 5, 7, 7, 7, 9, 11, and 11. In such instances it is essential that each score be included in the sum *as many times* as it appears in the data set. In our example, the score X = 7 must be counted three times, and when X = 11 the score must be counted twice. In other words, we must consider the *frequency* with which a score appears.

The mean may be calculated as follows:

(Formula 3.1)

$$\overline{X} = \frac{\Sigma(fX)}{N}$$

where $\overline{X}$ (read X-bar) is the mean; X is any score; f is the frequency of a score; and Σ (sigma) is the instruction to add. (That is, add whatever quantity is embraced by the summation command, Σ. In this case, we add all values of X.) Let us use this formula to compute the mean of the set of scores just given.

X (= score)	f (= frequency)	fX
3	1	3
5	1	5
7	3	21
9	1	9
11	2	22
	8	60 = Σ (fX)

$$\overline{X} = \frac{60}{8} = 7.5$$

This example illustrates one of the ways in which the mean is conceptually different from the median or mode: The mean represents the value (adjusted for frequency) of the scores. It does not represent position, nor does it represent frequency alone.

This emphasis on *value* is important to a conceptual understanding of the mean as the true value that represents a set of scores and from which all other scores can be viewed as deviations. Let us return to our simple data set, 3, 8, 0, -5, and 9. We have found the mean of this distribution to be 3. We can now define each score as a *deviation* from

Table 3.2. *Deviation Scores*

Raw Score X	Deviation Score $x = X - \bar{X}$
3	0
8	5
0	3
-5	-8
9	6
	$0 = \Sigma x$

the mean; we symbolize this deviation as $x = (X - \bar{X})$. Table 3.2 presents the data in their deviation-score form. The score of $X = 3$ has a deviation score of $x = 0$, because $(X - \bar{X}) = (3 - 3) = 0$; the score of $X = -5$ has a deviation score of $x = -8$, because $(X - \bar{X}) = (-5) - 3 = -8$; and so on. Notice in Table 3.3 that the sum of the deviations from the mean is zero; if the mean has been correctly computed, this will *always* be so. (This fact can be used to check on the accuracy of your work.)

The mean is analogous to the "center of gravity" of a distribution. If we conceive of our measurements as blocks on a seesaw, the mean is the point of balance (Figure 3.3). If we were to shift the fulcrum to any other point on the scale, the result would be imbalance. Figure 3.4 illustrates the mean-as-balance-point concept for another set of data.

This concept of the mean is very important to more advanced discussions of measurement and sampling. Suppose that we want to know the mean value of some large population and that we do not have the resources to measure the entire population. We therefore measure only a segment, or sample, of the population. Each of these sample measures deviates from the true population mean. And if our sample is large enough, we can assume that the errors in measurement will cancel each other out, and the net result, as reflected in the sample mean, will be zero error. Here the mean is the value that would appear if there was no sampling error, no measurement error.

Table 3.3. *Frequency Distribution (with Cumulative Frequencies) of 145 Homicide Rates*

Homicide Rate	f	Cum. f (low scores to high)	Cum. f (high scores to low)	
1-2	10	10		
3-4	28	38		
5-6	24	62	107	the N/2
7-8	15	(77) <-------	(83) <-----	case is
9-10	12	89	68	here
11-12	11		56	
13-14	11		45	
15-16	17		34	
17-18	9		17	
19-20	5		8	
21-22	3		3	
Total	145			

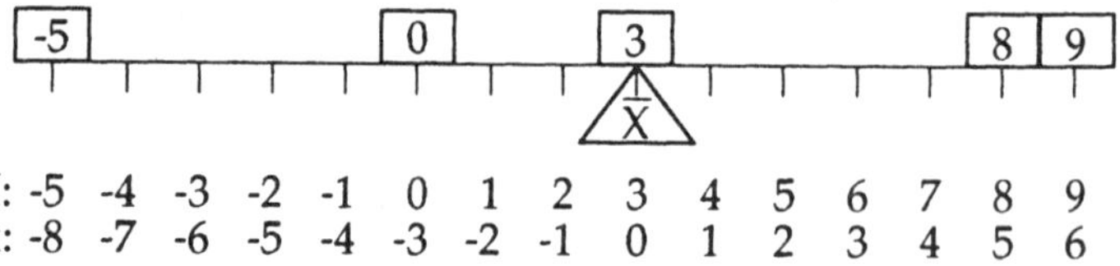

Figure 3.3. *The Mean as Center of Gravity*

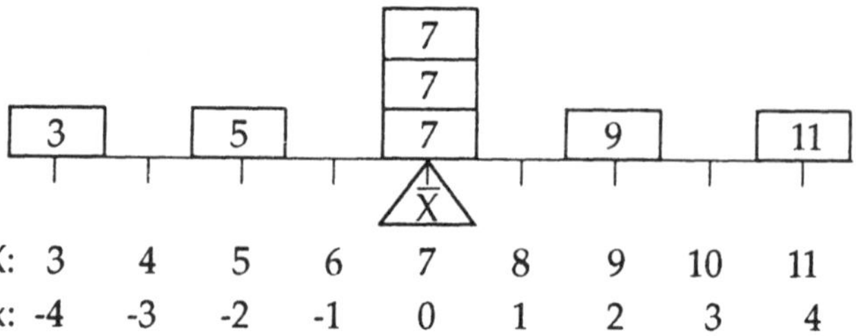

Figure 3.4. *Another Example of the Mean as Center of Gravity*

Grouped Data

The Mode

The procedure for finding the mode of a set of grouped data is similar to that described previously. We simply find the category or interval that has the greatest frequency. We then define the mode as that category (as in the ethnicity example), or if the data are quantitative, we define the mode as the midpoint of the category. In Table 3.3, we can see that the modal frequency is 28, which is associated with the modal category of 3-4. The midpoint of the category 3-4 is 3.5, so the mode of the distribution is 3.5.

The Median

The same logic of finding the central position (the median) governs the computation of the median for grouped data. Let us continue to work with data on homicide rates, as reproduced in Table 3.3. Because N = 145, the median is that point that has N/2 = 72.5 cases above and below it; we are, therefore, seeking the 72.5th case. If we begin to count the number of cases in each class interval and accumulate our tally, we can hope to find the 72.5th case. The first class interval, 1-2, has 10 cases and has brought us to the value of 2.5 (the upper limit of the interval 1-2 and the lower limit of the interval 3-4). Thus, we have accounted for 10 of the needed 72.5 cases; we still have a way to go. The second interval, 3-4, adds 28 cases for a cumulative total of 38 and has moved us to the true limit of 4.5. The third interval, 5-6, adds 24 cases for a cumulative total of 62 and has brought us to the true limit of 6.5. Looking ahead to the next interval, 7-8, we see that there are 15 cases, which is more than we need to reach our goal of 72.5 cases. We need only 10.5 of these 15 cases. In other words, we must go 10.5/15 of the distance into the interval 7-8. Remembering that this interval is two units large, we express this distance as

$$\text{distance} = \frac{10.5}{15}(2) = 1.4$$

The median can now be determined as the value of the last true limit which we fully accounted for, plus the additional distance needed from the median category. The last true limit we accounted for was 6.5, the added value is 1.4, and the median, therefore, can be expressed as follows:

$$\text{Mdn} = 6.5 + 1.4 = 7.9$$

This procedure can be summarized in the following computational formula:

(Formula 3.2)

$$\text{Mdn} = \text{LL} + \frac{N/2 - \text{cum. f}}{f_{\text{Mdn}}}(i)$$

where LL is the true lower limit of the median category; cum. f is the cumulative frequency up to but not including the median category; f_{Mdn} is the frequency of the median category; and i is the size of the median class interval.

In the previous example, we started from the smaller class intervals and worked toward the larger; that is, we started with the interval 1-2 and worked up. Alternatively, we could start at the highest interval, 21-22, and work down. If we do so, we have to adjust the procedure slightly: When we reach the true limit of the median category, we have to subtract some distance from the true limit. Expressed as a formula, the median can be computed as

(Formula 3.3)

$$\text{Mdn} = \text{UL} - \frac{N/2 - \text{cum. f}}{f_{\text{Mdn}}}(i)$$

where UL is the true upper limit of the median category. For the data from Table 3.3, we compute the median as follows:

$$= 8.5 - \frac{72.5 - 68}{15}(2)$$

$$= 8.5 - \frac{4.5}{15}(2)$$

$$= 8.5 - 0.6 = 7.9$$

which is identical to the previously computed value. (Until you become familiar with the procedure for calculating the median, it would be helpful to compute its value twice, once using the lower limit and once using the upper limit; this will provide you with a check on the accuracy of your work.)

> *Quick Quiz*
> **3.2**
>
> For the data from Quick Quiz 3.1 (A) and (C), compute the median.

Quartiles, Deciles, and Centiles

For grouped data, the following computational formulas may be used:

(Formula 3.4)

$$Q_1 = LL + \frac{N/4 - cum.f}{f_{Q_1}}(i) = UL - \frac{3N/4 - cum.f}{f_{Q_1}}(i)$$

(Formula 3.5)

$$Q_3 = LL + \frac{3N/4 - cum.f}{f_{Q_3}}(i) = UL - \frac{N/4 - cum.f}{f_{Q_3}}(i)$$

To determine Q_1 for Table 3.3, we must locate the 145/4 = 36.75th case. To determine Q_3, we need the 108.75th case. The procedures are as follows:

$$Q_1 = 2.5 + \frac{26.25}{28}(2)$$

$$= 2.5 + 1.875$$

$$= 4.375$$

$$Q_3 = 12.5 + \frac{8.75}{11}(2)$$

$$= 12.5 + 1.59$$

$$= 14.09$$

[NOTE: In both of the previous cases, we used the lower limit formula. You should verify for yourself the accuracy of this work by using the upper limit formula.] We can interpret these figures by saying that 25 percent of the 145 homicide rates fall below the rate of 4.375 (or that 75 percent fall above 4.375); and for Q_3, we can say that 75 percent of the homicide rates fall below 14.09 (or that 25 percent fall above 14.09).

We will not give specific formulas for each of the deciles, but it should be clear by now that the computational procedure for deciles is the same as that for the median and the quartiles. Let us compute D_1 and D_7 from Table 3.3 to illustrate.

$$D_1 = LL + \frac{N/10 - \text{cum. f}}{f_{D_1}}(i) \qquad D_7 = LL + \frac{7N/10 - \text{cum. f}}{f_{D_7}}(i)$$

$$= 2.5 + \frac{14.5 - 10}{28}(2) \qquad = 12.5 + \frac{101.5 - 100}{11}(2)$$

$$= 2.5 + .32 \qquad = 12.5 + .27$$

$$= 2.82 \qquad = 12.77$$

Thus, 10 percent of the 145 homicide rates fall below 2.82 and 70 percent of them fall below 12.77.

Centiles (or percentiles) are measures which divide a distribution into one hundred equal parts. The logic and procedures of calculation are as above. For example, we can find the 86th centile, the point below which 86 percent of the cases fall, as follows:

$$C_{86} = LL + \frac{.86N - \text{cum. f}}{f_{C_{86}}}(i) = 14.5 + \frac{124.7 - 111}{17}(2)$$

$$= 14.5 + 1.61 = 16.11$$

Quick Quiz
3.3

From Table 3.3, find (A) D_9 and (B) C_{16}.

The Mean

The principle underlying the computation of the mean for grouped data is identical to that for ungrouped data. In practice, one adjustment must be made. When data are grouped, the procedure for computing the mean assumes that within a given class interval, all scores fall at the midpoint of the interval. If we defined this midpoint as M, a computing formula for grouped data would be

(Formula 3.6)

$$\overline{X} = \frac{\Sigma(fM)}{N}$$

Table 3.4 illustrates this procedure, which provides a fairly simple and direct way to compute the mean. However, the values of (fM) can get rather large and cumbersome, and for this reason many people prefer an alternate computing procedure.

The method of the *guessed mean* is based on the center-of-gravity concept of the mean. It involves guessing where the mean might be, computing the deviations about this guessed mean, and making the necessary mathematical adjustment.

To use a very simple example with ungrouped data, suppose we have again the values 3, 8, 0, -5, and 9. Let us guess that the mean of this distribution is 6. If this guessed mean (symbolized as X') is correct, the sum of the deviations about the guessed mean (symbolized as x') should be zero. But in fact, $\Sigma x' = -15$ (Table 3.5). Because this sum, -15, is based on five scores, the mean deviation is -15/5 = -3. It follows, therefore, that our guessed mean must be adjusted by a value of -3. Thus, the correct value of the mean is our guessed mean *plus* any correction factor. (But note that the correction factor may be negative.) Symbolically,

$$\overline{X} = \overline{X}' + \frac{\Sigma(fx')}{N}$$

For our data, $\overline{X} = 6 + (-3) = 3$, which is, of course, the true mean of the distribution. It should be noted that this method will work with any guess. You may wish to verify for yourself that if the guessed mean was -8 or 145 or 2.917 or any other value, the correction factor of $\Sigma(fx')/N$ would still lead you to the true mean of 3.

Table 3.4. *The Mean and Formula 3.6*

Homicide Rate	M	f	fM
1-2	1.5	10	15.0
3-4	3.5	28	98.0
5-6	5.5	24	132.0
7-8	7.5	15	112.5
9-10	9.5	12	114.0
11-12	11.5	11	126.5
13-14	13.5	11	148.5
15-16	15.5	17	263.5
17-18	17.5	9	157.5
19-20	19.5	5	97.5
21-22	21.5	3	64.5
		145	1329.5

$$\overline{X'} = \frac{\Sigma(fM)}{N} = \frac{1{,}329.5}{145} = 9.17$$

Table 3.5. *Guessed Deviations*

Raw Score = X	Mean = $\overline{X}$	Guessed Deviation = x' = (X - $\overline{X'}$)
3	6	-3
8	6	2
0	6	-6
-5	6	-11
9	6	3
		-15 = Σx'

Coded Data

In actual day-to-day practice, procedures for computing the mean often involve the *coding* of data. Suppose you were asked to compute the mean of these three scores:

18,984,082   18,984,084   18,984,087

You could simply add the three values, divide this sum by 3, and obtain a mean of 18,984,084.33. With only three values to sum, this is a trivial problem. But if there were many such numbers, the addition task alone would be time-consuming and error-prone. An alternative is to adjust each raw score by some constant. In our example we could subtract 18,984,080 from each score. We could then compute the mean of our coded scores and finally readjust the coded mean by the constant value. Table 3.6 illustrates this procedure. In general, coding can be done by addition, subtraction, multiplication, division, or a combination of operations. There are two points to be remembered in all coding of data: (1) every raw-score value must be identically coded;

Table 3.6. *Coding*

Raw Score X	Coded Score (X - 18,984,080)
18,984,082	2
18,984,084	4
18,984,087	7
	13

Coded Mean = $\overline{X}$ = 13.3/3 = 4.33

True Mean = Coded Mean + Code Value
= 4.33 + 18,984,080
= 18,984,084.33

Table 3.7. *The Guessed Mean and Formula 3.7*

Homicide Rate	f	x	x'	fx'	
1-2	10	-6	-3	-30	
3-4	28	-4	-2	-56	-110
5-6	24	-2	-1	-24	
7-8	15	0	0	0	
9-10	12	2	1	12	
11-12	11	4	2	22	
13-14	11	6	3	33	
15-16	17	8	4	68	+231
17-18	9	10	5	45	
19-20	5	12	6	30	
21-22	3	14	7	21	
				$121 = \Sigma fx'$	

$$\overline{X} = \overline{X}' + \frac{\Sigma(fx')}{N} = 7.5 + \frac{121}{145}(2)$$

$$= 7.5 + 1.67 = 9.17$$

and (2) as the final step, data must be decoded, which means that the original coding procedure must be reversed.

In using coding to compute the mean for grouped data, it is a frequent practice to code the deviations from the mean. It is most common to *divide* each class deviation score by the size of the class interval. [NOTE: When we use this method, it is necessary that the intervals be of equal size.] The reason for this is to establish the neat and almost automatic sequence of 0, ±1, ±2, ±3, and so on, as values representing the *guessed deviations* (x') from the mean (Table 3.7). To compute the mean, each x' value is multiplied by its corresponding frequency; when the values of fx' are summed, divided by N, and then decoded (because the coding involved division by the size of the class interval, the decoding involves multiplication by the size of the class interval), we have a value that corrects the guessed mean. When the correction factor is added to the guessed mean, we have the true mean. In general, this procedure follows Formula 3.7,

(Formula 3.7)

$$\overline{X} = \overline{X}' + \frac{\Sigma(fx')}{N}(i)$$

where $\overline{X}'$, the guessed mean, is the midpoint of the class interval in which the mean is assumed to be; x' is a coded deviation score; and i is the size of the class interval.

In Table 3.7 we guessed the mean to be the midpoint, 7.5, of the category 7-8. (Again, note that *any* guessed midpoint would produce an identical result after coding and correction.) We next computed the deviations from the guessed mean, x = (X - X'), and coded these values of x by dividing by the size of the class interval (in this case, i = 2), obtaining x' = x/i.

You will find as you work with this method and if you fully understand the logic of what is being done, that it is not necessary to be concerned with the details of deviation scores, for once you have decided on a guessed mean, the x' scores will always follow the 0, ±1, ±2, and so on, in sequence.

Table 3.8 illustrates another application of this procedure. Carefully work your way through this and the other examples until you are certain that you understand both the logic and the procedure.

Notes on the Measures of Centrality

Weighted Means

Unlike modes and medians, means can be combined. The procedure for doing so is simple, but caution is required. For example, suppose one group of twenty subjects had a mean score of 74 on a test and another group of twenty had a mean score of 80. Because the Ns are of the same size, the *weight* of each mean is equal, and we can compute the grand mean as the mean of the two group means. That is, $\overline{X} = (74 + 80)/2 = 77$.

But suppose that the second group's mean is based on N = 50. Here the two groups are not equally weighted, because one mean is based on twenty scores and the other is based on fifty scores. Because the mean depends on *frequency* as well as on *value,* we must take this

Table 3.8. *Another Application of the Guessed Mean*

X	f	x′	fx′
66-70	3	-3	-9
71-75	11	-2	-22
76-80	18	-1	-18
81-85	30	0	0
86-90	20	1	20
91-95	13	2	26
96-100	5	3	15
	100	0	12

$$\overline{X} = \overline{X}' + \frac{\Sigma(fx')}{N}$$

$$= 83 + \frac{12}{100}(5)$$

$$= 83 + 0.6 = 83.6$$

into account. This is done by multiplying each group mean by its frequency; we then obtain ΣfX for each group, because

(Formula 3.8)

$$\Sigma(fX) = N\overline{X}$$

For the first group,

$$\Sigma(fX) = 20(74) = 1{,}480$$

For the second group,

$$\Sigma(fX) = 50(80) = 4{,}000$$

Table 3.9 *The Weighted Mean*

	f	x′	fx′
Group 1	20	74	1,480
Group 2	50	80	4,000
Totals	70		5,480

$$\text{Unweighted Mean} = \frac{74 + 80}{2} = 77 \quad \text{(incorrect)}$$

$$\text{Weighted Mean} = \frac{1{,}480 + 4{,}000}{20 + 50} \quad \text{(correct)}$$

Thus for the two groups combined, the grand sum is 1,480 + 4,000 = 5,480, and the grand mean is

$$\overline{X} = \frac{\Sigma(fX)}{N} = \frac{5{,}480}{70} = 78.3$$

Table 3.9 summarizes this procedure.

Effect of Extreme Scores

Because it depends on the value of each and every score in a distribution, the mean is strongly influenced by extreme scores. Consider the following distribution and its three measures of centrality:

4 5 5 6 6 6 7 7 89

Mode = 6 Median = 6 Mean = 15

Is the mean of 15 a representative value? Probably not, for it has been greatly influenced by the single extreme score of 89, a score that does not seem to be typical of the "usual" scores in the distribution. From this example we can see that when extreme scores are present, the mean may not be an appropriate measure of central tendency. Figure 3.5 illustrates how the mean is "pulled" in the direction of extreme scores. This figure also locates the approximate position of the mean, median, and mode in differently shaped distributions. Depending on the degree of *skewness*, that is, the extent to which the distribution is not symmetric, the mean may or may not be the appropriate measure of centrality.

Comparing Averages

It should also be noted that there are many instances in which a comparison of the same average over two distributions may be misleading. In Figure 3.5(e), for example, we might, upon learning that the two groups have identical means, conclude that the two groups are identical. But this would be an obviously incorrect conclusion. The identical means are simply a reflection of two very differently shaped distributions. In this instance we see the weakness of using only a measure of centrality to describe a distribution. (In Chapter 4 we shall see how distributions can be more completely described by reporting, along with a measure of centrality, a corresponding measure of dispersion.)

Which Average to Use?

Choosing an appropriate average to describe a set of data depends not only on the shape of the distribution (see previous paragraph) but also on the purpose to be served by the statistical measures used. It is essential to remember that statistical measures are only tools to aid us in our thinking, and proper use of these tools demands that we know why they are being used (not merely how to use them). Before we can decide which average to use as an indicator of the average homicide rate, we must have some understanding of why we want that particular piece of information. If we want to estimate the total number of murders, we should use the mean; if we want to know which homicide rate is most common, we should use the mode; if we want to locate our hometown's rate relative to all others, we should use the

(a) Normal Distribution
(e.g., IQ)

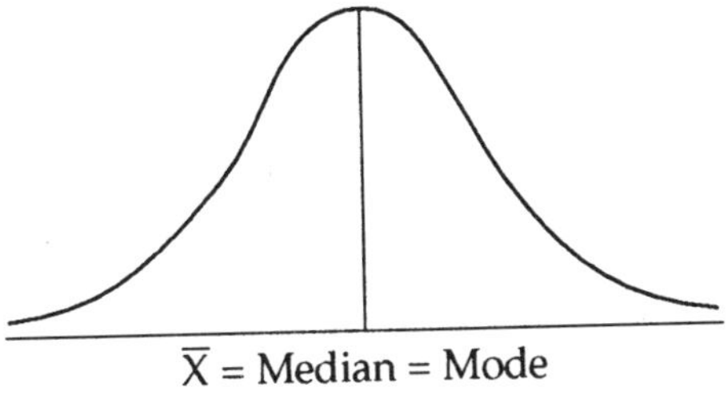

(b) Positively Skewed
Distribution
(e.g., income)

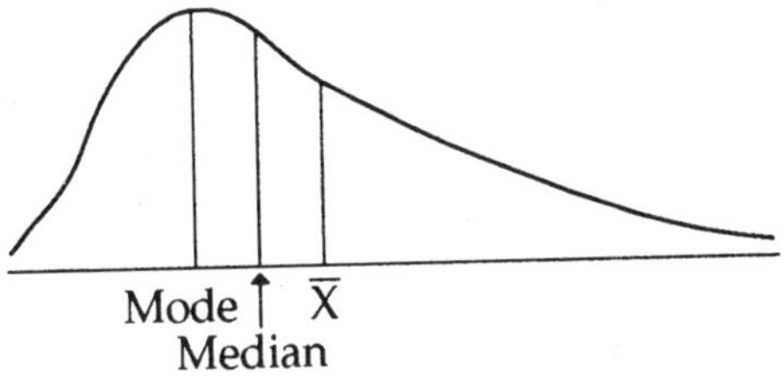

(c) Negatively Skewed
Distribution (e.g.,
grade-point average)

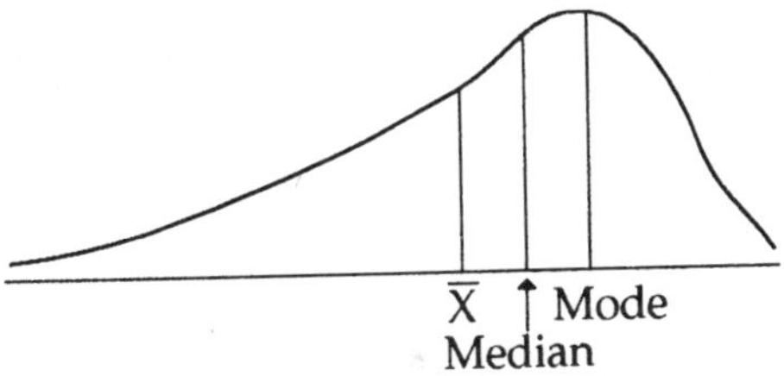

(d) Symmetric, Bimodal
Distribution

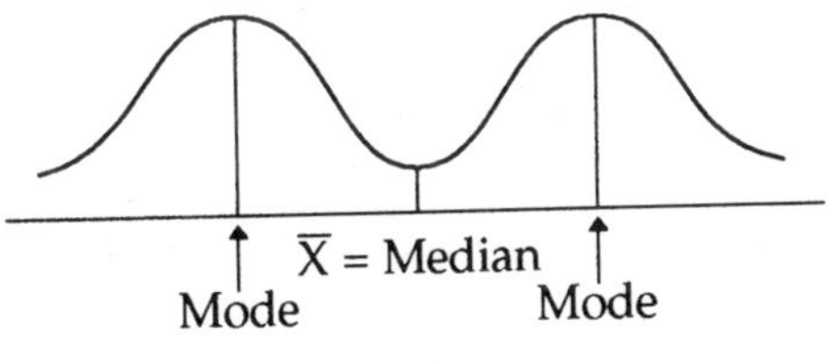

(e) Different
Distributions,
Identical Means

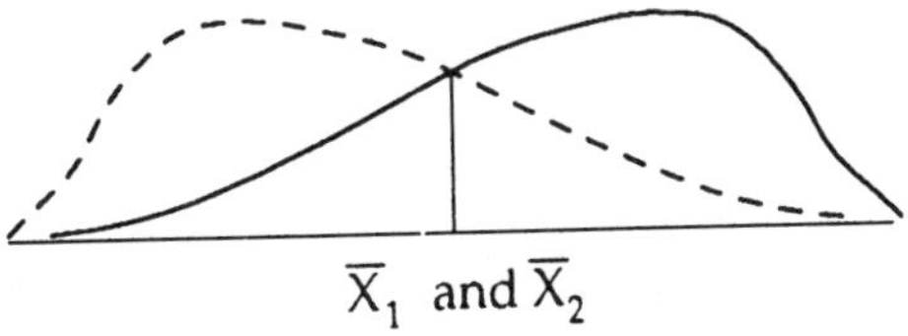

Figure 3.5. *Central Locations for Differently Shaped Distributions*

Table 3.10. *Summary of Characteristics of Mode, Median, and Mean*

	Mode	Median	Mean
Chief conceptual characteristic	Most *frequent* value in a distribution	Middle *location* in a distribution	Represents the *value* of every item in a distribution
Number in a distribution	One or more	One and only one	One and only one
Can it be arithmetically manipulated?	No	No	Yes
Applicable to which levels of measurement?	Nominal, ordinal, or interval (and ratio)	Ordinal or interval (and ratio)	Interval (and ratio) only

median (or one of its related quartiles). (Can you see why each average answers, in effect, a different question, tells us something different about the data? If not, you should review this chapter.)

In conclusion, Table 3.10 summarizes the major characteristics of the three averages.

An SPSS Example

SPSS also uses the FREQUENCIES (see Chapter 2) command to generate measure of centrality. In the following example, we will look at the age at which a person was married (AGEWED) for a sample of 353 adults.

The basic command, FREQUENCIES, is the same as in the previous chapter. What is different is the subcommands used to generate the specific statistics. In the following example, I have used the /STATISTICS subcommand to calculate the mean, median, and mode for the AGEWED variable; I also used /PERCENTILES to generate the first quartile (that is, the twenty-fifth percentile), the sixty-seventh percentile, and the ninth decile (that is, the ninetieth percentile).

The output first produces the frequency distribution for the named variable; the frequency table is immediately followed by the statistics that were requested.

AGEWED Example

```
FREQUENCIES AGEWED
 /STATISTICS = MEAN MEDIAN MODE
 /PERCENTILES = 25 67 90
```

AGEWED AGE WHEN FIRST MARRIED

Value Label	Value	Frequency	Pct	Valid Pct	Cum Pct
	14	1	.3	.4	.4
	15	1	.3	.4	.7
	16	8	2.3	2.9	3.6
	17	11	3.1	4.0	7.6
	18	33	9.3	12.0	19.6
	19	24	6.8	8.7	28.3
	20	32	9.1	11.6	39.9
	21	27	7.6	9.8	49.6
	22	24	6.8	8.7	58.3
	23	17	4.8	6.2	64.5
	24	19	5.4	6.9	71.4
	25	20	5.7	7.2	78.6
	26	11	3.1	4.0	82.6
	27	9	2.5	3.3	85.9
	28	7	2.0	2.5	88.4
	29	6	1.7	2.2	90.6
	30	8	2.3	2.9	93.5
	31	2	.6	.7	94.2
	32	5	1.4	1.8	96.0

(continued)

(continued)

	33	3	.8	1.1	97.1
	35	2	.6	.7	97.8
	36	1	.3	.4	98.2
	37	1	.3	.4	98.6
	38	1	.3	.4	98.9
	39	1	.3	.4	99.3
	43	1	.3	.4	99.6
	4	1	.3	.4	100.0
NAP	0	74	21.0	Missing	
DK	98	1	.3	Missing	
NA	99	2	.6	Missing	
		-----	------	------	
Total		353	100.0	100.0	

Mean 22.656 Median 22.000 Mode 18.000

Percentile	Value	Percentile	Value	Percentile	Value
25.00	19.000	67.00	24.000	90.00	29.000

Valid cases 276 Missing cases 77

Thus, we see that for this variable, AGEWED, the mean is 22.7 years. The median is 22, so we know that half of the sample were married before, and half after, the age of 22. And the age at which most people (33 people, to be exact) were married is 18 years. The twenty-fifth percentile (or first quartile) is found to be 19 years; in other words, about 25 percent of the subjects are less than 19 years of age and about 75 percent are older than 19. The ninetieth percentile (or ninth decile) is 29 years. These data were obtained from 276 subjects; 77 persons did not provide information about their age at marriage—some of them, undoubtedly, because they were not married.

Important Terms

Mode	Mean
Median	Summation command (Σ)
Quartile	Deviation score (x)
Decile	Guessed mean
Centile	Skewness

Suggested Readings

Anderson and Zelditch (1975: 65-79); Blalock (1979, Chap. 5); Kachigan (1986, Chap. 4); Ott et al. (1992, Chap. 4); Runyon and Haber (1984, Chaps. 2 and 3).

Quick Quiz Answers

Quick Quiz 3.1

(A) 16 (B) Brown (C) 102

Quick Quiz 3.2

(A) 17.5

(C) $\text{Mdn} = 99.5 + \frac{10.5}{19}(5) = 99.5 + 2.76 = 102.26$

Quick Quiz 3.3

(A) $D_9 = 18.5 - \frac{14.5 - 8}{9}(2)$

$= 18.5 - 1.44 = 17.06$

(B) $C_{16} = 2.5 + \frac{23.2 - 10}{28}(2)$

$= 2.5 + 0.94 = 3.44$

Important Symbols Introduced in This Chapter

f — f is the symbol for *frequency*, the number of times that a given score occurs.

N — N is the symbol for the *number* of cases. It is similar to frequency, but N usually refers to a total, while f usually refers to a subtotal, or a total within a category.

Mo — Mo is the symbol for the *mode*. The mode represents the score or category that occurs most frequently in a distribution of scores or categories.

Mdn — Mdn is the symbol for the *median*. The median is the value that occupies the middle position in a distribution of ordered scores.

Q — Q is the symbol for a *quartile*. Any distribution of ordered scores has three quartile points that divide the distribution into four equal parts. The first quartile is the point above the bottom 25 percent of the scores in the distribution; the third quartile is the point above the lower 75 percent of the scores. [NOTE: Related symbols are D (for *decile*) and C (for *centile*). Deciles divide a distribution into ten equal parts; centiles into one hundred equal parts. A *quintile* divides a distribution into five equal parts.]

X — This symbol is used to represent any given value or score in a distribution.

$\bar{X}$ — Read as X-bar; this is the symbol for the *mean*. The mean is the average that takes into account the numerical value of each score.

x — When used in the lower case, x represents a deviation *score*, that is, the difference between any given value of X and the mean.

Σ — The Greek letter *Sigma*, here used in the upper case, is a mathematical command to add the values that follow the Sigma. For example, ΣX means to add all values of X.

4

Measures of Dispersion

At the end of Chapter 3, we stated that by itself, a measure of central tendency is not sufficient to describe a set of data fully and properly. The reason for this is that such measures focus attention on only one aspect of the data, centrality, and in doing so suppress any information that shows the extent to which the data depart from centrality. An example should help to illustrate the importance of describing data by providing information about both centrality and dispersion. Consider the following sets of data:

A:	93, 93, 93, 93, 93
B:	92, 93, 93, 93, 94
C:	91, 92, 93, 94, 95
D:	89, 91, 93, 95, 97
E:	73, 83, 93, 103, 113

For each of these sets the mean (and median) is 93. If all we knew about the data sets was these average scores, we might readily conclude that the five groups were quite similar, if not identical. But clearly the groups are not identical, and not even similar in the more extreme comparisons (such as A vs. E). In group A, each score is identical to every other score; the chosen average is perfectly representative of the entire set; there is no deviation from centrality, no dispersion. In B, there is some variation in scores, but the mean (or median) is still quite representative; the amount of dispersion is slight. But in D, and especially in E, the scores diverge from each other and from the mean to a marked degree, and in these instances we can begin to question seriously how representative our average scores really are. From these simple examples we can see that we need more than a measure of centrality if we wish to describe a set of data fully and properly.

Ranges

The range is the simplest of all the measures. It is the distance between the highest score and the lowest score in a distribution in which the high and low scores are determined by the true upper and lower limits. (For a review of true limits, see Chapter 2.) Expressed as a formula

(Formula 4.1)

$$\text{Range} = (\text{True Upper Limit}) - (\text{True Lower Limit})$$

For example, we can find the range of the scores from the previous group C by determining the true limits of this distribution and subtracting. The true lower limit of 91 is 90.5; the true upper limit of 95 is 95.5. Therefore,

$$\text{Range} = 95.5 - 90.5 = 5.0$$

To say that the range of these scores is 5 is to say that the scores in this distribution all lie within a distance that is five units large. A glance at groups A and E tells us that the range of A is 1 and the range of E is 41. Knowing these ranges, we do not have to examine entire data sets to learn that group E is spread over a greater distance than is C, or that C covers more ground than does A. For grouped data, the computation is the same except that we use the true limits of the highest and lowest *categories*.

The range is easy to compute and comprehend, but it is a very crude measure of dispersion, and certain cautions are necessary when using the range. (To a greater or lesser degree, all measures of dispersion are subject to the following deficiencies.)

1. Most important, the range is greatly affected by extreme scores (for it is, after all, defined by the extreme scores). Because of this, a set of data whose elements are for the most part quite similar, such as 4, 5, 5, 5, 6, 6, 7, 36, can appear to be quite dissimilar if the range is used as measure of dispersion. In this

example, although most of the scores are actually quite close to one another, the relatively large range of 33 indicates a considerable amount of spread in the data; but most of this spread is due to the single score of 36, a score that may or may not be truly representative of the entire data set.

2. In general, ranges cannot be compared with each other unless they are based on a similar number of observations. For example, in Table 3.3 (page 42), the range of homicide rates is 22. But the range would probably be smaller than 22 if it was computed from a sample of only 15 cities instead of 145. The smaller sample has a smaller probability of including any given score, especially any given extreme score.
3. Like all measures of dispersion, ranges should have some standard of comparison. For example, it is not enough to state that the income range of a group of families is $18,000, for it probably makes an important difference if we are talking about a group whose incomes lie between $0 and $18,000, or a group whose incomes lie between $65,000 and $83,000.
4. Ranges do not give us any information about the pattern of variation. Figure 4.1 illustrates three distributions whose ranges are identical. But using only the range as a measure of dispersion does not permit us to distinguish which group has its scores concentrated at one extreme or the other or in the middle.

Because the range is especially subject to influence by extreme scores, many people prefer to use intermediate ranges that, by definition, eliminate from consideration and computation a proportion of the extreme scores. Quite common is the *interdecile* range, the distance between the ninth and first decile points:

(Formula 4.2)

$$\text{Interdecile Range} = D_9 - D_1$$

For example, in the previous chapter we computed the ninth and first deciles for the distribution of homicide rates; the corresponding values were 17.06 and 2.82. Thus, for these data, the interdecile range is 17.06 - 2.82 = 14.24. Compare this to the total range of 22.0. Note that the interdecile range eliminates from consideration the top 10 percent and the bottom 10 percent of scores, thereby focusing attention on the middle 80 percent of scores in a distribution.

Another commonly used range is the *interquartile range*, defined as the distance between the third and first quartiles of a distribution.

(Formula 4.3)

$$\text{Interquartile Range} = Q_3 - Q_1$$

This range excludes the extreme 50 percent of cases (25 percent from each extreme) and focuses on the middle 50 percent. For the homicide rate data, the interquartile range is expressed as follows:

$$Q_3 - Q_1 = 14.09 - 4.38 = 9.71$$

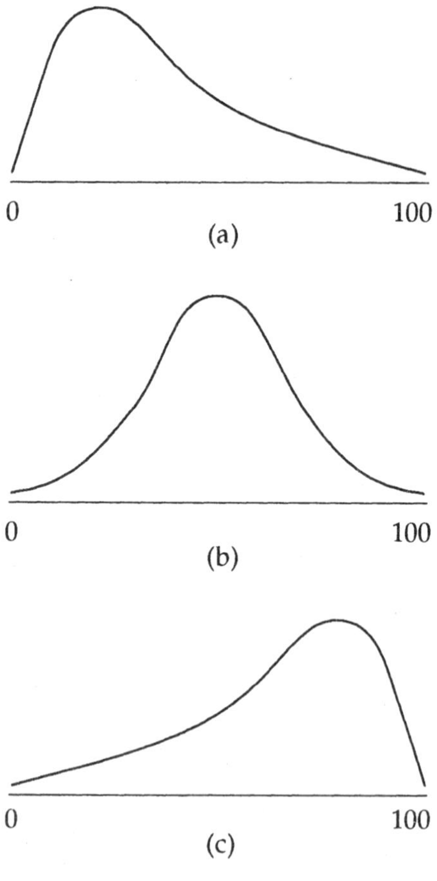

Figure 4.1. *Identical Ranges, Different Patterns of Dispersion*

The great virtue of intermediate ranges is that they reduce the influence of extreme scores. Thus, even though the total range of family incomes in the many large cities is well over several million dollars, we get a more realistic picture of typical family incomes by noting that the interdecile range is about, let us say, \$10,000 and the interquartile range is about, say, \$5,000. These intermediate ranges display the relative similarities of the incomes of most families, a pattern that is hidden by the total range.

Deviation Measures

The Average Deviation

Another way of viewing the concept of dispersion (or spread, deviation, variation) is to ask, Deviation from what? Variation about what? And how much dispersion? For example, let us take the set of scores from Table 4.1. If we use the mean ($\overline{X} = 7$) as our measure of centrality, we can ask, How much does each score deviate from the mean? The deviation score $x = (X - \overline{X})$ is recorded in column 2. Its sum, as we learned in Chapter 3, is zero. Clearly, because the value of Σx for every distribution is zero, we cannot use the sum of deviations as a measure of dispersion. But suppose we discarded the *sign* of the deviation (that is, we pay no attention to whether a score is above or below the mean, positive or negative) and consider only the *distance* that separates each score from the mean. This value, *the absolute value* of x, is represented by the symbol $|x|$ and is recorded in column 3. If we sum these absolute deviations from the mean, we obtain $\Sigma|x| = 12$, which is a measure of the total amount of deviation from the mean, disregarding signs. Because this value is based, in our example, on five scores, we can now define the *average* (mean) *deviation* from the mean ($AD_{\overline{X}}$) as

(Formula 4.4)

$$AD_{\overline{X}} = \frac{\Sigma(f|x|)}{N}$$

For these data, $AD_{\overline{X}} = 12/5 = 2.4$. This can be interpreted by stating that disregarding direction, the mean distance of each score from the mean is 2.4 units of measurement.

Table 4.1. *Dispersion Example*

X	x	$\lvert x \rvert$	x^2	d	$\lvert d \rvert$	d^2
4	-3	3	9	-2	2	4
5	-2	2	4	-1	1	1
6	-1	1	1	0	0	0
7	0	0	0	1	1	1
13	6	6	36	7	7	78
35	0	12	50	5	11	55
	$\overline{X} = 7$				Median = 6	

Although average deviation is usually understood to be deviation from the mean, we can also compute the average (mean) deviation from the median, or from any other point. To compute AD_{Mdn} we must first define d as the difference between any score and the median. (Note from column 5 that the sum of these scores is not zero; d will never be zero unless the mean and median are identical.) Again we compute the absolute value, $\lvert d \rvert$, as found in column 6, and sum. We can then define the average (mean) deviation from the median as

(Formula 4.5)

$$AD_{Mdn} = \frac{\Sigma(f\lvert d \rvert)}{N}$$

For these data, $AD_{Mdn} = 11/5 = 2.2$. This can be understood by stating that disregarding sign, the mean distance of each score from the median is 2.2 units of measurement.

You may note from this example that AD_{Mdn} is smaller than $AD_{\overline{X}}$. This will always be the case whenever a distribution is skewed. If a distribution is not skewed, that is, if it is symmetric, the mean and median will be identical and will equal $AD_{\overline{X}}$. This observation leads to the general rule that *whenever a distribution is markedly skewed, the median is the preferred statistic to use as a measure of central tendency* or as the basis for a measure of dispersion. This is so because the median is the point in a distribution that is closest (in terms of absolute value) to all other scores in the distribution.

The Standard Deviation

Because the average deviation is such an easy statistic to compute and understand, you may wonder why we do not make more use of it in social research, and why we must move on to an examination of other measures of dispersion. There are several reasons for this. First, for all practical purposes, the AD is a dead-end statistic. Once it is computed, there is little else that can be done with it. There are other measures that lend themselves to further and more useful statistical applications. Second, the interpretation of the AD, although quite clear, does not provide us with as much information about a distribution as do some other measures. Finally, there are certain mathematical properties of the *standard deviation* (properties that are beyond the scope of this book) that make it by far the preferred measure of dispersion.

Just as the average deviation is based on the concept of absolute deviations from some norm, the standard deviation is based on the concept of *squared deviations* from the mean. A return glance at Table 4.1 will help to clarify the very important *principle of least squares.* Column 4 contains the values of x^2, the squared deviations from the mean; column 7 contains the values of d^2, the squared deviations from the median. Note that $\Sigma x^2 = 50$ is less than $\Sigma d^2 = 55$. This will *always* be so unless the mean and median are identical, for the mean is that point in a distribution that minimizes squared deviations (just as the median is that point that minimizes absolute deviations). This is sometimes called the *least squares principle.*

The value Σx^2 is often referred to as the *sum of squares* and is sometimes symbolized as SS. We generally do not use SS as a measure of dispersion because this measure does not consider the number of cases upon which the sum of squares is based. But if we divide SS by the number of observations, we have an appropriate measure of the *mean squared deviations from the mean,* sometimes called the *mean square.* (The sum of squares, SS, will reappear as a crucial concept in our discussion of analysis of variance in Chapter 8.) The technical name for this value is the *variance*. It is symbolized as σ^2 (the lowercase Greek letter Sigma) or s^2, and its computational formulas are

(Formula 4.6)

$$\sigma^2 = \frac{\Sigma\,(x^2)}{N}$$

*(Formula 4.7)**

$$s^2 = \frac{\Sigma (x^2)}{n - 1}$$

For the data from Table 4.1 (assuming a population),

$$s^2 = \frac{50}{5} = 10.0$$

The standard deviation, σ or s, is simply the positive square root of the variance. Because the variance was computed by squaring, it is not unreasonable to "unsquare" this value. Thus, the formulas for the standard deviation are

(Formula 4.8)

$$\sigma = \sqrt{\frac{\Sigma x^2}{N}}$$

(Formula 4.9)

$$s = \sqrt{\frac{\Sigma x^2}{(n - 1)}}$$

---

*Statisticians usually (but not always) distinguish between values obtained from a *population* and values obtained from a segment or *sample* of a population. In notational terms this distinction is usually symbolized by using Greek letters for population values and Roman letters for sample values. Therefore, in Formula 4.6 the variance is symbolized as σ^2 (a lowercase Sigma squared) when it is based on population data,and as s^2 when based on sample data in Formula 4.7. (Note, too, that N is used for the size of a population and n for the size of a sample.)

Because sample statistics often have an error built into them, computational formulas are occasionally adjusted to account for such error. In the cases of the variance and standard deviation, this adjustment is made by using (n - 1) in the denominator instead of N. This increases slightly the value of the sample statistic, thus making it more accurate. Of course, if n is large, such an adjustment will be negligible, but when samples are relatively small, the adjustment should always be made.

For the data from Table 4.1 (assuming a population),

$$\sigma = \sqrt{\frac{50}{5}} = \sqrt{10} = 3.16$$

Thus, the standard deviation is somewhat analogous to the average deviation except that the standard deviation is based on squared deviations whose mean is then unsquared and the average deviation is based directly on absolute deviations.

The standard deviation and the variance are obviously closely related, but the relationship is not based simply on a square root sign. It will be shown that the standard deviation is a linear measure, that is, it measures distance and the variance measures area.

Computing Formulas, Ungrouped Data

The previous formulas for variance and standard deviation are useful to help us remember the conceptual meaning of the statistics in question. However, when the number of cases is large, computation becomes quite cumbersome. In such circumstances it is generally more useful to use the following formulas (even though they have no obvious meaning).

(Formula 4.10)

$$SS = \Sigma x^2 = \Sigma X^2 - \frac{(\Sigma X)^2}{N}$$

(Formula 4.11)

$$\sigma^2 = \frac{SS}{N} = \frac{\Sigma X^2}{N} - \left(\frac{\Sigma X}{N}\right)^2$$

(Formula 4.12)

$$s^2 = \frac{\Sigma X^2 - (\Sigma X^2/N)}{n - 1}$$

$$= \frac{295 - (35^2/5)}{5 - 1}$$

$$= 50/4 = 12.5$$

Table 4.2. *Computation of Variance and Standard Deviation*

X	X^2	Computation of SS	Computation of σ^2 and σ
4	16	$\Sigma x^2 = \Sigma X^2 - \frac{(\Sigma X)^2}{N}$	$\sigma^2 = \frac{295}{5} - \left(\frac{35}{5}\right)^2$
5	25		
6	36	$\Sigma x^2 = 295 - \frac{(35)^2}{5}$	$= 59 - 7^2$
7	49		$= 59 - 49$
13	169	$= 295 - \frac{1225}{5}$	$= 10$
35	295		
		$= 295 - 245$	$\sigma = \sqrt{10}$
		$= 50$	$= 3.16$

From these formulas the standard deviation can be readily computed simply by extracting the square root of the variance. A great advantage of these formulas is that they operate directly on the raw scores; they do not require the calculations of intermediate values such as means and deviations. Table 4.2 illustrates the application of the formulas to the data from Table 4.1. In this simple example, the computing formulas may seem overly complicated, but with a larger or more diverse data set, these formulas will save much time and work.

Quick Quiz
4.1

(A) For the following population data, compute SS, σ^2, and σ.
(B) Assume that the same data are obtained from a sample. Compute s^2 and s.

-1, 1, 2, 3, 5

Formulas for Grouped Data

When data are grouped, the procedure for computing these measures of variation is analogous to that used for the mean; that is, we use the same basic formulas but modify them to account for frequencies and the size of class intervals. Note that in the following formulas we again assume that the deviations are located at the midpoints of class intervals and are defined as deviations from a guessed mean.

(Formula 4.13)

$$SS = \Sigma fx^2 = \left[(\Sigma fx')^2 / N \right] (i^2)$$

(Formula 4.14)

$$\sigma^2 = \frac{\Sigma fx^2}{N} = \frac{\Sigma f(x')^2 - \left[(\Sigma fx')^2 / N \right]}{N} (i^2)$$

There are several points to note about these formulas. (1) From Formula 4.14 we can readily compute the standard deviation by extracting the square root of the variance. (2) We have not indicated a separate formula to distinguish sample data from population data. The reason for this is that we assumed that grouped data will always have a sufficiently large N, so that the correction factor of replacing N with (n - 1) is negligible and unnecessary. (3) In computational work, do not confuse the quantity fx'^2 with the quantity $(fx')^2$; remember that the former term refers to the frequency times the squared deviation; in the latter term the frequency is multiplied by the deviation and the product is squared.

The Standard Deviation and the Normal Distribution

We have now described several measures of variation based on deviation scores. The average deviation has little utility in modern statistical work. The sum of squares and variance are quite important and useful, and we will discuss these further in Chapter 8. In many respects, the standard deviation is the most important measure of dispersion. This importance comes from the special relationship that exists between the standard deviation and the normal distribution, a relationship that gives the standard deviation a very elegant and useful interpretation.

A normal distribution is one that is based on a theoretically infinite number of cases. It is unimodal and symmetric. When graphed as a frequency curve, this distribution resembles the familiar bell-shaped curve, which can be used as an approximation of the distribution of numerous variables: IQ scores, heights of American males, measurement errors, sampling distributions, and others. What is vitally important about the normal distribution is that *between any two points in a normal distribution we can specify the proportion of the corresponding area that lies under the curve.* This can be best illustrated by using as one point the mean of a distribution and as a second point some standard deviation unit. The normal distribution in Figure 4.2 has a mean of 0.00 and a standard deviation of 1.00. In this case, and in any normal distribution, the distance from the mean to +1s (or from the mean to -1s) includes 34.13 percent of the area under the curve. Therefore, the distance from +1s to -1s includes 68.26 percent of the area. The distance from the mean to +2s (or from the mean to -2s) includes 47.72 percent of the area under the curve; therefore, the distance from +2s to -2s includes 95.44 percent of the area. From the mean to +3s includes 49.85 percent of the area, and from +3s to -3s includes 99.72 percent. We can similarly define the area corresponding to the distance between any two points when those points are expressed as standard deviation units, which in this context are commonly known as z-scores.

A z-score is a measure of deviation from the mean, relative to the standard deviation; that is, it is a deviation score expressed in standard deviation units. (For this reason, it is also called a standard score.) Symbolically,

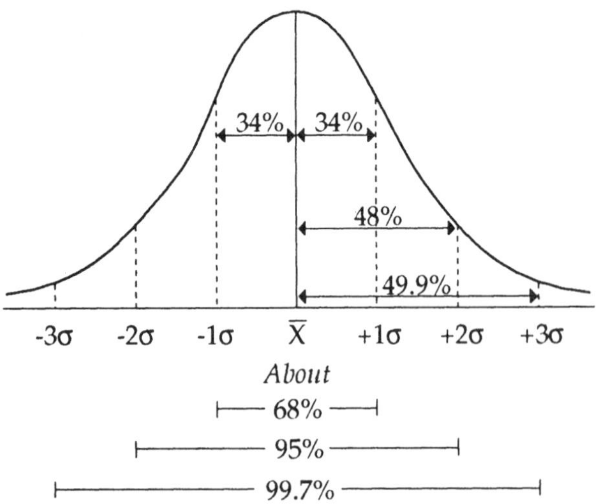

Figure 4.2. *The Standard Deviation and the Normal Distribution*

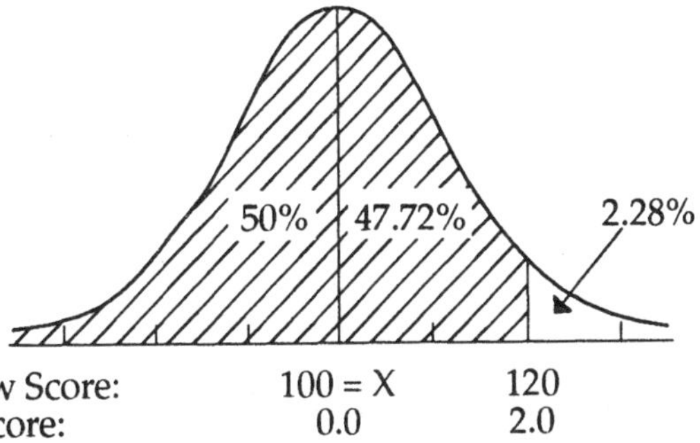

Figure 4.3. *Raw Scores and z-Scores, an Example*

(Formula 4.15)

$$z = \frac{X - \overline{X}}{\sigma} = \frac{x}{\sigma}$$

A z-score thus expresses any raw score as being a certain number of standard deviations above or below the mean.

For example, suppose we have an approximately normal distribution whose mean is 100 and whose standard deviation is 10. In this distribution we observe that a certain score is equal to 120. The score of 120 is thus twenty units above the mean. If we divide this deviation score, x = 20, by the standard deviation, we obtain a z-score of +2.00. In other words, the score of 120 lies two standard units above the mean. Because we already know something about the relationship between standard deviation units and the area under a normal curve, we can now determine rather accurately the location of the score of 120 relative to all other scores in the distribution. This location can be expressed as a centile. The exact centile locations are obtained from a table (Appendix Table A). But for the moment we do not need the table, since we know that a z-score of +2.0 corresponds to an area of 47.72 percent (from X to z). The score of 120 is thus above 48 percent + 50 percent = 98 percent of all scores in the distribution. Figure 4.3 describes this.

Following are other z-scores calculated for a distribution whose mean is 100 and whose standard deviation is 10.

Score	z	Area from $\bar{X}$ to z	Centile
100	0.00	.0000	50.00
105	+0.50	.1915	69.15
90	-1.00	.3413	15.87
87	-1.30	.4032	9.68
123	+2.30	.4893	98.93

Notice that the centile values are found in two different ways, depending on whether the z-score is positive or negative. If the z-score is positive, the area obtained from column B of Table A is *added* to 0.5000; if the z-score is negative, the obtained area is *subtracted* from 0.5000. To convince yourself of this, draw a normal curve, locate each of the given z-scores, and shade in the corresponding areas.

Similarly, we can find the area corresponding to the distance between any two points. For example, if we want to know what proportion of scores fall between 105 and 123, we simply subtract the corresponding areas (*not* z-scores). The area corresponding to a raw score of 123 is .4893 and the area corresponding to a raw score of 105 is .1915. Therefore, the area between 105 and 123 is .4893 - .1915 = .2978. (See Figure 4.4.) As noted, it is always useful to draw a figure that illustrates the problem. This will help to clarify where z-scores are in relation to the mean and whether to add or to subtract areas from each other or from .5000.

Quick Quiz
4.2

Given the data below, compute the appropriate z-score.

(A) X = 23, X = 20, s = 4
(B) X = 415, X = 500, s = 100
(C) X = 100, X = 70, s = 12

For simplicity's sake we have treated these z-scores as discrete values. (In other words, we have not considered true limits.) More frequently, however, we will treat scores as indicators of continuous values. When this is done, it is important to recall that true limits should be observed (see Chapter 2). For example, if the scores of 105 and 123 are assumed to reflect a continuous variable, to determine the area corresponding to the distance between these scores, we must deal with the lower limit of 105, which is 104.5 and the upper limit of 123, which is 123.5. The corresponding z-scores and areas are as given below and the area between 105 (actually 104.5) and 123 (actually 123.5) is .4906 - .1736 = .3170. In other words, nearly 32 percent of all scores fall between 104.5 and 123.5.

Raw Score	True Limit	z-score	Area
105	104.5	0.4	.1736
123	123.5	2.35	.4906

Quick Quiz
4.3

If an IQ test has a mean of 100 and a standard deviation of 15, what proportion of all scores fall between 90 and 120?

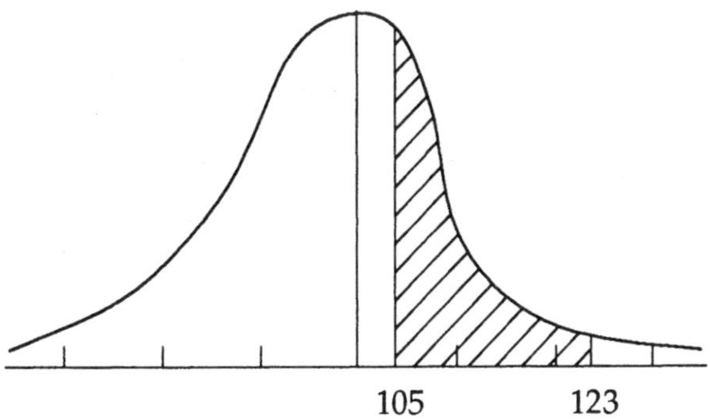

Figure 4.4. *The Area Between Two Scores*

An SPSS Example: z-Scores

[NOTE: In this chapter, we will not show you how to use SPSS to generate measures of dispersion, such as the standard deviation or variance. Suffice it to say that these statistics can be obtained from the FREQUENCIES procedure.]

To create z-scores, SPSS uses a procedure called DESCRIPTIVES. This procedure requires only a few very simple commands: a list of the variables that you wish to have converted to z-scores and the /SAVE subcommand. (It is this /SAVE subcommand that actually creates the z-scores.)

You must also ask for a LIST of the variables and their z-scores.

You will receive as output a list of the variables with their corresponding z-scores; you will also receive some basic descriptive statistics for the named variables.

In the following example, I have asked for the z-scores for the variables AGE and EDUC. Note that I have also asked only for the first 5 cases. (If I did not specify only the first 5 cases, I would have received information for all 353 cases in my sample.)

DESCRIPTIVES Example

DESCRIPTIVES AGE EDUC /SAVE

File: GENERAL SOCIAL SURVEY (NORC) 1990

Number of valid observations (listwise) = 353.00

Variable	Mean	Std Dev	Min	Max	Valid N	Label
AGE	44.52	17.91	18	89	353	AGE OF R
EDUC	12.98	2.91	4	20	353	HGST YR OF SCH

(continued)

(continued)

The following Z-Score variables have been saved on your active file:

From Variable	To Z-Score	Label	Weighted Valid N
AGE	ZAGE	Zscore: AGE OF RESPONDENT	353
EDUC	ZEDUC	Zscore: HIGHEST YEAR OF SCHOOL COMPLETED	353

LIST VARIABLES = AGE ZAGE EDUC ZEDUC /CASES FROM 1 TO 5

AGE	ZAGE	EDUC	ZEDUC
65	1.14374	16	1.03912
55	0.58540	8	-1.71367
53	0.47373	14	0.35092
68	1.31125	12	-0.33728
69	1.36708	12	-0.33728

Number of cases read: 5 Number of cases listed: 5

Look at the last part of the output. The first subject is someone who is 65 years old and who has sixteen years of education. For AGE, the raw score of 65 corresponds to a z-score of 1.14; that is, this person is a little more than one standard deviation above the average (mean) age for the entire sample. This person's EDUC score, expressed as a standard score, is +1.04; again, this person is about one standard deviation above the mean on the EDUC variable. If the table is converted to percentiles, this person could be described as being at about the eighty-fifth percentile in EDUC.

Important Terms

Range
Interdecile range
Interquartile range
Average deviation
Standard deviation
Principle of least squares
Sum of squares
Variance
z-score

Suggested Readings

Levin and Fox (1991, Chap. 5); Mueller, Schuessler, and Costner (1970: 152-179); Phillips (1988, Chap. 4).

Quick Quiz Answers

Quick Quiz 4.1

X	x	x^2	X^2
-1	-3	9	1
1	-1	1	1
2	0	0	4
3	1	1	9
5	3	9	25
10	0	20	40

$\overline{X} = 2$

(A) SS = 20. If we use Formula 4.10,

$$SS = 40 - \frac{10^2}{5} = 40 - 20 = 20$$

$$\text{and } \sigma^2 = 20/5 = 4 \text{ and } \sigma = \sqrt{4} = 2$$

(B) $s^2 = 20/(5-1) = 5$ and $s = \sqrt{5} = 2.24$

Quick Quiz 4.2

(A) $z = \frac{23 - 20}{4} = \frac{3}{4} = 0.75$

$$(B)\ z = \frac{415 - 500}{100} = \frac{-85}{100} = -0.85$$

$$(C)\ z = \frac{100 - 70}{12} = \frac{30}{120} = +2.50$$

Quick Quiz 4.3

$$z_{89.5} = \frac{89.5 - 100}{15} = \frac{-10.5}{15} = -0.70 \text{ (Area = .2580)}$$

$$z_{120.5} = \frac{120.5 - 100}{15} = \frac{20.5}{15} = +1.37 \text{ (Area = .4147)}$$

The total area is .2580 + .4147 = .6727. Thus, 67 percent of all scores fall between 89.5 and 120.5. (See following illustration.)

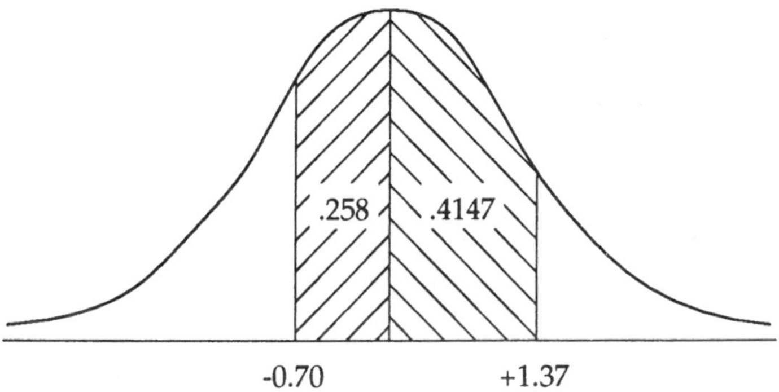

5

Bases of Statistical Inference, I: Probability and the Logic of Hypothesis Testing

In the first four chapters of this book we discussed simple descriptive statistics. In this chapter and subsequent chapters we shall deal with inferential statistics. Descriptive statistics provide us with a quantitative "picture" of some aspect of the world. Such statistics may be drawn from populations or samples and, strictly speaking, apply only to the population or sample from which the statistic was derived. For example, the decennial census of the United States gives us many descriptive measures of the American population. These census data apply only to the United States and cannot be used to describe any other population. Inferential statistics also give us a picture of some aspect of the world. But inferential statistics differ from descriptive statistics in that the former enable us to generalize beyond the data at hand. For example, public opinion polls such as those of Gallup or Harris measure the opinions of approximately 1,500 people and from the descriptive measures derived from the sample *infer* a description of the opinions of the entire American population. What makes such inferences possible? How can we trust that the opinions of 1,500 people will accurately reflect the opinions of millions? The answers to such questions lie with the concepts of probability and sampling, the subjects of this and the next chapter.

Probability: A Way of Viewing the World

1. The early morning weather forecast states that there is a 30 percent chance of rain today.
2. At the pregame coin toss, the team captain calls heads but knows that tails is equally likely to occur.
3. On a multiple-choice test with four options, a student who doesn't know the answer makes a pure guess, "c."
4. At the roulette table a chip is placed on number 13.

These are but a few of the many events in our day-to-day lives that are affected by the "laws" of probability. When situations involving probabilities are stated this way, they do not seem difficult to grasp. The statistician, however, uses the language of mathematics, and the previous statements as rendered by a statistician might look like this:

1. Pr(rain) = .30 [and, by implication, Pr(no-rain) = .70]
2. Pr(heads) = .50 [and, by implication, Pr(tails) = .50]
3. Pr(right) = .25 [and Pr(wrong) = .75]
4. Pr(13) = .0263 [and Pr(not 13) = .9737]

Such probability statements are used for two purposes. First, they help us to make *inferences* about events that have not yet occurred; they do this, of course, by telling us how likely it is that the event in question will occur. Second, they help us to make certain kinds of *decisions* concerning those events. In example 1, we might make the following inference: In the past one hundred days when weather conditions were similar to those of today, it rained thirty of the days; therefore, it is reasonable to infer that the chances of rain today are 30/100 = 0.30 = 30 percent. We can then use this inference to make a decision: Shall we take an umbrella or not? The decision we actually make will be based on many factors besides the probability statement itself, such as whether we are wearing good or old clothes, whether the corn on our big toe is hurting, how much of a risk we are willing to take that we won't get wet, and the like. In example 2, the inference is simpler: When a fair coin is tossed, heads will come up as often as tails. The decision is equally simple: If the coin is fair, it really doesn't matter whether one calls heads or tails, and whichever choice is made will be perfectly idiosyncratic. In example 4 the inference might be, "I have one chance in thirty-eight of winning, so the odds against me are thirty-seven to one." The decision to bet or not to bet will again depend on many other factors. (But we might point out that because the house usually pays off at thirty-five to one when the true odds are thirty-seven to one, the only rational decision is to not play roulette except for amusement.)

How do we know that there is a 30 percent chance of rain today or a 50 percent chance of observing a head when a coin is tossed? One way of knowing about the behavior of the coin toss is *empirical observation*, from which we obtain *empirical probability*. We could, for example, take a coin and toss it once, twice, a hundred times, and we could ask twenty friends to do the same. If we observe the result, or *outcome*, of each of these 2,000 tosses, or trials, we would undoubtedly see something like this:

Number of heads = 1,000	Number of tails = 1,000
$\text{Pr (heads)} = \frac{1{,}000}{2{,}000} = .5$	$\text{Pr (tails)} = \frac{1{,}000}{2{,}000} = .5$

We might not get exactly 1,000 heads—there might be 1,013 heads and 987 tails—but the figure would be fairly close to 1,000. Because of this empirical observation that the number of heads is essentially equal to the number of tails, we could be quite confident that if we were to toss the coin another 2,000 times we would again get a result very close to a fifty-fifty split. In fact, this particular observation is so common in our experience that we rarely consider it.

Now suppose that at 6:00 A.M. every day we noted the temperature, wind velocity and direction, humidity, barometric pressure and activity, and other meteorological data. We then note whether it rains that day. After many, many such days we might begin to detect certain weather patterns. Soon we would be able to make predictions about the day's weather. We do so, in part, on the basis of the empirical probabilities that were established by previous observation. In this sense we see that empirical probability enables us to make guesses or predictions about some unknown event on the basis of known past events.

Just as much of the physical world is governed by probability, so it is with the social world. If I buy a five-year term insurance policy, I am "betting" that I will die within five years. My insurance premium is the amount of my bet, and the face value of the policy is the amount of the insurance company's wager. The ratio of the two bets gives the odds that I will die, and these odds are set by the company's actuarial tables, which from past experience show that a certain number of men in my age group die within five years.

In a similar fashion, a personnel manager wants to know whether the person to be hired will be a success or failure on the job. Therefore, she asks whether, in the past, people with certain background characteristics had better success records than persons with different background characteristics. In effect, she uses previous empirical observation to determine the probability of a future event. And on the basis of her inference, she decides to hire or not to hire the applicant.

A prison warden must decide whether to recommend parole for an inmate. Although there are many individual factors to consider, the final decision might be determined, in part, by the warden's formal or informal calculation of empirical probabilities for recidivism.

Just as we can calculate to some degree the probabilities concerning a coin toss, a throw of the dice, human death, and parole violations, so can we determine probabilities for other spheres of human activity. Indeed, the sociological concepts of norm and role might be thought of in probabilistic terms. A role can be defined as an expected pattern of behavior, and if we know that someone is playing a role, we can make certain predictions about that person's behavior. For example, if someone is occupying the role of teacher, it can be predicted that he will more often give than receive information in the classroom. Such predictions are not usually formalized into quantitative probability statements; they generally remain informal and subjective. But they do exist and we do use them to guide us in our everyday behavior. We could even argue that the social order is nothing more than a set of informal probability statements.

Order implies *predictability* and *interdependence*. The opposite condition of chaos implies the lack of predictability, independence. If social interaction is not ordered, we often say it is random, or subject to laws of chance. But the real world in which we live is neither completely ordered nor completely random. No one can predict another's behavior with 100 percent accuracy, and no one could survive if the correct prediction rate were zero. The sociologist's real world lies somewhere between perfect order and complete chaos. It is a probabilistic world. It is so because our knowledge of the world is never complete, is always subject to uncertainty, randomness, fate, chance, or probability.

Thus, any event (including a statistical event) is the result of two broad factors, those that are known and those that remain unknown. The former are called determining factors, the latter, chance factors.

For example, what causes delinquency? Some plausible causes are broken homes, association with delinquents, inadequate superego, failure in school, and so on. To a greater or lesser extent, delinquency is dependent on these factors, among others. But can we list *all* of the others? And do *all* children from broken homes become delinquents? Do *all* children from unbroken homes remain nondelinquent? Of course not. And this is where the unknown factors, or chance, come in. Chance is a residual category that includes all of the causes that we cannot specify. It is a measure of our ignorance. This ignorance need cause us no shame, because it is also important to know that-which-we-don't-know.

Having said all of this, we will now make what seems to be a totally contradictory statement: Under certain conditions *chance itself behaves in regular patterns.* Such conditions resemble games of chance. This is so because "for statistical purposes chance factors are presumed to be (1) very numerous, (2) relatively minute, (3) independent of one another and (4) very largely unidentifiable and, therefore, not measurable; consequently, (5) they work collectively—as far as we know—to produce equally likely events" (Mueller, Schuessler, and Costner 1970: 210).

Basic Rules of Probability

We have just seen that if it is possible to measure past outcomes, it is possible to calculate empirical probabilities. We do this by following several basic rules of probability.

Rule 1: The probability of any simple event (E) can be expressed as a ratio of the frequency (n) of any event to the total number (N) of trials in which the event might occur. This can be expressed as

(Formula 5.1)

$$Pr(E) = \frac{n}{N}$$

For example, suppose we record the sex of a random sample of 800 births in a given community. We note 412 girls and 388 boys. We can then make a prediction concerning the probability of a girl being born in that community. It is

$$\text{Pr (girl)} = \frac{412}{800} = .515$$

Often we are not interested in simple events but in events that occur together, such as rolling two dice. We may want to know the probability of rolling "snake-eyes" (two one-spots). This leads us to

Rule 2: The probability of a *compound event* (that is, of two or more *independent* events occurring together) is equal to the product of probability of the individual events. This can be expressed as

(Formula 5.2)

$$\text{Pr}(E_1 \textit{ and } E_2) = \text{Pr}(E_1) \times \text{Pr}(E_2)$$

In our example, the probability of rolling a one-spot with the first die is 1/6 and the probability of rolling a one-spot with the second die is also 1/6. Therefore, the joint or compound probability is

$$\frac{1}{6} \times \frac{1}{6} = \frac{1}{36} = .028$$

Finally, we are sometimes interested in the probability of any one of several specified events. For example, there are six ways of rolling a 7 with a pair of dice: 1 + 6, 2 + 5, 3 + 4, 4 + 3, 5 + 2, and 6 + 1. If we are only interested in the event of a 7, regardless of how that 7 was achieved, we use the following rule for *alternative and mutually exclusive events.*

Rule 3: The probability of one of two or more mutually exclusive outcomes is equal to the sum of the probabilities of the individual outcomes. This can be expressed as

(Formula 5.3)

$$\text{Pr}(E_1 \textit{ or } E_2 \textit{ or} \ldots E_n) = \Sigma \text{Pr}(E)$$

Each of the six ways of rolling a 7 has an individual probability of 1/36. Therefore, the probability of rolling a 7 is

$$\text{Pr}(7) = \text{Pr}(1,6) + \text{PR}(2,5) + \text{Pr}(3,4) + \text{Pr}(4,3) + \text{Pr}(5,2) + \text{Pr}(6,1)$$

$$= \frac{1}{36} + \frac{1}{36} + \frac{1}{36} + \frac{1}{36} + \frac{1}{36} + \frac{1}{36}$$

$$= \frac{6}{36} = \frac{1}{6} = .167$$

A slight modification of Rule 3 is necessary if we are working with alternative events that are not mutually exclusive. (Two events are mutually exclusive if the occurrence of one precludes the occurrence of the other. On a single roll of a die, each of the six outcomes is mutually exclusive of the others.) We can see an example of two outcomes that are not mutually exclusive in the following example. What is the probability of drawing a red card (heart or diamond) *or* a face card (J,Q,K) from a deck of fifty-two cards? Because there are twenty-six red cards, Pr(red) = 26/52 = 1/2 = .5, and because there are twelve face cards, Pr(face) = 12/52 = .23. But notice that six of the cards are *both* red and face. This means we have counted them twice (once as red, and once as face). To correct this obvious error, we must subtract the probability of this joint occurrence, as follows:

$$\text{Pr(red } \textit{or} \text{ face)} = \text{Pr(red)} + \text{Pr(face)} - \text{Pr(red } \textit{and} \text{ face)}$$

$$= \frac{26}{52} + \frac{12}{52} - \left(\frac{26}{52}\right)\left(\frac{12}{52}\right)$$

$$= \frac{38}{52} - \frac{6}{52} = \frac{32}{52} = .62$$

Thus, there is a 62 percent chance of drawing a card that is *either* a red card *or* a face card.

Probability and Social Science

By now you may be asking yourself what the relationship is between social science research and dice and card games of chance. The following two simple problems (p. 88) should help you to answer such a question. At first glance it may seem that these two problems have nothing in common. One involves a trivial situation, while the other deals with a vital socioeconomic issue; one problem deals with a game of chance, the other involves the game of life. While recognizing that Problem B is greatly oversimplified, let us examine how the use of probability statistics can help us solve both problems.

Problem A

Suppose we toss twenty coins. What is the probability of observing ten heads?

Problem B

Suppose a certain large city has an equal number of female and male workers. An employer is suspected of gender bias because, of his twenty employees, only seven are female. Is it reasonable to accuse the employer of gender bias?

One way of solving Problem A is by empirical observation. We could toss twenty coins many, many times, each time counting and tallying the number of heads. If we were to do this 1,000 times, we would observe results similar to those in Table 5.1. But we do not really want to take the time to toss 1,000 coins, and we already know that the "random" tosses of a coin are subject to very predictable behavior in the long run and on the average. This behavior is defined mathematically by the *binomial probability distribution*. A binomial situation is one in which each trial (1) is identical to every other trial; (2) is independent of, that is, unaffected by, every other trial; (3) has two and only two possible outcomes, the probability of each being known. In coin tossing, each toss is considered to be identical; each toss is independent of the other tosses; each toss has only two possible outcomes (head or tail) and Pr(head) = Pr(tail) = 5. Mathematically, the binomial distribution is defined by

(Formula 5.4)

$$\Pr(n) = \frac{N!(p^n)(q^{n-1})}{n!(N - n)!}$$

where n = the number of successes; N = the total number of trials; p = the probability of a success on a single trial; and q = (1 - p). [NOTE: N!, or N-factorial, is the product of N(N - 1)(N - 2) ... (3)(2)(1). Zero factorial, 0!, is defined as equal to one. A detailed discussion of Formula 5.4 is beyond the scope of this book. For further information, see Blalock (1979) or Mueller, Schuessler, and Costner (1970).]

When formula 5.4 is applied to Problem A, N = 20, p = .5, n = 10, q = (1 - .5) = .5, and

$$\Pr(10 \text{ heads}) = \frac{20!(.5^{10})(.5^{10})}{10!(20 - 10)!} = .176$$

Table 5.1. *A Sampling Distribution of the Probability of Obtaining a Given Number of Heads When Twenty Coins Are Tossed*

Number of Heads	Binomial Distribution	Normal Approximation
0	*	*
1	*	*
2	*	*
3	.002	.001
4	.005	.005
5	.015	.015
6	.037	.036
7	.074	.073
8	.120	.120
9	.160	.162
10	.176	.174
11	.160	.162
12	.120	.120
13	.074	.073
14	.037	.036
15	.015	.015
16	.005	.005
17	.002	.001
18	*	*
19	*	*
20	*	*
Total	1.002**	0.998

* Less than .001

** Does not equal 1.00 due to rounding error.

Thus, the probability of observing exactly ten heads when twenty coins are tossed is about 18 percent.

Let us now turn to Problem B. Each time a person is hired could be considered a trial, and each time a female is hired could be termed a "success." (Of course, these terms are arbitrary; we could just as well define a success as the hiring of a male.) Because the city's population contains an equal number of eligible men and women, the theoretical probability of hiring a woman, all other things being equal, is 1/2, or .5. Therefore, N = 20, p = .5, n = 7, q = .5, and

$$\Pr(7) = \frac{20!(.5^7)(.5^{13})}{7!(20 - 7)!} = .074$$

Thus, if *only chance* factors are operating, there is but a 7 percent probability of the employer hiring exactly seven women. Shall we conclude that hiring seven or fewer women is evidence of discrimination? Not yet—we must also consider the more extreme situations: six women hired, five women hired, and so on (including zero women hired). For if hiring only seven women constitutes discrimination, certainly hiring a smaller number than seven also constitutes discrimination. In other words, we are interested in the probability of an alternative, not mutually exclusive, event. We are interested in Pr(7 or 6 or 5 or 4 or 3 or 2 or 1 or 0) which is

$$(.074 + .036 + .015 + .005 + .002 + .0002 + .00002 + .000002) = .132.$$

What have we shown? If the situation described in Problem B is purely a matter of chance (that is, if it is independent of any external factors such as discriminatory hiring practices), the outcome of hiring seven or fewer women would occur, on the average and in the long run, 13.2 percent of the time. If Pr(7 or fewer) = .132, is this evidence of discrimination? The answer to this question cannot be derived from statistics, for we are now left with a question of judgment. Is something that can happen statistically only 13 percent of the time an unusual event, so unusual that we are ready to say that it could not have happened by chance? Again, we have a question of judgment, a question that our statistics cannot *prove*, but to which they can bring *evidence*. It is usually, but not always, the case in sociological work to consign an event to the realm of improbability only if its probability is .05 or less (generally expressed as $p < .05$). If we apply this convention, we would conclude that there is not sufficient statistical evidence to reject the *chance model*.

The Binomial Distribution and the Normal Curve

Any binomial distribution that is based on a sufficiently large N (20 or more) bears a striking resemblance to a normal distribution. Even when N is as small as 10, the resemblance between the two distributions is quite close if both p and q are approximately .5. Furthermore, the mean and the standard deviation of a binomial distribution are easily computed from the following formulas:

(Formula 5.5)

$$\overline{X} = Np$$

(Formula 5.6)

$$\sigma = \sqrt{Npq}$$

Consider again our example of tossing twenty coins. In Figure 5.1 we can perhaps intuitively "see" that the mean of the distribution is ten. But can you easily "see" the standard deviation? I can't. So let us use Formulas 5.5 and 5.6 to understand what is happening.

$$\overline{X} = 20(.5) = 10.0$$

$$\sigma = \sqrt{20(.5)(.5)} = \sqrt{5} = 2.24$$

The data from Problem B are based on the same values of N and p, so the mean of the distribution is also 10 and its standard deviation is 2.24.

Notice that we have now described our data as being approximately normal and that we know the mean and the standard deviation. We can, therefore, reconceptualize the entire problem as one involving z-scores.

However, we first must notice that the binomial distribution differs from the normal distribution in that the former is discrete; that is, it takes on only the whole numbers 1, 2, 3, . . . 19, 20. But the normal distribution is continuous; it can take on any value from 0.00 to 20.00, including 1, 2.24, 3.14159, 18.9999, and $\sqrt{2}$. Because we are using a continuous curve (the normal distribution) to approximate a discrete distribution (the binomial), we must make a slight adjustment in our thinking: We must use the *true* upper and lower limits of any discrete number to define its location in the continuous distribution. Thus, the discrete number 7 is represented in its continuous form by all values between 6.5 and 7.5. (You might wish to review the discussion of true limits on pages 20-23.)

To solve Problem B, we must find the probability of observing 7.5 or fewer women in a group of twenty employees. Using z-scores (see Formula 4.15),

$$z = \frac{7.5 - 10}{2.24} = \frac{-2.5}{2.24} = -1.12$$

Turning to Appendix Table A, we see that the area corresponding to a z-score of ±1.12 is .3686 of the total area under the normal curve. Therefore, the area beyond z = -1.12 is .5000 - .3686 = .1314. Thus, we again see, using z-scores, that the probability of hiring seven or fewer women is about 13 percent.

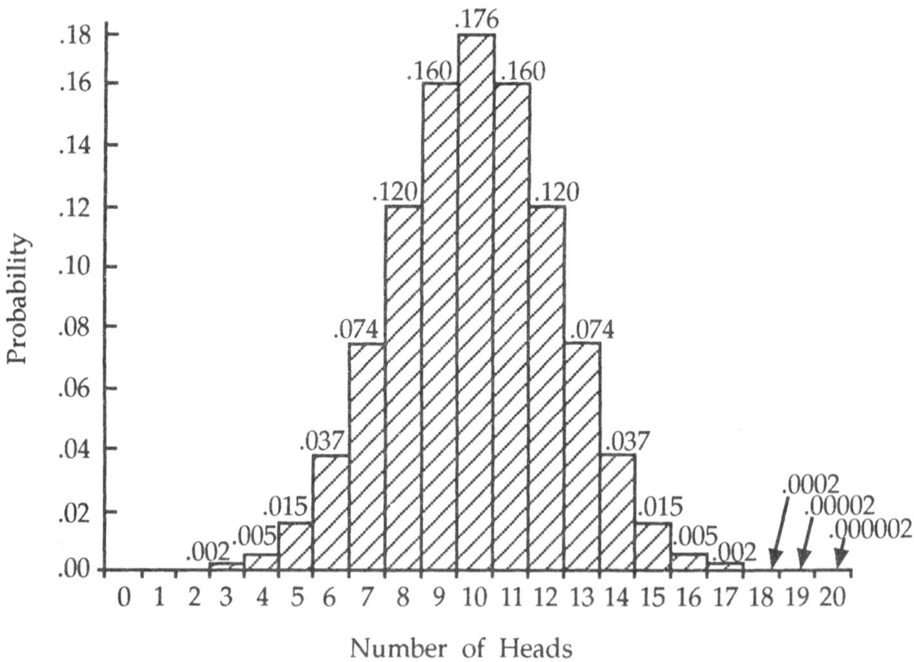

Figure 5.1. *The Probability of Observing a Given Number of Heads When Twenty Coins Are Tossed*

Probability and the Logic of Hypothesis Testing

Let us now develop what we have learned thus far into some general principles for conducting statistical tests of hypotheses. Our first task will be to select an appropriate hypothesis. There can be a variety of hypotheses for any research problem. In tossing twenty coins we could hypothesize (1) the outcome will be ten heads, (2) the outcome will be eleven heads, or (3) the outcome will be between eight and twelve heads, and so on. Any of these alternative hypotheses are plausible, but, statistically speaking, most are very difficult to test. (The reason for this difficulty is beyond the scope of this discussion.) There is, however, one general hypothesis that we can test. It is the hypothesis that says that the observed event occurs in conformity with a chance model. For example, Figure 5.1 describes a chance model of the possible outcomes when twenty coins are tossed. Of specific interest, this chance model tells us that the mean number of heads when twenty coins are tossed is ten. We can then formulate the following research question: Is the number of heads actually observed *reasonably similar* to the number of heads that we should expect to observe? Stated more formally, because the true *population* mean is 10, we hypothesize that our *sample* mean will also be 10. This type of statement, which says that the sample value is no different from the population value, is called a *null hypothesis* (H_0), or the hypothesis of no difference. But the practical meaning of the term *null hypothesis* lies in the fact that it is the hypothesis we hope to nullify, that is, to disprove. Strictly speaking, the null hypothesis is the only hypothesis that can be statistically tested. For our example, the null hypothesis might be stated in any of the following ways:

1. H_0: The sample mean is no different from the population mean.
2. H_0: $\overline{X} = 10$
3. H_0: $\overline{X} - \mu = 0$

Note that we use the symbol $\overline{X}$ for the sample mean and μ, the Greek letter Mu, for the population mean. Very often, we use a sample mean to estimate the population value.

In addition to stating the null hypothesis, researchers will also specify an alternative, or research, hypothesis. In our example, the research hypothesis (H_1) might be stated as

1. The sample mean is different from (or is greater than or less than) the population mean;
2. $\overline{X} \neq 10$, or the sample mean is not equal to 10;
3. $\overline{X} - \mu \neq 0$, or the sample mean minus the population mean is zero;
4. $\overline{X} - \mu < 0$, or the difference between the sample mean and the population mean is less than zero (is negative);
5. $\overline{X} - \mu > 0$,

and so on. Note that the null hypothesis is *always* a statement of no meaningful difference or of no meaningful relationship and that the alternative hypothesis is *always* a statement of some difference or of some relationship.

The null hypothesis is based on a known, or accurately estimated, characteristic of a population. We observe this characteristic in a sample. If the two observations yield contradictory values, we *reject* the null hypothesis. If the two observations do not show contradictory values, we *do not reject* the null hypothesis.

When does the sample observation contradict the null hypothesis? When it is highly improbable. How improbable? There is no statistical law that defines what is probable or improbable, but as stated earlier, statisticians generally consider that an event is statistically improbable only if it is among the extreme 5 percent of possible outcomes. This 5 percent value (or 1 percent or 10 percent, as the case may be) is called alpha (symbolized by the Greek letter α) and represents an important concept in statistical decision making: We are willing to assume a level of risk in that we may consider an outcome to be *improbable* when it is, in fact, *probable*. The technical name for such an error is a *Type I Error*. In a sampling distribution, alpha defines the *region of rejection*, or the proportion of the distribution that contains the specified highly improbable outcomes. In other words, alpha defines the probability of a Type I Error. In contrast, the *Type II Error* occurs when a null hypothesis that is actually false is not rejected.

The problem of Type I and Type II errors is analogous to the problem faced by a jury in a criminal case. The defendant is either guilty or not guilty. The jury may render a verdict of either guilty or not guilty. If the defendant is indeed guilty, and if that is also the jury's finding, there is no error. Similarly, if the defendant is truly not guilty and the jury so finds, there is no error. But if the defendant is guilty and the jury finds him not guilty, an error has been made, and if the defendant is truly not guilty and the jury finds him guilty, an error is made. Of the two errors, which is worse? In our system of justice with its notion of innocent until proven guilty, the latter error is usually deemed to be worse, so the legal system is designed to minimize that type of error. Consequently, our whole legal system is designed to protect the innocent, even if this means that an occasional guilty party will go unpunished. The statistical analogues to the guilty-not-guilty problem are Type I and II errors, which are described in Table 5.2.

One-Tail and Two-Tail Tests

Returning to Problem A, if we toss a coin twenty times in order to determine whether it is fair (not subject to any controlling force except chance), we will regard any outcome in the vicinity of ten heads as probable and any outcome in the vicinity of zero heads or twenty heads as improbable. In statistical terms such a test of a hypothesis is called a *two-tail test*, that is, a test in which either extreme outcome will lead us to reject the null hypothesis. In Problem B we are not interested in both extremes; we are only interested in one extreme, that in which women are underrepresented. A research hypothesis that tells us to look for one extreme outcome or the other, but not both, is a directional hypothesis, and the statistical tests used in such circumstances are called *one-tail tests*. Figure 5.2 illustrates directional or nondirectional hypotheses. In a one-tail test, alpha, the region of rejection, is located entirely at one end (or in one "tail") of the sampling distribution. In a two-tail test, alpha is divided in half, and there are, in essence, two regions of rejection, one in each tail and each having a value of $\alpha/2$.

Table 5.2. *Type I and Type II Errors*

		The Null Hypothesis Is	
		True	**False**
The Decision Concerning H_0 Is to	**Reject**	Type I Error	Correct Decision
	Not Reject	Correct Decision	Type II Error

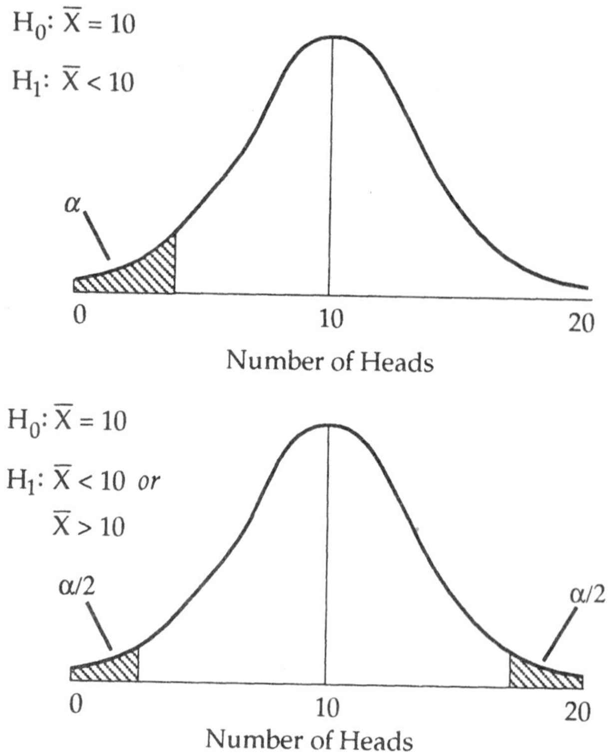

Figure 5.2. *One-Tail Test (Top) and Two-Tail Test (Bottom)*

We have in the previous few pages described the fundamentals necessary to conduct a statistical test. These are

1. A *null hypothesis*, a statement that specifies some aspect of a population that is known or assumed to be true. It is this hypothesis that is actually subject to the statistical test.
2. A *research hypothesis*, a statement that contradicts the null hypothesis. This hypothesis is not directly tested, but we often accept its validity if the null hypothesis has been rejected.
3. A *region of rejection*, alpha (α), which specifies the risk that we will incorrectly reject the null hypothesis. Before testing, the researcher must decide whether alpha should be located in one or in both tails of a distribution; this decision depends on whether the research decision is directional or nondirectional.

4. A *test statistic* that is computed from data taken from a sample. The z-score is but one example of a test statistic; many others will be described in Chapters 7-11.

Let us illustrate these elements of a statistical test with our problem concerning discriminatory hiring. Our null hypothesis is that there is no difference between the observed sample mean ($\overline{X} = 7$) and the theoretically expected population mean ($\mu = 10$). Stated formally,

$$H_0: \overline{X} - \mu = 0$$

Our research hypothesis is that the difference between $\overline{X}$ and μ is significantly different from zero. More specifically, we might be willing to specify a *directional* hypothesis because we suspect our sample data to reveal a bias against women. Stated formally, an alternative might be

$$H_1: \overline{X} - \mu < 0$$

In this instance, we will conduct a one-tail test. Our selection of alpha is arbitrary, but we shall follow a common convention and let $\alpha = .05$. As our test statistic, we have chosen to use the z-score. We are now ready to conduct our test of significance, and we shall evaluate the test in terms of the following *decision rules*.

Reject H_0 if the observed value of z is greater than the critical value obtained from Appendix Table A. (For our data, the critical value for a one-tail test, when $\alpha = .05$, is 1.645.) *Do not reject* H_0 if the critical value is less than 1.645.

As we have already seen, the computed value of z is -1.12. The magnitude of z is thus less than that of the critical value. Following our decision rule, we do not reject the null hypothesis. Because the null hypothesis was not rejected, we conclude that an observed sample mean of 7 could have occurred by chance and that there is no statistical evidence of discrimination.

If our sample mean had been 5 rather than 7, then the value of z would be obtained as follows:

$$z = \frac{5.5 - 10}{2.24} = \frac{-4.5}{2.24} = -2.01$$

In this instance, we would reject the null hypothesis because the observed value of z is greater than the critical value (the value obtained from Appendix Table A).

> *Quick Quiz*
> **5.1**
>
> From some population that consists of an equal number of males and females, a sample of n = 36 is drawn. (A) How many females would you expect to be included in the sample? (B) What is the probability that the sample will have 12 or fewer females?

Important Terms

Probability (p)	Alpha (α)
Empirical probability	Region of rejection
Chance factors	Type I error
Three rules of probability	Type II error
Binomial distribution	One-tail test
Null hypothesis (H_0)	Two-tail test
Research hypothesis (H_1)	

Suggested Readings

Arney (1990, Chaps. 5 and 6); Blalock (1979, Chaps. 9 and 10); Ott, et al. (1992: 167-200); Mueller, Schuessler, and Costner (1970: 207-237).

Quick Quiz Answers

Quick Quiz 5.1

(A) $\overline{X} = np = 36(.5) = 18$

(B) $s = \sqrt{npq} = \sqrt{9} = 3$

$$z = \frac{12.5 - 18}{3} = -1.83$$

$$p = .0336$$

6

Bases of Statistical Inference, II: Sampling and Estimation

In Chapter 5 we learned how to use the laws of probability to assist us in making decisions about observed events. The examples used in Chapter 5 provided all of the information needed to reach those particular conclusions. In sociological research, however, we frequently do not have access to all of the necessary information. For example, we might want to know what the American people think about nuclear disarmament. Depending on how we define "American people," this population could have as many as 250,000,000 people. It would require extraordinary resources to gather so much information, and such tasks are attempted only once every ten years. Given that no one but the Bureau of the Census has the capacity to study the entire population of 250,000,000 American people, does this mean that our original question cannot be answered, cannot even be asked? It does not, for we can, with a very high degree of confidence and with only a small amount of error, obtain the answer to our question by using data from a sample of the larger population. From the sample data, we can make inferences about the population. And the inferences we make will not be at all haphazard.

It is not unusual for us to understand our world by making inferences, or generalizations: Having touched one hot stove, we are unlikely to touch another; finding several rotten apples, we may reject the entire barrel; noticing that some Europeans eat with their forks in their left hands, we conclude that all Europeans do the same. Such inferences are reasonable. They help us to make sense out of what would otherwise be a chaotic universe. They guide our behavior.

But obviously, such generalizations are not always valid. A sensible person will reshape generalizations in the light of new information. A prejudiced person will use generalizations to reshape information. If a person is refused employment because of ethnic differences between employer and employee, shall we conclude that all or even most members of the employer's ethnic group are prejudiced? If my wallet is taken by a bearded youth, shall I infer that most bearded youths are thieves?

One of the functions of statistical sampling is to help us distinguish between valid and invalid generalizations; indeed, this is probably its most important function. But two other important functions should be mentioned. As indicated, sampling permits us to save our resources of time, energy, money, and personnel. Except for census purposes, there is no need to survey 250,000,000 people when we can get the same information from 1,500 people. Finally, sampling is at times necessary if the very process of measurement alters or even destroys what is being measured. For example, politicians are often the subject of "voter recognition" studies. In such studies, potential voters are asked, "Do you recognize the name of John Doe? Who is he?" But people who do not recognize Doe may be moved by the question and by their ignorance to seek information about Doe. In this example, simply asking the question alters, or may alter, a portion of the respondents.

Populations and Samples

A population, or universe, is any category about which an inference is made. A sample is a category within a population from which measurements are obtained. It is imperative that a population be well defined; that is, the elements that constitute a population must be clearly specified. A population may be of any size, and it is generally determined by the research problem at hand. For example, given a particular research problem, any of the following may be considered as a population: (1) all American citizens age eighteen or older, (2) all registered voters in Tennessee, (3) all Democrats who voted in the previous presidential election, (4) all undergraduate students now registered at this school, (5) all sophomore females at this school, and so on.

Some authors distinguish between the target, or theoretical, population and the sampled population. The target universe is the universe we are seeking to know, such as the official list of all registered voters in Chicago. Although this universe is reasonably well defined, it probably is difficult to obtain an accurate list of this population because within any given time span a certain number of people die or move out of or into the city or for some other reason do not appear or mistakenly appear on the official voter list. But it is this list that defines the sampled universe and distinguishes it from the target universe.

A *sample* is a specified portion of the universe. Samples are of many kinds but can generally be classified as *random* (or scientific or probability) or *nonrandom*. A random sample *is not* an accidental sample, that is, one that "just happens." Rather, it is random in the sense that every element in the population has a known, and often equal, chance of being included in the sample that is eventually drawn from the population. Let us illustrate this important point by means of an example. Suppose you wanted to draw a sample of 500 voters from your congressional district. You might simply go to the largest city and stop the first 500 people you meet on the street. Or your might knock on 500 doors in a nearby neighborhood. From a naive point of view, one might argue that it is a matter of chance which 500 people you happen to meet; but it is also true that these 500 are likely to be *unrepresentative* because they are found in a city, not in a rural area. Thus, the people who do not come to the city, or even to that part of the city, have no chance of being included in the sample. These 500 people are unrepresentative of their district because not everyone in the district had an equal chance of being included in the sample. This bias may not have been intended; nonetheless it is real and present. A truly random sample minimizes the danger of such biased selection by using the laws of probability as the basis of sample selection. Thus, a sample is random if, and only if, it is selected by a process that is *statistically random*.

The most obvious type of random sample is the *simple random* sample. For instance, if we wanted to draw a sample of five students from a class of twenty-five, we could write each of the twenty-five names on a slip of paper, place the slips in a hat, thoroughly mix, and blindly select five.* Note that this procedure guarantees that each person has an equal and known probability of being included in the sample: Pr(inclusion) = 5/25 = .20. We might note as a further

*To be technically correct, after we select each slip of paper we should return it to the hat before drawing the next slip because we must theorctically assume that the relevant population is infinitely large.

technical point that every possible sample of n = 5 has an equally likely chance of being selected.

A variation of the simple random sample is the interval, or systematic, sample. If the sampling units are arranged in some kind of unbiased order, such as an alphabetical list of all students in a university, we can draw a reasonably representative sample simply by selecting every n-th name from the list, after a random starting point. (Some people argue, however, that an alphabetical list is confounded by ethnicity and may, therefore, be biased.)

Most social research problems involve populations much too large to permit us to draw names from a hat, but the principles of more advanced sampling techniques have the same end.

In research situations in which a crucial variable can be specified in advance, a *stratified random sample* will frequently be used. For example, if we are sampling political attitudes in a town where voters are 50 percent Republican, 35 percent Democrat, and 15 percent other, we might wish first to divide the total population into three groups, or strata, and then sample from each group. This procedure has two strong points in its favor. (1) It ensures that our final sample will accurately reflect the population in terms of the political party variable; and (2) it enables us to achieve this with a smaller total sample size than would be required by simple random sampling. Figure 6.1 presents a schematic representation of a stratified sample.

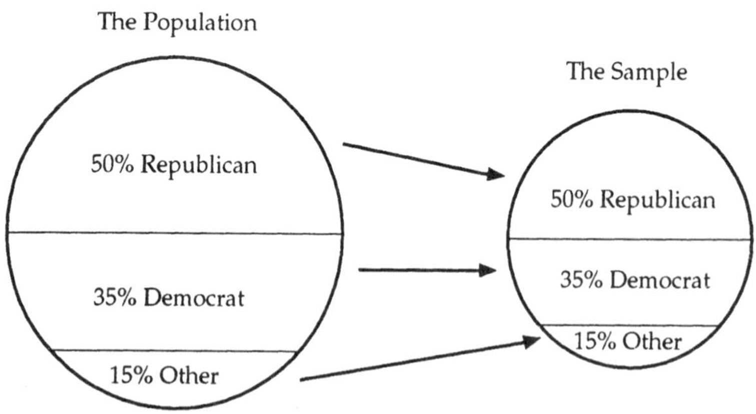

Figure 6.1. *A Stratified Sample*

When the geographic area that includes the population is very large, researchers will often use an *area probability sample.* National polls, for example, would be too expensive to conduct if the researchers had to rely on samples drawn from all fifty states. Therefore, the country is divided into smaller geopolitical areas, and a sample of the area is drawn. These areas may then be divided into yet smaller areas such as counties or census tracts, and another sample is drawn. After several such steps, the final sampling units are drawn. In this type of sample, the first stage of sampling involves very large units, and it is only at the final stage that discrete individuals are chosen.

To the sociologist, sampling is especially important in the construction of research designs. To the statistician, sampling is important as a basis for inference. We sociologists who use statistics must appreciate both points. Most important, we must understand that a sample statistic can be seen as a sample value that, because it is only one value of many possible values (that is, the sample is but one of many possible samples), may or may not be truly representative of the corresponding population value. It is our task to develop means to determine how representative our statistics really are. To do so, we must first understand the concept of a sampling distribution.

The Sampling Distribution of a Statistic

For the sake of familiarity, let us return to our example of tossing twenty coins (see pages 86ff). Table 5.1 presented the probabilities of obtaining each of the twenty-one possible outcomes (from zero heads to twenty heads). The sum of these probabilities must equal 1.00. Using Table 5.1, we can directly tell the probability of observing a given number of heads when twenty coins are tossed. Thus, Pr(8) = .120 and Pr(15) = .015. With a little manipulation, we can also quickly determine the probability of observing any set of heads; thus, the probability of five or fewer heads is

$$\text{Pr}(5 \text{ or } 4 \text{ or } 3 \text{ or } 2 \text{ or } 1 \text{ or } 0) = .015 + .005 + .002 + (\,^*\,) = .022$$

and the probability of observing between eight and twelve heads is

$$\text{Pr}(8 \text{ or } 9 \text{ or } 10 \text{ or } 11 \text{ or } 12) = .120 + .160 + .176 + .160 + .120 = .736$$

---

*The probability of two, one, or zero heads is so small as to be negligible.

Quick Quiz
6.1

When twenty coins are tossed, what is the probability of observing (A) at least fourteen heads; (B) between nine and eleven heads?

A listing of all possible outcomes of any event is known as a *sampling distribution*. Thus, Table 5.1 gives the sampling distribution of the number of heads when twenty coins are tossed. Sampling distributions are calculated on the basis of a very large number, theoretically infinite, of the events in question. The importance of a sampling distribution is that it lists all possible outcomes and their probabilities and thus enables us to determine which of the outcomes are likely to occur and which are not. Because any and every sample statistic belongs to some sampling distribution, it is possible to determine how representative any sample statistic is as long as we know its sampling distribution. For instance, suppose we sample 1,500 families from a population of all American families and from each of these families we obtain a measure of family income. Can we be sure that our sample statistic is a reasonably accurate representation of the true population value? Figure 6.2 pictures the median income in the population and in each of three samples. But suppose there were more than three samples in Figure 6.2. Suppose there were hundreds and hundreds: Try to imagine *all possible samples* and all possible sample medians. If we could develop a list of all possible sample medians, what would we have? The sampling of distribution of the median family income for a sample of 1,500. If we could have such a sample distribution, we could easily tell whether any given sample was indeed representative, just as we could with our twenty coins. But in doing research we usually do not have a list of all possible samples, for, in fact, we usually draw only one sample. However, if we can locate that one sample relative to a *theoretical* list of all possible samples, we could determine the statistical probability that our observed sample reflects the true population value. Exactly how this is done is described in Figure 6.2.

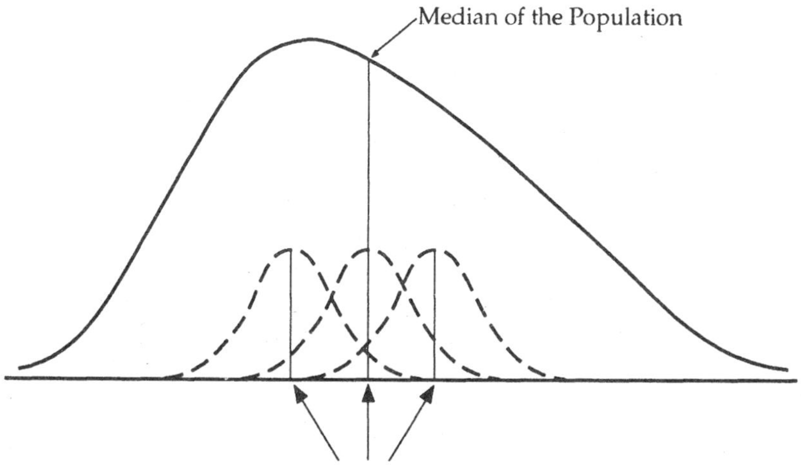

Figure 6.2. *A Population Value and Three Possible Sample Values*

How Big Must a Sample Be?

One of the most frequent questions asked by students concerns the size of a sample. "I want to do a survey of student attitudes on campus. How many students do I interview?" This type of question is common and important. If you have noticed the fine print at the bottom of newspaper reports of sample surveys, you may have seen statements that give the sample size. The size is rarely less than 400 people, and more frequently it is around 800. Rarely is it larger than 1,500 people. The appropriate size of any sample is a function of a number of factors, all of which are related to the fact that any sample necessarily involves some degree of measurement error. What researchers must decide is how much error is tolerable.

For very large (theoretically, infinitely large) populations, selecting an appropriate random sample of size n involves (1) making a determination about the width of the *confidence interval* about the sample statistic, and (2) selecting an *acceptable margin of error*. Further, a distinction is made if one is (3) estimating the *proportion* of the population containing the relevant measure—for example, "What proportion of the voters favor Candidate X?"—or (4) calculating a *mean*. The formulas are

(Formula 6.1)

$$n = (p)(1\text{-}p)\left(\frac{z}{\text{M.E.}}\right)^2 \qquad \text{[for a proportion]}$$

(Formula 6.2)

$$n = \left(\frac{(z)(s)}{\text{M.E.}}\right)^2 \qquad \text{[for a mean]}$$

where z is determined by the confidence interval (e.g., for a 95% CI, z = 1.96); p is the population proportion (which, if not specifically known, can safely be estimated as 0.5); **s** is the standard deviation of the sample; and M.E. is the tolerable margin (or amount) of error (usually somewhere between 3 and 5 percent for proportions).

An Adjustment for Small Populations

When the population is not very large (theoretically, for any finite population) the value of n computed in Formulas 6.1 and 6.2 should be adjusted as follows:

(Formula 6.3)

$$n^* = \frac{n}{1 + (n/N)}$$

where n* is the adjusted sample size and N is the size of the finite population.

Suppose we are interested in the proportion of respondents who favor a certain political candidate. If we wish to use a 95 percent CI, then we must use z = 1.96. If we wish to allow a 3 percent margin of error and if we assume nothing about the proportion in the population, the necessary sample size is determined as follows:

$$n = (.5)(.5)[1.96/.03]^2 = 1{,}067.11$$

Thus, a sample of 1,067 cases would be appropriate for any theoretically very large (i.e., infinite) population.

However, many populations are not infinitely large. For example, if our population consists of a finite number, say N = 8,000 registered voters, then

$$n^* = n/[1 + (n/N)] = 1{,}067/[1 + (1{,}067/8{,}000)]$$

$$= 1{,}067/1.1335 = 941.33$$

Thus, we need a sample of 941 cases in order to have a 95 percent confidence interval and to be within a 3 percent margin of error.

Estimation

Up to this point we have discussed only a few of the obvious advantages of using a sample as the basis for statistical study. However, one noticeable disadvantage of sampling is that it inevitably involves a loss of information; consequently, measurements based on sample data contain some error. Because a sample is only an approximation of a population, one of the fundamental questions raised by sampling is, How much error is contained in sample statistics?

Let us suppose that we have a population consisting of the homicide rates of 145 SMSAs (see Table 2.1, p. 20). From this population we draw a random sample of size n = 30 (Table 6.1). We compute a mean from this sample and find $\overline{X} = 8.37$. How certain can we be that this sample mean accurately represents the population mean? How much confidence can we have in our sample statistic? Is it possible, because of an unknown bias or bad luck, that we have drawn a sample that does not represent the population? To answer such questions, we must reflect on both the sampling distribution of our sample statistic, in this case the sampling distribution of the mean, and on a new concept, the *standard error* of the sample statistic.

Let us put aside for a moment the previous problem. Instead, let us imagine a very different and very large population such as all children currently enrolled in the seventh grade in a large school system. From this population we draw a sample of 100 cases and obtain measures of some variable such as IQ. We observe that this sample has a mean of 98.7 and a standard deviation of 17.8. Now we draw a second sample, also of n = 100. For this second sample we find a mean of 102.6 and a standard deviation of 14.2. We continue to draw new samples, each with an n = 100, and obtain the same descriptive statistics for each sample. We repeat the process until we have 100 (or even 1,000) samples, with 100 sample means and 100 sample standard deviations (see Table 6.2).

Table 6.1. *Random Sample of Thirty Homicide Rates*

5	2	10	12	13
10	15	8	5	3
12	5	2	3	4
11	14	18	4	7
10	15	5	5	7
7	19	10	5	5

$\overline{X} = 8.37$
$s = 4.75$

Table 6.2. *Partial List of 100 Sample Values*

Sample Number	$\overline{X}$	s	x
1	98.7	17.8	-1.3
2	102.6	14.2	+2.6
3	105.5	15.9	+5.5
.	.	.	.
.	.	.	.
.	.	.	.
99	91.3	18.2	-8.7
100	109.4	15.3	+9.4

The Standard Error

If we consider these 100 means as a sample (that is, as a sample of sample means), we can compute the mean of the sample means. Let us guess that this "grand mean" has a value of 100.0. This value is now our best estimate of the true population mean. (The true population mean cannot be known, of course, as long as we rely on sample data.) Next, we can see that each of the 100 sample means deviates from the grand mean by a certain amount—some are above 100.0, some are below. Because we can compute deviations of sample means from the grand mean, we can also compute a standard deviation of all the sample means about the grand mean. This type of standard deviation has a special name—the *standard error.* (In our example, we are concerned with the standard error of the mean, but note that many other statistics have standard errors. We could, for instance, compute 100 medians and then determine the standard error of the median.) Now assume that this special standard deviation, the standard error of the mean, has a value of 2.5. Figure 6.3 illustrates this point. The larger curve represents the population. (Its mean is actually unknown, but for the sake of clarifying what follows, let us suppose that we know that the true population mean is 98.5). The smaller curve represents the distribution of 100 sample means; its mean, as we have seen, is 100.0. There is about this estimated mean of 100.0 a standard error of 2.5. Because this standard error is a standard deviation, it can be interpreted in relation to the normal curve, just as any other standard deviation. To be more precise, the distance from the estimated mean to ± 1 standard error will include the true population mean 68 percent of the time. In other words, 68 percent of all sample means lie within one standard error of the true population mean; conversely, because the grand mean of all sample means is the best estimate of the population mean, we can also say that the true population mean will fall within the range $\{\overline{X} \pm s_{\overline{X}}\}$ 68 percent of the time. Further utilizing our knowledge of the normal distribution, we can also be certain that the distance, $\{\overline{X} \pm 2s_{\overline{X}}\}$ will include the true population mean 95 percent of the time, and $\{\overline{X} \pm 3s_{\overline{X}}\}$ will include the true population mean 99 percent of the time. [NOTE: To be precise, instead of $\overline{X} \pm 2s_{\overline{X}}$, use $\overline{X} \pm 1.96s_{\overline{X}}$; and instead of $\overline{X} \pm 3s_{\overline{X}}$, use $\overline{X} \pm 2.58s_{\overline{X}}$.]

If the sample mean is seen as a *point estimate* of the true population mean, the standard error provides us with information about the accuracy of that estimate. It does this by changing our estimated value of the population value from a single point (the sample mean) to a range of scores about which we can make a probability statement concerning the likelihood that the range includes the true population mean. This latter type of estimate is called an *interval estimate.*

In the example of 100 sample means, we found a grand mean of 100.0 and a standard deviation of 2.5. We can, therefore, make the following estimates:

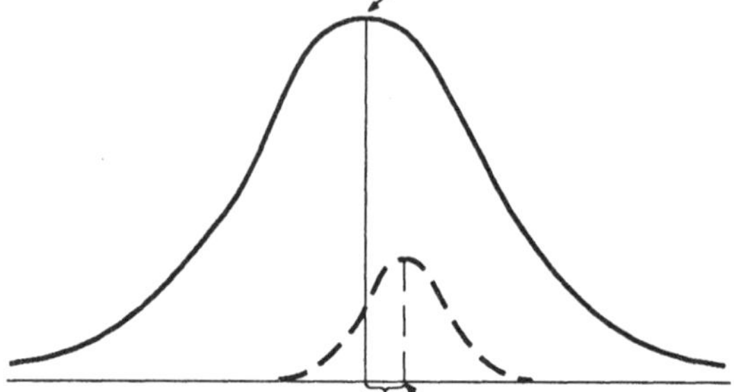

Figure 6.3. *The Sample Mean and Sampling Error*

1. We can say that the true population mean will fall within the range {100.0 ± 2.5} 68 percent of the time.
2. We can say that the true population mean will fall within the range {100.0 ± (2.5)(1.96)} 95 percent of the time.
3. We can say that the true population mean will fall within the range {100 ± (2.5)(2.58)} 99 percent of the time.

These interval estimates are often called *confidence intervals* (CI) because they enable us to say, for example, that we are 95 percent confident that the true population mean lies within two standard errors of the sample mean. In our example, we are 95 percent confident that the true mean lies within the range 100.0 ± 4.9, or between 95.1 and 104.9.

In the real-world situation, of course, we do not collect 100 sample means in order to determine the standard error of the mean. We have only one sample with one sample mean. How, then, do we obtain our best estimate of the true population mean, and how do we establish interval estimates (or confidence intervals)? Fortunately, this task is relatively simple, for the standard error is directly related to the sample size and standard deviation in the following way:

(Formula 6.4)

$$s_{\bar{X}} = \frac{s}{\sqrt{n}}$$

where s is the sample standard deviation and n is the sample size. An alternative computing formula, perhaps simpler for computing the standard error, is

(Formula 6.5)

$$s_{\bar{X}} = \sqrt{\frac{\Sigma x^2}{n(n-1)}}$$

where Σx^2 is the sum of squares and n is the sample size. Given this information, we can compute a standard error on the basis of a single sample, and from this we can readily set the 68 percent, 95 percent, or 99 percent confidence intervals.

Let us now return to our example from Table 6.1. Given the sample of n = 30, we can use as our point estimate of the mean the sample mean of 8.37. The sample of thirty homicide rates has a standard deviation of 4.75. Therefore, for these data, the standard error of the mean is

$$s_{\bar{X}} = \frac{4.75}{\sqrt{30}} = 0.87$$

To establish the 95 percent confidence interval around the sample mean, we simply do the following:

$$\begin{aligned} 95\%\ CI &= \bar{X} \pm 1.96\ (s_{\bar{X}}) \\ &= 8.37 \pm 1.96\ (0.87) \\ &= 8.37 \pm 1.71 \end{aligned}$$

Therefore, we are 95 percent certain that the true population mean lies within the range of 6.66 to 10.08.

There is yet another way of looking at confidence intervals. We can pose the following problem as our example: What is the probability that the true population mean lies within some specified range? If we let alpha be the probability that our observed sample mean will fall outside of some specified range, the problem can be represented graphically (Figure 6.4). The shaded areas represent the unlikely outcomes. In this case, what is unlikely is that the true population mean will fall in one of these areas. The unshaded areas represent the more probable outcomes; in this case, the probable outcome is that the true population mean will be here. The level of probability is set by

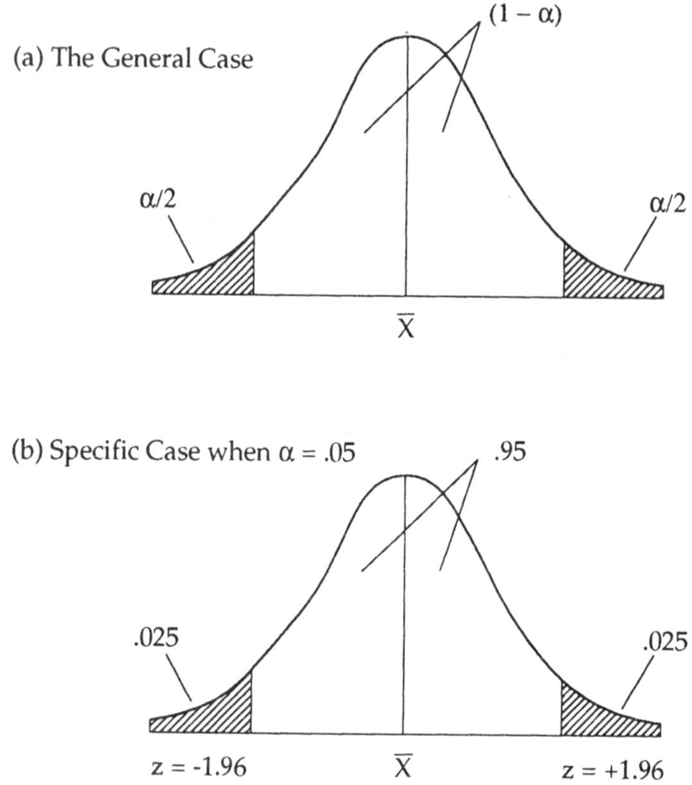

Figure 6.4. *Probability and Confidence Intervals*

alpha. In this sense the establishment of a confidence interval is analogous to a hypothesis test.

We have in this discussion dealt with only three confidence intervals (68 percent, 95 percent, and 99 percent). We can, however, establish whatever confidence intervals we wish. The procedure involves the use of z-scores. You may have noticed that the values 68 percent, 95 percent, and 99 percent correspond to the areas under the normal curve that are bounded by the z-scores of $\pm$ 1.00, $\pm$ 1.96, and $\pm$ 2.58 respectively. Therefore, it follows that if we wanted to construct another confidence interval, say 80 percent, the procedure would be to find the z-score whose positive and negative values correspond to 80 percent of the area under the curve. This value is $z = \pm 1.28$, and the 80 percent confidence interval is $X \pm 1.28s_{\bar{X}}$.

Sample Size and the Standard Error

It should be obvious from Formula 6.4 that as the sample size gets larger, the standard error will get smaller. This is true regardless of how large the population may be. Mathematically, this is obvious because increasing the size of n will result in a larger divisor in the formula and a correspondingly smaller quotient. In logical terms this means that increasing the sample size is an excellent way to increase the reliability of a sample statistic. Increasing the size of n decreases the size of the standard error, which in turn decreases the size of any given confidence interval; this means that we become increasingly certain about the accuracy of our sample statistics. Figure 6.5 may help to clarify this point. Figure 6.5(a) describes a population. In 6.5(b), each element in the sample corresponds to an element of the population, so the two distributions are identical and the standard error equals the standard deviation. In 6.5(c), the increased n results in a smaller standard error. Finally, in 6.5(d), there is no standard error at all. Because the sample is identical to the population, there is no sampling error.

Quick Quiz
6.2

(A) Compute the standard error of the mean for each of the following:

(1) $n = 64$; $s = 16$ (2) $n = 640$; $s = 16$
(3) $n = 6{,}400$; $n = 16$ (4) $n = 400$; $s = 250$

(B) For the data from the sample of thirty homicide rates, determine the 99 percent confidence interval.

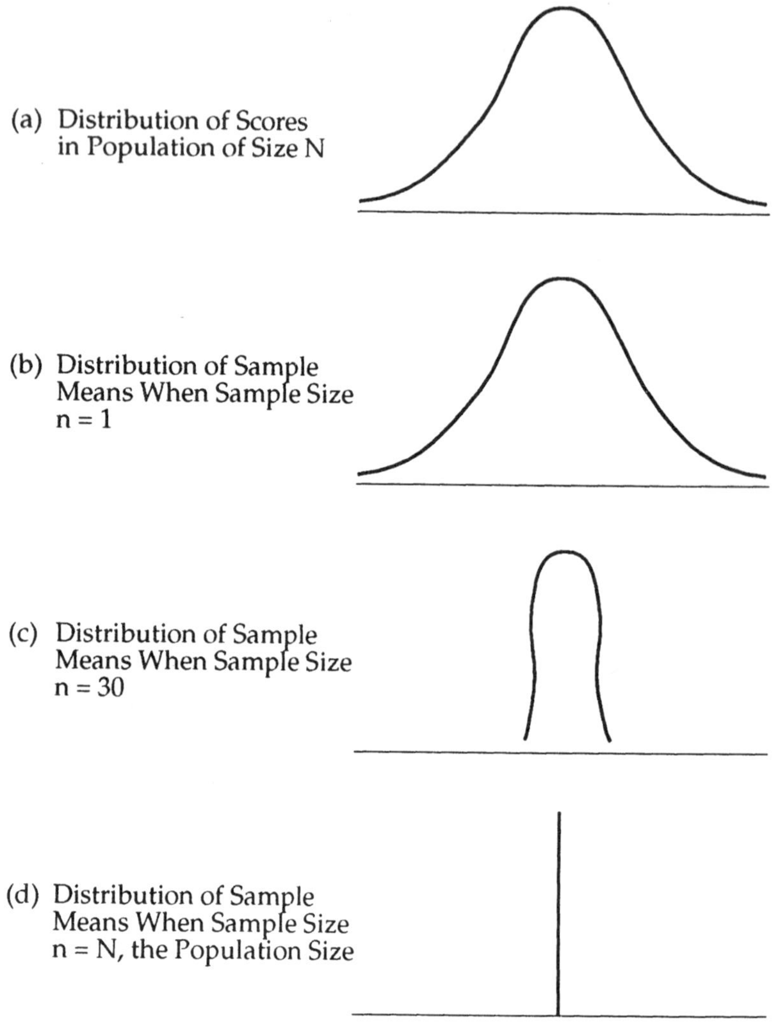

Figure 6.5. *Sample Size and Standard Error*

Estimation from Finite Populations

Although we have not emphasized the point, the previous discussion of estimation assumes in theory that the population in question is infinitely large. But the sociologist rarely deals with an infinitely large population. So in practical terms, we must assume only a "very large" population. The definition of "very large" is arbitrary, and most populations with which we work are sufficiently large so that violation of the assumption does not damage our results. But *if we are dealing with relatively small populations* such as the population of 145 homicide rates, and *especially if the ratio of sample size (n) to population size (N) is large,* that is, when n/N = .20 or greater, a certain adjustment should be made in the calculation of the standard error. In such circumstances, the correct formula is

(Formula 6.6)

$$s_{\bar{X}} = \frac{s}{\sqrt{n}}\sqrt{1 - \frac{n}{N}}$$

The reason for this adjustment is as follows. If the ratio of n/N is small, we would expect the standard error to be relatively large; and if the ratio is large, we would expect the standard error to be relatively small; and if the ratio n/N = 1, we would expect the standard error to be zero (because if the sample is 100 percent of the population there can be no sample error). We can illustrate this by recomputing the standard error for the sample of thirty homicide rates.

$$\begin{aligned} s_{\bar{X}} &= \frac{4.75}{\sqrt{30}}\sqrt{1 - \frac{30}{145}} \\ &= (.87)(\sqrt{.7931}) \\ &= (.87)(.89) \\ &= 0.77 \end{aligned}$$

Thus, we see that the adjusted standard error is smaller than the originally computed value (.77 < .87). This adjustment will, of course, also affect the size of our confidence intervals. For example, the 95 percent confidence interval, originally determined to be from 6.66 to 10.08, now becomes

$$95\%\ \text{CI} = 8.37 \pm 1.96(.77) = 8.37 \pm 1.51$$

or from 6.86 to 9.88. The confidence interval has become a bit smaller.

Important Terms

Population	Sampling distribution
Sample	Standard error
Random sample	Point estimate
Stratified sample	Interval estimate
Area probability sample	Confidence interval

Suggested Readings

Blalock (1979, Chaps. 12 and 21); Knoke and Bohrnstedt (1991, Chap. 6); Levin and Fox (1988, Chap. 9).

Quick Quiz Answers

Quick Quiz 6.1

(A) Pr = .06 (B) Pr = .50

Quick Quiz 6.2

(A) (1) 2.0 (2) 0.63 (3) 0.20
(4) 12.5

(B) $99\%\ CI = \pm 2.58 s_{\overline{X}}$

$= 8.37 \pm (2.58)(0.87) = 8.37 \pm 2.24$

7

Testing for the Difference Between Means

A common problem in social research involves the determination of whether two or more groups are meaningfully different on some variable. Are homicide rates higher in the North or South? Do minority-group children learn more in integrated or segregated classrooms? Is family income higher among whites than among blacks? Are children reared in permissive environments more neurotic than children reared in strictly controlled environments? In this chapter we will discuss some statistical ways of answering such questions. (It should be clear by now that these questions will usually not be answered in a simple yes-no fashion, but rather in terms of probability statements.)

The t-Test

If the populations in question are small enough, we can answer many such questions by simple enumeration. Thus, if we determine the homicide rate for every northern city and every southern city, we could simply compute the mean rate for each region and give a rather definite answer. But most social research involves collection of data from samples, not from populations, and in Chapter 6 we saw that any sample, no matter how carefully drawn, is subject to some error. Therefore, if we find that a sample of children from permissive home environments has a mean neuroticism score of 56.0 and that a sample from rigid home environments has a mean score of 58.6, and if we realize that each sample mean is subject to some sampling error, can we safely conclude that the two means are truly different? Or is it possible that the observed difference is simply a function of sampling error?

In statistical terms, the problem is this: If we have two samples, each drawn from some population, can we determine whether the two population means are identical or different? Let us illustrate with a specific example. Table 7.1 presents data on the homicide rates for a random sample of thirty-six eastern and thirty western cities. (Note that the following procedure requires a minimum sample size of thirty. If any sample is less than thirty, another technique, described further on, must be used.) From the table we see that the sample of thirty-six eastern cities has a mean homicide rate (a point estimate) that is higher than the mean rate for the sample of thirty western cities. But we know that each of these means is subject to some sampling error, error which can be probabilistically measured by the standard error. Using data from Table 7.1, we can compute the standard error of each sample and establish the 95 percent confidence interval for each sample. An interval estimate of the true population mean of the eastern cities is

$$\begin{aligned} 95\%\ \text{CI} &= \overline{X} \pm 1.96\,(s_{\overline{X}}) \\ &= 9.75 \pm (1.96)\left(\frac{5.67}{\sqrt{36}}\right) \\ &= 9.75 \pm 1.84 \end{aligned}$$

Table 7.1. *Homicide Rates of Thirty-Six Eastern and Thirty Western Cities*

			Eastern			
3	13	15	12	6	17	$\overline{X} = 9.75$
12	21	2	3	14	7	$s = 5.67$
4	4	2	9	16	4	$s^2 = 32.14$
6	15	14	5	2	10	$s_{\overline{X}} = 0.94$
15	18	13	5	3	10	$n = 36$
5	16	16	14	16	4	
						95% CI is from 7.91 to 11.59
			Western			
11	3	10	4	16	11	$\overline{X} = 8.73$
8	4	9	5	5	13	$s = 4.19$
7	13	10	4	11	6	$s^2 = 7.58$
3	16	5	5	17	10	$s_{\overline{X}} = 0.77$
15	11	5	7	6	12	$n = 30$
						95% CI is from 7.23 to 10.23

and an interval estimate of the true population mean of the western cities is

$$95\%\ CI = 8.73 \pm 1.96\left(\frac{4.19}{\sqrt{30}}\right)$$
$$= 8.73 \pm 1.50$$

Notice that the point estimate of the eastern rate falls within the interval estimate of the western rate (and vice versa). Figure 7.1 may help to clarify this observation. From this illustration we can see that it is reasonable to find a sample mean of 8.73 (the western mean) within the interval estimate of the eastern mean; it is also reasonable to find a sample mean of 9.75 (the eastern mean) within the interval estimate of the mean for western areas. This line of reasoning leads us to the inference that the two sample means may plausibly reflect two population means that, we may assume, are virtually identical.

If the interval estimate for eastern cities did *not* include the point estimate for the western cities (and if the interval for the western cities did not include the eastern sample mean), we could reasonably conclude that the two sample means represented two population means that were distinctly and truly different from one another. (Such a situation is described in Figure 7.2 on page 122.)

The "Student's t" statistic is a measure that in similar logical fashion tells us whether two sample means reflect two distinct population means. Stated differently, the t-test is a test for the significance of the difference between two sample means. It tells us whether an observed difference is a "true" difference or is merely a difference that could have occurred "by chance."

(For the student who by now may be somewhat bored by statistics, we offer the following brief and irreverent digression. "Student" was the pen name of W. S. Gosset. Gosset was either a brewer who knew statistics, or a statistician who worked for a brewery. In planning to brew beer, he had to deal with the fact that the grains were often of different quality, that different water temperatures resulted in different brews, and so on. However, the statistics of his day did not permit him to do the kind of scientific brewing that he wanted. Consequently, Gosset began to develop statistics that would do the trick; the t-test is the most famous of these. Gosset is long dead but that brewery still uses his method to prepare its beer, which is among the most famous in the world.)

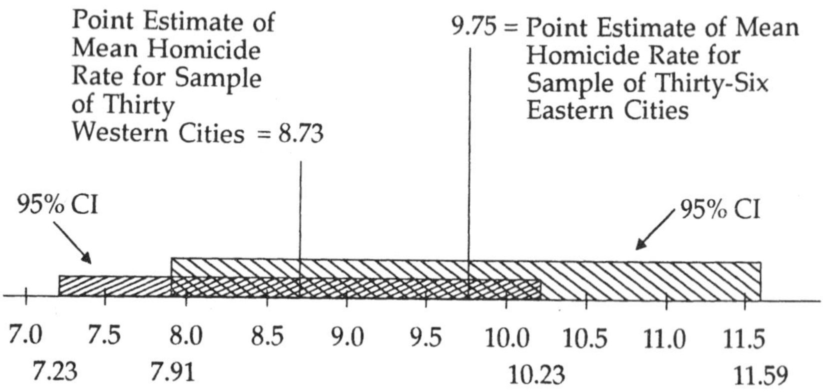

Figure 7.1. *Point and Interval Estimates from Table 7.1*

Suppose we have two populations, one composed of children reared in a permissive environment, the other composed of children from a more rigid environment. We draw a sample from each population and record the *difference between the two sample means*, $\overline{X}_1 - \overline{X}_2$. We then draw another pair of samples and record the difference between means. We do this again and again and again. If we do this often enough, we can build up a picture of the sampling distribution of the difference between means, $\overline{X}_1 - \overline{X}_2$. (A sampling distribution, as we learned in Chapter 6, is a list of all possible outcomes of a statistical event.) This list of all possible differences is normal in form and has its own mean ($\mu_1 - \mu_2$) and its own standard error ($\sigma_{\overline{X}_1 - \overline{X}_2}$).

If we now think of the difference between the two observed sample means as a score, a score that may deviate from the true population mean, we can define the t-statistic as

(Formula 7.1)

$$t = \frac{\overline{X}_1 - \overline{X}_2}{\sqrt{\frac{s_1^2}{n_1} + \frac{s_2^2}{n_2}}} = \frac{\overline{X}_1 - \overline{X}_2}{s_{\overline{X}_1 - \overline{X}_2}}$$

That is, t is equal to the *difference between means* divided by the *standard error of the difference.* You may notice that the formula for t is analogous to the formula for z-scores (Formula 4.15). As a matter of fact, when the sample sizes are sufficiently large (greater than 30) the sampling distribution of t is virtually identical to the sampling distribution of z. (The t-test also assumes that the population variances are equal.)

Suppose our two samples of children had the characteristics described above. We can proceed to test the hypothesis that there is no difference between the two sample means; this hypothesis is our null hypothesis. Stated more formally, our test consists of the four following elements:

1. *A null hypothesis,* H_0: $\mu_1 - \mu_2 = 0$.
2. *An alternative hypothesis,* H_1: $\mu_1 - \mu_2 < 0$ *or* $\mu_1 - \mu_2 > 0$.
3. *A specified level of alpha:* Here, let $\alpha = .05$; two-tail test.
4. *Decision rules:* Reject H_0 if the observed value of t is greater than $\pm$ 1.96; do not reject H_0 if the observed value is less than $\pm$ 1.96.

Inserting the sample data into Formula 7.1, we find

$$t = \frac{56.0 - 58.6}{\sqrt{\frac{6.2^2}{100} + \frac{8.3^2}{95}}} = \frac{-2.6}{\sqrt{.3844 + .7252}}$$

$$= \frac{-2.6}{\sqrt{1.1096}} = \frac{-2.6}{1.05} = -2.47$$

Because our observed value of t exceeds the critical value of $\pm$ 1.96, we can reject the null hypothesis, and by implication we can reasonably assume that there is evidence that the two samples were drawn from two populations whose means are truly different. Figure 7.2 illustrates this example. Notice that the 95 percent confidence interval surrounding $\overline{X} = 56.0$ *does not* include $\overline{X} = 58.6$, and the interval around 58.6 does not include 56.0. In other words, if one of the observed sample means does reflect a true population value, the other sample mean could not have come from the same population.

> *Quick Quiz*
> **7.1**
>
> Compute and interpret t for the data from Table 7.1. Let α =.05, two-tail test.

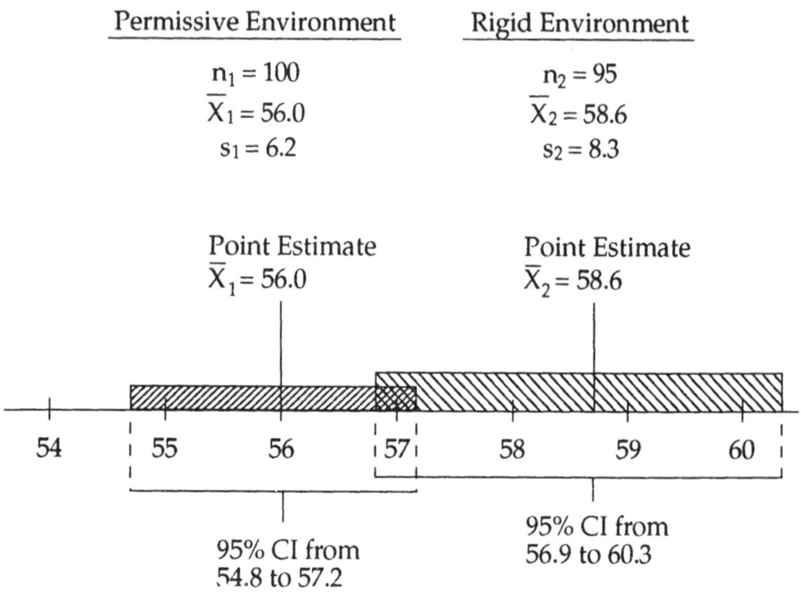

Figure 7.2. *Point and Interval Estimates, Another Example*

Small-Sample t-Test

In the previous section we assumed that sample sizes were large (that is, both values of n are greater than 30). The reason for this is that the t distribution is virtually identical to the unit normal (or z) distribution when the samples are large. However, if the sample size is small, an adjustment must be made in the calculation of t. For small samples the formula is

(Formula 7.2)

$$t = \frac{\overline{X}_1 - \overline{X}_2}{\sqrt{\dfrac{n_1 s_1^2 + n_2 s_2^2}{n_1 + n_2 - 2}}\sqrt{\dfrac{n_1 + n_2}{n_1 n_2}}}$$

In the small-sample case, the t distribution does not correspond to the z distribution. Furthermore, as the sizes of the samples change, the shape of the t distribution also changes; thus, there is not one t distribution but many. In statistical terminology, this happens because the *degrees of freedom* associated with t are a direct function of sample size.

Degrees of Freedom for t

We must again digress for a moment, this time to take up the concept of degrees of freedom, a concept that is related to many statistical problems. We have seen that we can use sample statistics to estimate true population values (commonly called *parameters*). In this chapter we are using a sample mean to estimate a population mean, and a sample standard deviation to estimate a population standard deviation. There are no restrictions placed on the data when computing a mean; in other words, each of the several values that compose the mean is "free to vary." For example, if N = 5, the five numbers may take on *any* values, and we can still compute the mean no matter how great or small the five values are. However, when we compute a standard deviation, the data are not completely free. One restriction is imposed, namely that

$$s_{\overline{X}} = \Sigma(X - \overline{X}) = 0$$

that is, the sum of the deviations about the mean must be zero. We then say that this restriction uses up one degree of freedom.

Let us use another example, hypothetical, to illustrate degrees of freedom. Suppose we have five numbers and for some strange reason we *require* that their mean be 10. How many of the five values are free to vary? To answer this, examine the four sets of data below. Note that each group has a mean of 10.

	(a)	(b)	(c)	(d)
	7	6	25	6.8
	8	9	-14	13.7
	9	14	10	19.5
	10	3	-6	17.1
	?	?	?	?
$X =$	50	50	50	50
$\overline{X} =$	10	10	10	10

In each instance, the first four numbers are "free"—they may take on any value. But once these four numbers have assumed some value, the fifth term, the "?" term, is not free; it is determined. In (a), the fifth number must be 16. If it is any other number, the requirement that the mean is 10 cannot be met. In (b), the fifth value must be 18; in (c), 35; and in (d) it must be -7.1. It is in this sense that the computation of a sample standard deviation uses up one degree of freedom.

In computing the t statistic we make use of not one but two standard deviations, one from each sample. Therefore, the degrees of freedom for the t-test are

(Formula 7.3)

$$df(t) = (n_1 - 1) + (n_2 - 1) = n_1 + n_2 - 2$$

Because the small sample test involves degrees of freedom and different t distributions, we cannot use Appendix Table A to obtain the critical values. Critical values for t are obtained from Appendix Table B.

Small-Sample t: An Example

Suppose an experiment yields the following data:

Experimental Group	Control Group
$n_1 = 16$	$n_2 = 25$
$\overline{X}_1 = 117$	$\overline{X}_2 = 112$
$s_1 = 14$	$s_2 = 12$

We wish to test the hypothesis that there is no difference between means. If we use a one-tail test with alpha = .05,

$$t = \frac{117 - 112}{\sqrt{\dfrac{16\,(14^2) + 25\,(12^2)}{16 + 25 + 2}}\sqrt{\dfrac{16 + 25}{16 \times 25}}}$$

$$= \frac{5}{\sqrt{\dfrac{3{,}136 + 3{,}600}{39}}\sqrt{\dfrac{41}{400}}}$$

$$= \frac{5}{\sqrt{172.72}\sqrt{.1025}} = \frac{5}{13.14\ (.32)} = 1.19$$

With df = (16 + 25 - 2) = 39, the critical value obtained from Appendix Table B is 1.68. (Actually, that is the value for df = 40, which is the closest value indicated in the table.) Our observed value is less than the critical value, so we do not reject the null hypothesis. In other words, we conclude that the two sample means are *not* different; given the size of the samples, a difference such as the one we observed could have occurred by chance.

Quick Quiz
7.2

Given the following data, test the null hypothesis that there is no difference in levels of anxiety between sophomores and seniors. (Let alpha = .01 and use a one-tail test.)

Anxiety Scores	
Sophomores	Seniors
$\bar{X} = 49$	$\bar{X} = 43$
s = 6	s = 5
n = 12	n = 16

The t-Test for Matched Samples

In both the large-sample and the small-sample t-tests, we assume that the two samples are *independent;* that is, we assume that whether a given unit is selected for inclusion in one sample has no bearing whatsoever on the selection of a given unit for the second sample. However, there are many instances in sociological research for which this assumption does not hold. In a study of husbands' and wives' attitudes, for example, the inclusion of one spouse in a sample

Table 7.2. *Violent Crime Rate (Rounded) for Fifteen Cities*

City	Year 1	Year 10	D = Difference	D^2
New York	1,060	1,480	420	176,400
Chicago	920	1,170	250	62,500
Los Angeles	950	1,060	110	121,000
Philadelphia	420	750	330	108,900
Detroit	1,220	1,680	460	211,600
Houston	610	690	80	6,400
Baltimore	2,060	1,770	-290	84,100
Dallas	470	1,000	530	280,900
Washington	1,510	1,560	50	2,500
Cleveland	630	1,010	380	144,400
Indianapolis	580	340	-240	57,600
Milwaukee	220	290	70	4,900
San Francisco	1,300	1,200	-100	10,000
San Diego	200	370	170	28,900
San Antonio	380	590	210	44,100
			2,430	1,235,300

Mean Difference: $\overline{D} = \dfrac{2{,}430}{15} = 162$

Standard Deviation: $s_D = 297.00$
Standard Error: $s_{\overline{D}} = 76.7$

implies the inclusion of the other spouse; or, in a study of homicide rates in large cities over a ten-year period, the inclusion of a city in the first time sample implies that the same city will also be in the second time sample. Such samples are said to be *matched,* or correlated. Matched samples are dealt with more efficiently by a special version of the t-test.

Table 7.2 lists the violent crime (murder, rape, robbery, and assault) rate for fifteen large cities in two different years. The table lists the differences (D) between the rate for each city in both years, the standard deviation of D, the mean difference ($\overline{D}$), and the standard error of $\overline{D}$. The value of t is then defined as a ratio of the mean difference to the standard error of the difference, as in Formula 7.4:

(Formula 7.4)

$$t = \frac{\bar{D}}{s_{\bar{D}}}$$

The degrees of freedom for this variation of the t-test are (n - 1), where n is the *number of pairs* from which differences are obtained. For the data from Table 7.2,

$$t = \frac{162}{76.7} = 2.11$$

Our null hypothesis is that there is no difference between means. If we specify a one-tail test with α = .01, and with df = (15 - 1) = 14, the critical value obtained from Appendix Table B is 2.62. Our observed value of t falls short of the critical value; therefore, we *do not reject* the null hypothesis. (Had we established a level of α = .05, our decision would have been to *reject* H_0. Here we see the importance of specifying alpha in advance of the statistical test.)

An SPSS Example of the t-Test

Using the T-TEST procedure in SPSS, I want to determine if the mean score for those who voted for George Bush is different from the mean score for those who voted for Michael Dukakis in 1988. Next, I want to look at the difference between working- and middle-class respondents (disregarding lower- and upper-class respondents) with regard to their TV viewing hours. What follows is an SPSS run that uses the procedure T-TEST to analyze the difference between the mean POLVIEWS scores for the 1988 voters and then the mean hours of TV viewing for lower- and upper-class respondents.

These commands indicate that we are going to look at the two groups of voters—those who supported Bush and those who supported Dukakis—with respect to their political views of themselves as liberal or conservative. Here, remember that POLVIEWS is coded as a seven-point scale, with a value of 1 being most liberal and 7 being most conservative. [NOTE: I am assuming here that POLVIEWS can be treated as an interval-level variable.]

Next, we will issue commands that request the determination of the difference between the mean number of TV hours viewed by lower- and upper-class respondents. The values in parentheses (1,4) specify that only the two groups coded as 1 (lower class) and 4 (upper class) are to be enumerated. If we had not included the parenthetical information, the t-test, by default, would have been computed for groups coded as 1 and 2.

POLVIEWS and TVHOURS Examples:

```
10 T-TEST  GROUPS = PRES88
11  /VARIABLES = POLVIEWS
```

t-tests for independent samples of PRES88: VOTE FOR DUKAKIS OR BUSH

GROUP 1 - PRES88 EQ 1: DUKAKIS
GROUP 2 - PRES88 EQ 2: BUSH

Variable	Number of Cases	Mean	Standard Deviation	Standard Error
POLVIEWS THINK OF SELF AS LIBERAL OR CONSERVATIVE				
GROUP 1	76	3.5000	1.438	0.165
GROUP 2	125	4.6800	1.202	0.108

		Pooled Variance Estimate			Separate Variance Estimate		
F Value	2-tail Prob.	t Value	Degs of Freedom	2-tail Prob.	t Value	Degs of Freedom	2-tail Prob.
-1.43	.078	-6.26	199	.000	-5.99	137.32	.000

TVHOURS and CLASS Example:

```
12 T-TEST  GROUPS = CLASS (1,4)
13  /VARIABLES = TVHOURS
```

(continued)

(continued)

t-tests for independent samples of CLASS SUBJECTIVE CLASS IDENTIFICATION

GROUP 1 - CLASS EQ 1: LOWER CLASS
GROUP 2 - CLASS EQ 4: UPPER CLASS

Variable	Number of Cases	Mean	Standard Deviation	Standard Error
TVHOURS	HOURS PER DAY WATCHING TV			
GROUP 1	13	3.5385	2.222	0.616
GROUP 2	7	2.2857	1.496	0.565

		Pooled Variance Estimate			Sep. Variance Estimate		
F Value	2-tail Prob.	t Value	Degs of Freedom	2-tail Prob.	t Value	Degs of Freedom	2-tail Prob.
2.21	341	1.33	18	.200	1.50	16.84	.153

Important Terms

The t-test (for large and small samples, and correlated data)
Standard error of the difference
Degrees of freedom

Suggested Readings

Blalock (1979, Chap. 13); Freeman (1965: 199-209); Knoke and Bohrnstedt (1991, Chap. 7); Mueller, Schuessler, and Costner (1970: 404-419); Ott et al. (1992, Chap. 8).

Quick Quiz Answers

Quick Quiz 7.1

$$t = \frac{9.75 - 8.73}{\sqrt{\frac{5.67^2}{36} + \frac{4.19^2}{30}}} = \frac{1.02}{\sqrt{.8930 + .5852}}$$

$$= \frac{1.02}{\sqrt{1.4782}} = \frac{1.02}{1.2158} = 0.84$$

Because the observed value of t does not exceed the critical value of ±1.96, we *do not reject* the null hypothesis; we conclude that the two sample means reflect two population means that are not different. The observed difference between the sample means could have occurred by chance; the difference is not statistically significant.

Quick Quiz 7.2

$$t = \frac{49 - 43}{\sqrt{\frac{12(6^2) + 16(5^2)}{12 + 16 - 2}}\sqrt{\frac{12 + 16}{12 \times 16}}}$$

$$= 2.78$$

The observed value of t exceeds the critical value (which is 2.48), so we can *reject* the null hypothesis and conclude that the two means are truly different; the observed difference is not a function of sampling error; it could not have occurred by chance.

8

Analysis of Variance

In the previous chapter we described a procedure, the t-test, for testing whether a difference between *two* means is significant. The next logical questions is, What do we do when we have *three or more* means? One apparent answer is to repeat the t-test, taking two means at a time until all possible comparisons have been made. Thus, if we have five groups of subjects, we would conduct ten separate t-tests to find out which pairs of means are significantly different. Running that many tests can be tedious, but there are two other more important reasons why this procedure is generally not accepted by most statisticians. (1) If we run a large number of tests of significance, we can expect as a matter of chance that a certain proportion of these tests, a proportion defined by alpha, will be significant. For example, if we conduct one hundred t-tests, the laws of probability tell us that five of these tests will be statistically significant at the .05 level and one will be significant at the .01 level. Multiple tests, therefore, increase the likelihood of making an incorrect decision concerning the null hypothesis. (2) In more sophisticated research designs where there are two or more independent variables, we must acknowledge the fact that these variables can and do *interact* with one another. Because the t-test does not "partial out" these interaction effects, it will necessarily produce results that are not free from this bias.

The procedure known as *analysis of variance* (ANOVA) is used when we wish to make comparisons among three or more means. In this text we will examine only the most elementary form of ANOVA, simple, or *one-way*, analysis of variance. One-way ANOVA is used when there is only one independent variable but three or more categories of that variable. (If there are two independent variables, a technique called two-way ANOVA is used; this and other techniques,

Table 8.1. *Data for Analysis of Variance Example: Three Schools, Nine Students*

	Scores of Students from		
	School A	School B	School C
	-10	0	+10
	-10	0	+10
	-10	0	+10
$\Sigma X =$	-30	0	+30
$\overline{X} =$	-10	0	+10

such as multiple analysis of variance, are described in advanced texts [Edwards 1974; Winer et al., 1991].)

Like the t-test, ANOVA requires that the dependent, or criterion, variable be capable of at least interval measurement. ANOVA also assumes that our samples of subjects have been randomly selected from a distribution that is approximately normal in shape. Further, we must assume that the variances of the two samples are approximately equal. The independent, or predictor, variable may be at any level of measurement, even nominal.

The t-test focuses attention on the means of samples; ANOVA looks instead at the patterns of variability in the individual scores that make up the samples. It looks at this variability as it is found in two different ways: *within* categories of the independent variable and *between* those categories.

Consider the following example. Suppose there are three schools (A, B, and C). From each of the three schools we randomly select three students and measure these nine subjects on some variable, obtaining the data in Table 8.1.

There are several important things to notice in Table 8.1. First, the means of the three groups appear to be quite different, ranging from -10 to +10. Thus, between (grammatically, among) the groups there appears to be some difference in the average (mean) scores of the subjects. Second, within each of the groups the scores are identical;

that is, there is no variation whatsoever within groups. Finally, note that the overall mean, $\overline{X}_T$, for all nine subjects combined is 0.00.

In this example, the term *variation* refers not merely to the general meaning of dispersion or variability but also to the technical definition of variation as the *sum of squares*, SS (also known as Σx^2, a term that we have already used repeatedly). In the context of ANOVA, we will need to compute several forms of SS. First we need the *total* sum of squares.

(Formula 8.1)

$$SS_T = \Sigma (X - \overline{X}_T)^2 = \Sigma x^2$$

This formula asks that we (1) take each individual score, (2) subtract from it the overall mean score, (3) square the difference, then (4) add the squared values. For our nine subjects,

Score	Score - Mean	(Score - Mean)^2
-10	-10	100
0	0	0
+10	+10	100

Note, however, that three subjects have a score of -10 and three have a score of +10; thus, for all nine subjects, the total sum of squares is (100 + 100 + 100 + 0 + 0 + 0 + 100 + 100 + 100) = 600.

The total sum of squares is made up of two parts: the *within-groups* sum of squares (SS_w) and the *between-groups* sum of squares (SS_b). SS_w is determined by taking each individual score, subtracting its group mean, squaring, and summing all of the squared values. Stated differently, SS_w is the sum of the squared deviations of each individual score from its own sample (category, group) mean. A logical formula for SS_w is presented as Formula 8.2, but an easier way to compute this value is given as Formula 8.3.

(Formula 8.2)

$$SS_w = \Sigma(X - \overline{X}_c)^2$$

where $\overline{X}_c$ is the mean of the category in which the raw score is located. For our data,

X	$X - \overline{X}_c$
-10	0
0	0
+10	0

(Remember that there are three subjects with each of the previous scores.) Our within-groups sum of squares is thus 3(0) + 3 (0) + 3(0) = 0.00.

(Formula 8.3)

$$SS_w = \Sigma\left[\Sigma nX^2 - \frac{(\Sigma X_w)^2}{n}\right]$$

In Formula 8.3, the quantity within the square brackets is computed for *each* group. For our example,

X	nX^2	$(\Sigma X_w)^2$	$\frac{(\Sigma X_w)^2}{n}$	$\Sigma nX^2 - \frac{(\Sigma X_w)^2}{n}$
-10	300	900	300	0
0	0	0	0	0
+10	300	900	300	0

When we sum the last column, we again get $SS_w = 0.00$.

The final sum-of-squares value needed is SS_b, the between-groups sum of squares. Because we have already figured the *total* SS to be 600 and the *within-groups* SS to be 0, it follows that the *between-groups* SS must be 600 - 0 = 600. However, let us also look at how this value, SS_b, might be computed on its own. Conceptually, the between-groups sum of squares is the difference between each sample mean and the overall mean. That is,

(Formula 8.4)

$$SS_b = \Sigma((\overline{X}_s - \overline{X}_T)^2 n)$$

where $\overline{X}_s$ is a sample mean and n is the number of cases in a given category. For our data,

$$SS_b = (10 - 0)^2 3 + (0 - 0)^2 3 + (-10 - 0)^2 3$$
$$= 300 + 0 + 300 = 600$$

An alternative computing formula is

(Formula 8.5)

$$SS_b = \Sigma\left[\frac{(\Sigma X)^2}{n} - \frac{(\Sigma X_T)^2}{N}\right]$$

where n = the number of cases in a category; N = the total size of all samples combined; and ΣX_T is the sum of *all* raw scores. For our data,

$$SS_b = \left(\frac{30^2}{3} + \frac{0^2}{3} + \frac{30^2}{3}\right) - \frac{0^2}{9} = 600$$

The logic of ANOVA can be seen by another example. Suppose we have four income groups (I, II, III, and IV). A sample of n = 5 is taken from each group. These twenty subjects are then given an instrument that measures some attitude on an interval scale. Table 8.2 gives two possible outcomes of such a study. In 8.2(a) we observe four means that correspond exactly to the four means of 8.2(b). But would you be more inclined to conclude that one set of means is truly different and that the other set is different only by chance? You might if you looked at the pattern of variation. In 8.2(a) the scores that go into Group I have only a small amount of within-groups variation; they tend to cluster together. The same is true of the scores that compose the other three within-groups means. This clustering of scores is statistically measured by the variance s^2. This clustering phenomenon is shown graphically in Figure 8.1(a). Here the circles tend to cluster around 80, the stars around 86, and so on. Because the pattern of dispersion as measured by the variance is small, we have greater confidence in the accuracy and reliability of the sample mean. (Recall the discussion of sampling error in Chapter 6.)

Now focus attention on Table 8.2(b). Again we have the same means. But notice the patterns of dispersion. The scores do not cluster closely about the mean; rather, they range widely. In Figure 8.1(b) we see that there is great overlap among the constituent elements of the four categories. A statistical measure of the variance within each of the four income groups would be quite large relative to the groups in (a). Consequently, we would have less confidence in the sample means

Table 8.2. *Comparison of Four Samples*

(a) Small Variation Within Four Income Groups

Income Group:	I	II	III	IV
	80	81	84	91
	81	82	86	87
	81	82	87	88
	79	85	87	89
	79	80	86	90
Group Mean =	80	82	86	89

(b) Large Variation Within Four Income Groups

Income Group:	I	II	III	IV
	85	76	87	79
	80	92	95	98
	75	86	80	99
	73	82	92	77
	87	74	76	92
Group Mean =	80	82	86	89

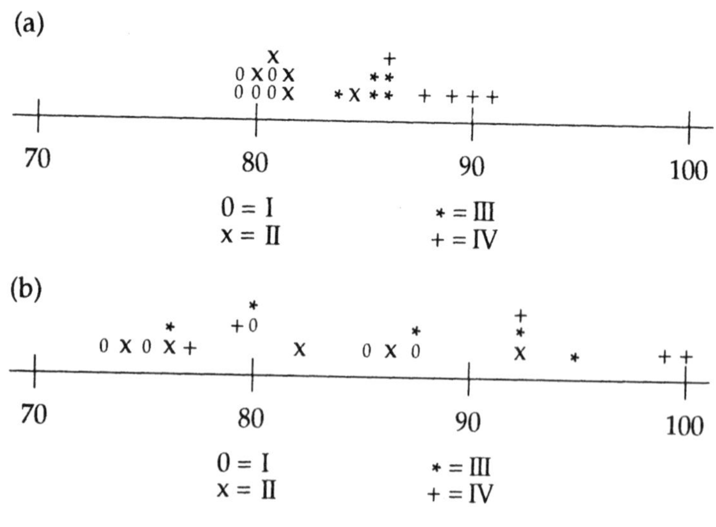

Figure 8.1. *Schematic Representation of Table 8.2*

of (b) as reliable indicators of true population means. We would be more likely to attribute differences among means to sampling error than to true differences.

Carefully examine Table 8.2 and Figure 8.1. Together they should help you to understand the concept of analysis of variance. Even if you do not grasp all of the mathematics of ANOVA, you should be able to develop a mental picture of ANOVA. It is a technique that provides a statistical answer to the question, Does a pattern of dispersion, as measured by the variance, indicate that sample means are truly different, or does it indicate that the difference is due to chance or to sampling error?

We can think of our problem in yet another way. Let us focus attention less on the sample means and more on the sample variance. We can first speak of the total variance, s_T^2. (In the language of ANOVA, the variance is sometimes referred to as the *mean square*—short for "mean squared deviations.") In our example, we could compute the total variance by using Formula 4.7 (see p. 68). Here,

(Formula 8.6)

$$s_T^2 = \frac{\Sigma x^2}{n - 1}$$

In the present case, we would first find the grand mean of all twenty scores, determine the deviation of each score from the grand mean, square these deviations, sum them, and divide by (n - 1). This procedure yields the total variance.

The total variance can, in turn, be divided into two components. The first is the *within-groups variance,* s_W^2. This value is obtained by computing the variance *within each* sample, then finding the mean variance for *all* samples. In terms of a simple computational procedure,

(Formula 8.7)

$$s_W^2 = \frac{\Sigma s^2}{k}$$

where s^2 is a sample variance and k is the number of samples.

The second component of the total variance is the *between-groups variance,* s_B^2. The between-groups variance is obtained by using the difference between each sample mean and the grand mean as a deviation score, x, which is squared, weighted for sample size (n), summed, and then divided by (k - 1). Thus

(Formula 8.8)

$$s_b^2 = \frac{\Sigma(x^2 n)}{k - 1}$$

where the deviation score, x, is the difference between a sample mean and the grand mean; n is the number of cases in a category; and k is the number of categories.

The actual analysis of variance is then computed by means of the F ratio, or F-test, which is simply a ratio of the between-groups variance to the within-groups variance.

(Formula 8.9)

$$F = \frac{s_b^2}{s_w^2}$$

For this F-test the null hypothesis states that the two variances, s_b^2 and s_w^2, are equal, and that both are equal to the true population variance. If the two sample variances are indeed equal, or close to equal, the ratio of one to the other will be approximately 1.00. But if s_b^2 is greater than s_w^2, the F-ratio will become considerably larger than 1.00; this indicates the null hypothesis cannot be accepted. [Note that the value of F can never be negative. It may vary between zero and infinity.]

Let us now illustrate the analysis of variance with a specific example. Suppose we draw a sample of n = 6 students from each of k = 4 schools. Each student is measured on some standard achievement test and results are obtained (see Table 8.3). First we calculate the within-groups variance and then we calculate the between-groups variance:

$$s_w^2 = \frac{2.0 + 2.4 + 4.3 + 2.0}{4}$$

$$= \frac{10.7}{4} = 2.675$$

x = Sample $\overline{X}$ – Grand $\overline{X}$	x^2	n	x^2n
-1.625	2.64	6	15.84
1.375	1.89	6	11.34
-0.125	0.02	6	0.12
0.375	0.14	6	0.84
	Total		28.14

$$s_b^2 = \frac{28.14}{4 - 1} = 9.38$$

Finally we compute the F-ratio:

$$F = \frac{s_b^2}{s_w^2} = \frac{9.38}{2.675} = 3.51$$

The F-ratio is larger than 1.00. However, before we can determine whether this F is statistically different from one that could have occurred by chance, we need one further piece of information: the *degrees of freedom* associated with each variance. (The reason for this is that, as with the t distribution, there is not one F distribution but many; in fact, there is a different sampling distribution of F for every different combination of degrees of freedom.) The degrees of freedom associated with the between-groups variance are determined by

(Formula 8.10)

$$df_b = k - 1$$

and the degrees of freedom associated with the within-groups variance are found by

(Formula 8.11)

$$df_w = N - k$$

where N is the total number of subjects. The total degrees of freedom for the analysis of variance are thus N - 1. For our data, $df_b = 4 - 1 = 3$ and $df_w = 24 - 4 = 20$. To interpret F, we use the table of critical values of F (Appendix Table C) for df = 3 and 20. The critical value read from

Table 8.3. *Data for Analysis of Variance: Four Schools, Twenty-Four Students*

	School 1	School 2	School 3	School 4
	15	17	17	15
	14	17	15	17
	15	19	13	19
	16	19	18	18
	17	20	18	16
	13	16	18	17
ΣX:	90	108	99	102
$\overline{X}$:	15.00	18.00	16.50	17.00
s^2:	2.00	2.40	4.30	2.00
Grand Mean = $\overline{X}_T$ = 16.625				

Table C (with $\alpha = .05$) is 3.10. Because our observed value of F is larger than this critical value, we *reject* the null hypothesis, and by implication, we conclude that there is a true difference between the sample means. Had we set the level of alpha at .01, the critical value from Table C would have been 4.94; we would not have rejected the null hypothesis and it would have been reasonable to assume that the observed differences between sample means could have occurred by chance.

This introductory discussion of ANOVA has been kept deliberately simple, and we have stressed the logical understanding of ANOVA rather than the mathematical procedures in the hope that you will grasp the underlying meaning of this type of analysis. However, for purposes of computation we suggest a procedure that works directly from the raw data and does not require the computation of variances. This procedure makes extensive use of the quantity s_x^2, also known as the *sum of squares,* or SS. Again, there are three values: the total sum of squares, the between-groups sum of squares, and the within-groups sum of squares.

The *total sum of squares* is found by computing the grand mean, $\overline{X}_T$, then measuring the deviation of each score from the grand mean, squaring these deviations, and summing. (This procedure was described earlier in Formula 8.1.) It can also be expressed as a computing formula:

(Formula 8.12)

$$\Sigma x_T^2 = SS_T = \Sigma X^2 - [(\Sigma X)^2/N]$$

For the data from Table 8.3,

$$SS_T = (15^2 + 14^2 + 15^2 + ... + 16^2 + 17^2) - \frac{399^2}{24}$$

$$= 6{,}715 - 6{,}633.375 = 81.625$$

The *between-groups sum of squares* is found by squaring the difference between the mean of each group and the grand mean, multiplying this by the sample size of the group, and summing across all groups. (This procedure is contained in the numerator of Formula 8.8.) Using Formula 8.4 for our data,

$$SS_b = (15 - 16.625)^2 + (18 - 16.625)^2$$

$$+ (16.5 - 16.625)^2 + (17 - 16.625)^2$$

$$= 15.844 + 11.344 + 0.094 + 0.844 = 28.126 = 81.625$$

Notice that the two procedures for computing SS_b yield identical values (within rounding error).

The *within-groups* sum of squares could simply be obtained by subtracting SS_b from SS_T, because

$$SS_T = SS_b + SS_w$$

This would give us a value for SS_w of

$$SS_w = 81.625 - 28.125 = 53.5$$

However, it is wise to compute SS_w independently, as a useful check on the accuracy of our work. This can be done using Formula 8.3.

$$SS_w = \left(1{,}360 - \frac{90^2}{6}\right) + \left(1{,}956 - \frac{108^2}{6}\right)$$
$$+ \left(1{,}655 - \frac{99^2}{6}\right) + \left(1{,}744 - \frac{102^2}{6}\right)$$
$$= 10 + 12 + 21.5 + 10 = 53.5$$

With these independently computed values of the various sums of squares we can verify that $SS_T = SS_b + SS_w$, because

$$28.125 + 53.5 = 81.625$$

Finally, the *degrees of freedom* for SS_T are (N - 1), because in computing the grand mean, we must use up one degree of freedom. The degrees of freedom for SS_w are (N - k), because we use up one degree of freedom in computing the mean of each group. And the degrees of freedom for SS_b are the number of groups less one, or (k - 1).

It is a common practice in research writing to summarize all of this information in an ANOVA table such as Table 8.4. The ANOVA table lists the various sources of variation (within and between), the respective df values, the SS values, and finally a value called the *mean square* (MS), which is simply SS/df, and which is the variance. The F statistic is nothing more than a ratio of two variances, the variance between groups of subjects and the variance within groups. When working from an ANOVA table such as Table 8.4, the F statistic can be defined as

(Formula 8.13)

$$F = \frac{MS_b}{MS_w}$$

To determine whether F is statistically significant, use Appendix Table C. In Table 8.4, we see that the computed value of F will occur with a probability of less than 5 percent. Therefore, we can reject the null hypothesis that there is no difference between the two variances; by inference, we can then reasonably assume that there is at least one pair of means that contains a statistically significant difference.

This text presents only a short introduction to ANOVA. But one question needs to be briefly addressed. In the preceding example, we can conclude that there is at least one pair of means that is different. Look again at Table 8.4. Clearly School 1, which has the lowest mean

Table 8.4. *Analysis of Variance for Table 7.4*

Source	df	SS	MS
Between Groups	3	28.125	9.375
Within Groups	20	53.5	2.675
Total	23	81.625	

$F = 3.50$
$p < 0.05$

score (15.00), must be different from School 2, which has the highest mean score (18.00). But what about the other differences? Is the mean score of School 1 different from that of School 3? Is School 2 different from School 4? Simple ANOVA does not answer these questions. However, there are techniques that do answer such questions, and you may refer to more advanced texts to pursue such issues.

An SPSS Example: ANOVA

SPSS computes a simple one-way analysis of variance by using the command ONEWAY. Following that keyword, you must first name the variable that you wish to examine (in this example, POLVIEWS—here treated as an interval variable), then the variable that will be used to categorize the data (here, that variable is HELPSICK—one's attitude regarding government contributions to medical care). In the following example, we have also requested the computer to print the labels for the variables and to provide us with some general descriptive statistics.

Example: ONEWAY (ANOVA)

```
ONEWAY POLVIEWS BY HELPSICK (1,5)

  /FORMAT=LABELS   /STATISTICS=DESCRIPTIVES
File:   GENERAL SOCIAL SURVEY (NORC) 1990
```

(continued)

(continued)

------ ---------ONEWAY----------------

Variable POLVIEWS THINK OF SELF AS LIBERAL OR CONSERVATIVE By Variable HELPSICK SHOULD GOVT HELP PAY FOR MEDICAL CARE?

ANALYSIS OF VARIANCE

SOURCE	D.F.	SUM OF SQUARES	MEAN SQUARES	F RATIO	F PROB.
BETWEEN GROUPS	4	98.5354	24.6339	13.5869	.0000
WITHIN GROUPS	834	1512.0915	1.8131		
TOTAL	838	1610.6269			

GROUP	COUNT	MEAN	STD DEV	STD ERROR
GOVT HELP	253	3.7549	1.5234	.0958
Grp 2	222	4.1396	1.2668	.0850
AGREE BOTH	261	4.3333	1.2710	.0787
Grp 4	67	4.7761	1.1784	.1440
SELF HELP	36	4.9722	1.3199	.2200
TOTAL	839	4.1704	1.3864	.0479

GROUP	95 PCT CONF INT FOR MEAN
GOVT HELP	3.5663 TO 3.9436
Grp 2	3.9721 TO 4.3072
AGREE BOTH	4.1784 TO 4.4882
Grp 4	4.4887 TO 5.0635
SELF HELP	4.5256 TO 5.4188
TOTAL	4.0765 TO 4.2644

The ANOVA table tells us that there is at least one pair of subjects whose POLVIEW scores are statistically different. (More elaborate

SPSS procedures can help us identify whether there are more pairs that are different. Here, however, we can get a clue as to which pairs might be different by examining the confidence intervals. Notice that the CI for the first group does not contain the confidence interval for any other of the four remaining groups. This suggests that the first group, those who believe the government should provide medical care, is different from every other group. The CI of Group 2 does overlap with the CI for the third group but not with the CIs of the fourth or fifth groups; this suggests that Group 2 is not different from Group 3 in terms of POLVIEWS, but is different from Groups 4 and 5.)

Important Terms

Analysis of variance	Total variance
Sum of squares (SS)	Within-groups variance
Within-groups sum of squares	Between-groups variance
Between-groups sum of squares	Mean square (MS)
F-ratio	

Suggested Readings

Arney (1990, Chap. 13); Levin and Fox (1991, Chap. 9).

9

Measuring the Association Between Two Nominal Variables

The Concept of Statistical Association

In the first few chapters of this book we studied various statistics that describe a set of data. Those measures of centrality and dispersion were applied to a single-variable, or univariate, data set. We saw, for example, ways of computing mean family income or modal religious preference. As important as such univariate descriptive measures are, their utility is clearly limited, since so many sociological problems usually call for a type of analysis far more complex than that which can be provided by the simple description of a single variable. Such analyses must also tell us how two or more variables are related to each other. In this chapter and Chapters 10-12 we will examine some of the many measures that sociologists use to assess the relationships between two variables. Such measures are called measures of relationship, association, or correlation. In general, we shall say that *"two qualities are associated when the distribution of values of the one differs for different values of the other"* (Weiss 1968: 158). In statistical language, the opposite of association is *independence*. We can illustrate these concepts of association and independence by using the data from Tables 9.1 and 9.2. In Table 9.1, the variables of sex and preference for Brand X are independent, or not associated: Proportionately as many males as females prefer Brand X. However, in Table 9.2 the variables are associated: As we go from the category male to the category female, the proportion of people preferring Brand Y *changes* from 40 percent to 10 percent. This example illustrates another way by which we define association and

Table 9.1. *Sex and Preference for Brand X (Percentage Distribution)*

		Sex	
		Male	Female
Prefer Brand X	Yes	40	40
	No	60	60
	Totals	100	100

Table 9.2. *Sex and Preference for Brand Y (Percentage Distribution)*

		Sex	
		Male	Female
Prefer Brand Y	Yes	40	10
	No	60	90
	Totals	100	100

independence. *If subgroup proportions of variable A differ within a given subgroup of variable B, we have association. If such subgroup proportions do not differ, we have independence.*

There are a great many things in the world that seem to be related to or associated with each other. As we noted earlier, height and weight are generally related so that in any population the tall people tend to weigh more than the short people. (The word *tend* is used to emphasize the point that the relationship is not perfect—some tall person may indeed weigh less than some short person.) Intelligence and academic success also are related to one another, as are religious preference and suicide rates, and a host of other variables.

To say that two variables are related is not necessarily to say that the two are causally related. That is, if we find that two variables, A and B, are related, it does not mean that A causes B or that B causes A or that they are both caused by a third variable, C. In fact, no *causal* inference can be drawn from a statistical measure of relationship. Causality is fundamentally a logical rather than a statistical problem; however, we can and do use the statistical method to help us develop our logical arguments, and there are certain advanced statistical techniques that we can use to detect causality.

To illustrate this distinction between association and causation, let us suppose that we found a statistically significant relationship between the number of storks in given geographic areas and the human birthrates of those areas: The more storks in an area, the higher the human birthrate. Such an association, however statistically accurate, does not mean that babies "cause" storks, or that storks "cause" babies (although a popular myth does support the latter explanation). To explain this relationship, we would have to look beyond the statistical measure. We might better explain the relationship by noting that storks are more frequently found in rural, as opposed to urban, areas and that rural populations typically have higher birthrates than do urban populations.

Users of the statistical method of analysis are not content with merely assuming the existence of a relationship; they want to know, in quantifiable terms, precise information about the relationship between phenomena. Most measures of relationship give us two such pieces of information. First, they tell us the *direction* of the relationship, that is, whether the phenomena in question vary directly (positively) or inversely (negatively) with one another. An example of a direct or positive relationship is the one usually found between income and education. Typically, as one of these variables increases, the other also increases; as measured income level increases, so too, generally, will measured education level. An example of an inverse, or negative, relationship might be found between social class position and rate of juvenile arrests: the higher one's social class, the lower one's rate of arrests. Inverse relationships are those in which one variable increases in magnitude while the other variable decreases. Statistical measures that tell us the direction of a relationship conventionally do so by the simple procedure of using a plus (+) or minus (-) sign before the statistic. The second piece of information we get from most statistical measures of relationship is an indication of the *strength* of the relationship. The indication of strength comes from the size of the computed statistic. Most measures of relationship vary between zero and one: A score of zero reflects the absence of a relationship or no association; a score of one (either +1.00 for a direct relationship or -1.00 if the relationship is inverse) reflects a complete or perfect relationship.

There are many ways that we can use statistics to determine whether two variables are related to each other in any meaningful fashion. Weiss (1968: 161) has suggested five general procedures that can be used to identify relationships between variables.

1. *Departure from independence between two factors.* We imagine what the data would be like if there were no association. Then we say that there is association to the extent that the observed data depart from this....
2. *Magnitude of subgroup differences.* Assuming that there is association, its degree may be measured by direct comparison of subgroup proportions with each other....
3. *Summary of pair-by-pair comparisons.* Another approach would be to think of forming all possible comparisons of one member of the population with another. In each of these comparisons, we should decide whether the two factors under study occurred together or did not. We should then summarize the results of all these pair-by-pair comparisons, and association would be measured by the preponderance of one type of pair....
4. *Proportional reduction of probable error.* We might imagine that we are called on to predict whether factor A exists or not, first without information regarding B, and then with information regarding B. The more we are helped by information regarding B, the more association we are willing to admit....
5. *Extent to which increments in one factor occur together with increments in the other factor.* We might take as our meaning of association the extent to which increase in the one factor is accompanied by increase in the other, or decrease in one by decrease in the other....

Further discussion of these five procedures will be provided at appropriate points in the next few chapters. We begin with an illustration of procedure 2.

Percentage Difference

A discussion of percentage difference as a measure of association was implicit in our discussion of the concept of association. Percentage differences are quite easy to determine: *Within* a category of the *dependent* variable, we compute the percentage difference (if any) between categories of the *independent* variable. If the difference is 0, we can conclude that the two variables are not associated, as in Table 9.1. If the difference is 100, the variables are perfectly associated. Differences between 0 and 100 indicate intermediate degrees of association. (This conceptualization of percentage difference applies only to a 2 × 2 table, that is, a table with two rows and two columns. For larger tables, modification of the preceding technique is necessary.)

Because of its ease of computation and its simple, obvious interpretation, percentage difference has much to recommend it as a measure of association. Its major weakness is that it does not tell us how much of an observed difference constitutes a meaningful difference. To compute this, we must turn to other measures.

Chi-Square: A Test of Statistical Independence

The Chi-square test is one of the most prominent and frequently used statistical tests in sociological literature. With care, it is relatively easy to compute; but before we turn to the computation of Chi-square, let us first come to an understanding of the logic that provides the basis for this statistic. Suppose we have two coins, a nickel and a dime. If we toss each coin twenty times and if the coins are unbiased (that is, if they are "fair" coins, not subject to any controlling force except chance, i.e., *independent*), we could theoretically expect each coin to show ten heads and ten tails. From our earlier discussion of probability (Chapter 5), we know that we will not necessarily get a ten-ten split. Many other outcomes are plausible. For example, we might obtain thirteen heads from the nickel and eight heads from the dime. This outcome is presented in Table 9.3. Clearly, the coins have not adhered perfectly to the theoretically expected ten-ten outcome. Or, in more technical terms, we can suggest that the coins have departed from the *model of statistical independence.* But is this departure sufficiently large to be meaningful? Can it occur by chance? Is this difference between what we observed and what we expected to observe really big enough to make a difference? Should we begin to wonder if one or both of the coins is not statistically independent; if one or both are biased? A return glance to Chapter 5, especially Figure 5.1, may help you to answer this question *without* using Chi-square. Indeed, we will not now provide the Chi-square solution to this problem but will first look at another example more likely to confront a sociologist.

Suppose we are interested in the relationship (if any) between religious preference and political preference (both nominal-level variables). We might suspect, for example, that members of certain religious groups are more likely to vote for candidates from a particular political party. To test this notion, we might draw a random sample of two hundred people, ask them the relevant questions, and obtain the results given in Table 9.4. If we convert the raw frequencies from Table 9.4 to percentages (this is the second procedure suggested by Weiss), we might begin to suspect that there is some departure from the model of statistical independence: It *seems* that Catholics prefer the Democratic party and, to a lesser extent, that Protestants prefer the Republican party. But are we ready to make a judgment on the basis of what *seems* to be? Can we come to a more definitive solution? We can, and we do so by using Chi-square. But first we must face a relatively simple logical problem, a logical problem with a mathematical solution.

Table 9.3. *Hypothetical Coin-Tossing Results*

	Nickel	Dime	Totals
Heads	13	8	21
Tails	7	12	19
Totals	20	20	40

Table 9.4. *Religious and Political Preferences (Hypothetical Data)*

		Religious Preference						
		Protestant		Catholic		Other		Totals
		N	(%)	N	(%)	N	(%)	
	Democrat	30	(30)	40	(57)	10	(33)	80
Party	**Republican**	40	(40)	20	(29)	10	(33)	70
Preference	**Independent**	30	(30)	10	(14)	10	(33)	50
	Totals	100	(100)	70	(100)	30	(99)	200

In the previous discussion on coin tossing, we saw an example of a situation in which we know something about the expected outcomes. On the basis of previous knowledge and experience we know that unbiased coins should yield, on the average and in the long run, an equal number of heads and tails. But in the present situation can we hold any expectations about religious and political preferences? Can we suggest any plausible strategies for determining the appropriate expected frequencies for Table 9.4? One suggestion is to assume that the 200 subjects distribute themselves equally throughout the nine cells of the table. Thus, we would expect to find a value of 22.2 in each cell—a pure "chance" relationship. But this strategy cannot be applied. It forces us to ignore reality because in this instance, we know certain facts which contradict the possibility of equal cell values. For example, we already know that there are 80 Democrats in our sample. The assumption of equal-expected cell frequencies, as described previously, would wrongly lead us to conclude that there were not 80, but 66.6 Democrats (22.2 + 22.2 + 22.2), equally divided among Protestants, Catholics, and others. Because it is foolish to assume 66.6 Democrats when we *know* there are 80, we must seek another strategy for determining expected cell frequencies.

A more appropriate strategy is one that makes full use of what we do know about our data. We know that there are 200 subjects, of whom 80 are Democrats, 70 are Catholics, and so on. Let us consider these *marginal values*. (Marginal values are the column and row subtotals in any tabular distribution.) If chance factors only are operating, we would expect to find no differences in political preference within any of the religious categories. (And alternatively, we would expect to find no differences in religious preference within any of the political categories.) Now let us note that the *proportion* of Democrats in our total sample is 80/200, or 0.40. Similarly, the proportion of Republicans in our sample is 70/200, or 0.35. Therefore, because we have 100 Protestants in our sample, the expected number of persons who are both Protestant *and* Democrat is 100(.4) = 40. The expected number of Catholic-Democrats is 70(.4) = 28, and the expected number of Other-Democrats is 30(.4) = 12. In similar fashion we can calculate the remaining expected cell frequencies. The results of these calculations are found in Table 9.5.

It should be noted that identical results could be obtained by reversing the variables, that is, by first determining the proportions of Protestants (0.50), Catholics (0.35), and others (0.15) and then

Table 9.5. *Expected Cell Frequencies Based on Data from Table 9.4*

		Religious Preference			
		Protestant	Catholic	Other	Totals
	Democrat	40	28	12	80
Political	Republican	35	24.5	10.5	70
Preference	Independent	25	17.5	7.5	50
	Totals	100	70	30	200

multiplying by the numbers of Democrats, Republicans, and Independents. You might want, as an exercise, to verify this.

We shall now examine a way of computing expected cell frequencies, which is, for most people, simpler than the procedure previously employed. In many instances, though not in the present example, this simpler method is also more accurate because it minimizes rounding error. However, before proceeding, please review this section to make certain that you understand the logic of determining expected cell frequencies. The procedure described next is a rote procedure that you should not use unless you understand the reason for doing so.

Suppose we have a very simple 2 × 2 table whose cell values, marginal totals, and grand total are identified by the letters a, b c, d, k, l, m, n, and N (Table 9.6). *The expected values for any cell can be obtained by multiplying the marginal totals associated with that cell and dividing that product by the grand total,* as shown in Table 9.7. This procedure applies not only to 2 × 2 tables, but to tables with any number of rows and columns. Verify this procedure for the data in Table 9.4; your results should be identical to those in Table 9.5.

We now have the basis for developing a measure of statistical independence. From our expected frequencies we know how the data should "behave" in a pure chance situation, that is, in a situation of statistical independence. Comparing these expected values with a set of actually observed values will tell us the extent to which our observed data depart from the chance model. But how shall we construct an appropriate statistic? We can quickly see that it would not be sufficient simply to compute the deviation between observed frequencies (f_o) and expected frequencies (f_e), because some deviations will be positive and others negative, and these will cancel each other

Table 9.6. *Schematic Representation of a 2 × 2 Table*

$\frac{km}{N}$	$\frac{lm}{N}$	m
$\frac{kn}{N}$	$\frac{ln}{N}$	n
k	l	N

Table 9.7. *Expected Frequencies for Table 9.6*

a	b	m
c	d	n
k	l	N

out. Therefore, we need to eliminate the *sign* of the deviation. One way to do this is to *square* each deviation. (If we square a negative number we get a positive number.)

There is one final factor to consider. In examining the table of expected frequencies, we note that each cell in the table can carry a different "weight." Therefore, we must adjust each squared deviation in an appropriate manner. We do this by dividing each squared deviation by the corresponding f_e. This step gives us, for each cell, the mean squared deviation of the observed from the expected frequencies. Repeating this procedure for each cell, we then sum across all cells. The result is a statistic that indicates the extent to which our observed frequencies fit a model of statistical independence. This statistic is Chi-square (χ^2), and it can be simply presented by the formula

(Formula 9.1)

$$\chi^2 = \Sigma \frac{(f_o - f_e)^2}{f_e}$$

where Σ is the summation command, f_o is an observed frequency, and f_e is an expected frequency.

Let us now proceed to a solution of the question we posed earlier: Are religious and political preferences related? A simple work table (Table 9.8) can be used to give us the necessary figures. From this table we see that the computed value of Chi-square is 14.57. You might ask, 14.57 what? There is no simple answer to such a question. The Chi-square statistic has no clear conceptual meaning except to say that as χ^2 gets larger, there is greater departure from the chance model. Remember that Chi-square is defined as the *sum of the mean square deviations of observed from expected frequencies.* So the computed value of Chi-square is but an indication of the magnitude of these mean square deviations. The greater the magnitude, the greater the departure from a chance model. But again, how much of a difference is a meaningful difference? How large must a difference be before we reject the model of statistical independence? To answer these questions and to interpret Chi-square, we still need several pieces of information. Specifically, we must have information about the

Table 9.8. *Work Table for Computing Chi-Square Using Data from Table 9.4*

f_o	f_e	$(f_o - f_e)$	$(f_o - f_e)^2$	$(f_o - f_e)^2/f_e$
30	40	-10	100	2.50
40	28	12	144	5.14
10	12	-2	4	0.33
40	35	5	25	0.71
20	24.5	-4.5	20.25	0.83
10	10.5	-0.5	0.25	0.02
30	25	5	25	1.00
10	17.5	-7.5	56.25	3.21
10	7.5	2.5	6.25	0.83
				14.57 = χ^2

Table 9.9. *Critical Values of Chi-Square for Various (α) and for Varying Degrees of Freedom*

df	α = .10	.05	.02	.01
1	2.71	3.84	5.41	6.64
2	4.61	5.99	7.82	9.21
3	6.25	7.81	9.84	11.34
4	7.78	9.49	11.67	13.28
5	9.24	11.07	13.39	15.09

sampling distribution of the Chi-square statistic. (For a review of sampling distribution, see Chapter 6.) The relevant information about the sampling distribution of Chi-square is presented in Appendix Table D. A small portion of that table is reproduced here as Table 9.9.

A quick glance at Table 9.9 tells us that we need one final piece of information: the degrees of freedom associated with the computed statistic. As you will recall from Chapter 6, it is necessary to consider the degrees of freedom for any sampling distribution that changes its shape as the degrees of freedom change. Chi-square is one such distribution. The approximate shapes of the sampling distributions of Chi-square when df = 1 and when df = 10 are presented in Figure 9.1. You may notice that as df gets larger, the shape of the Chi-square distribution begins to approximate a normal curve.

For the Chi-square statistic, degrees of freedom are determined by the formula

(Formula 9.2)

$$df = (r - 1)(c - 1)$$

where r = the number of rows and c = the number of columns in the contingency table. Why is the degrees of freedom for Chi-square defined as (r - 1) (c - 1)? An illustration may help. Recall our coin-tossing example from the beginning of this section. We may set up this problem as in Table 9.10. If we accept certain "givens," namely that the marginal totals are 20, 20, 21, and 19, we may ask, How many of the cells within the table are "free to vary?" If we look at a table

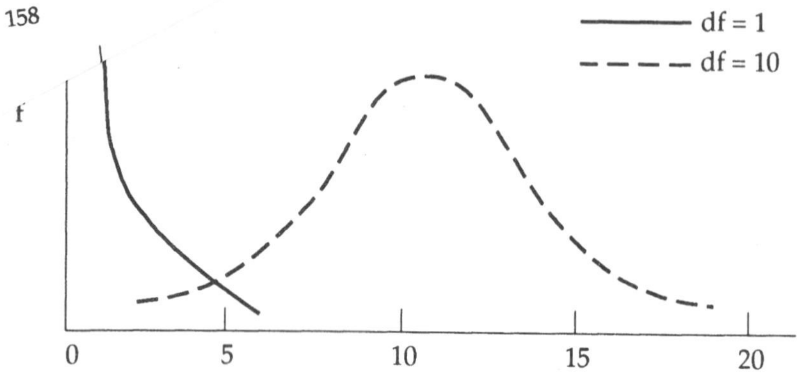

Figure 9.1. *Approximate Shape of the Chi-Square Distribution When df = 1 and When df = 10*

whose marginals are fixed but whose cell values are left open (Table 9.11), we can see that it is possible to enter into any *one* of the cells any value between zero and the corresponding minimal value. However, once we enter a value, for example, as in Table 9.12, *every other value is fixed* as well. If 13 is entered in the upper-left cell, as in Table 9.12, or in any other cell, and if the corresponding row marginal is 21, the upper-right cell must have the value of 8. The other two cells are similarly fixed. In this sense, only one of the four cells is "free to vary"; the other three cells are fixed. (Convince yourself that this procedure for determining degrees of freedom holds true for any table of r rows and c columns.) Therefore, the degrees of freedom for our coin-tossing example are

Table 9.10. *Coin-Toss Example*

	Nickel	Dime	Totals
Heads	13	8	21
Tails	7	12	19
Totals	20	20	40

Yates's Correction

In the special case of the 2 × 2 table (or when df = 1), the computation of Chi-square presents a particular problem because of the fact that although the theoretical distribution of Chi-square is continuous (that is, it is able to take on any value within limits), the actual values of the Chi-square statistic are discontinuous, or discrete.

This problem can be quite crucial when df = 1, as well as and especially when any expected frequency is relatively small (less than 10). A full discussion of this problem can be found in other texts (for example, Blalock 1979; Ott et al. 1991); it will not be discussed here. For our purposes, we will simply note the problem and offer the appropriate computational formulas.

The following is a general formula that incorporates Yates's correction:

(Formula 9.3)

$$\chi_y^2 = \Sigma \frac{(|f_o - f_e| - 0.5)^2}{f_e}$$

where $|f_o - f_e|$ is the absolute value (that is, the difference without regard to a positive or negative sign) of the deviation between observed and expected frequencies. In the special case of a 2 × 2 table such as Table 9.6, a useful computing formula is

$$\chi_y^2 = \frac{N(|ad - bc| - N/2)^2}{k \times l \times m \times n}$$

Fisher's Exact Test

In cases where f_e is very small (less than 5), even Yates's correction can produce a misleading decision. Therefore, when $f_e < 5$ we must use a technique known as Fisher's exact test. We will not compute Fisher's test here, but you should note it as a special case which you might confront in some sociological literature. See Blalock (1979) or Siegel (1956) for a detailed discussion of this procedure.

Quick Quiz
9.2

Given the following computed values for Chi-square, levels of α, and degrees of freedom, would you accept or reject the null hypothesis (the hypothesis of statistical independence)?

	χ^2	α	df
(A)	5.00	.05	1
(B)	5.00	.01	1
(C)	8.14	.05	3
(D)	2.96	.05	2
(E)	13.08	.01	4
(F)	13.08	.05	6

Quick Quiz
9.3

Compute Chi-square for Table 9.10. If $\alpha = .05$, what is your decision regarding the null hypothesis?

Cell Collapsing

There is one further problem concerning the use of Chi-square that should be mentioned. In some cases, even if N and df are relatively large, we may encounter a situation in which several cells have a small value of f_e. Instead of applying Yates's correction, an alternative strategy is to collapse, or combine, cells. This can be done *as long as the collapsing procedure makes sense.* Suppose that our original table of religious and political preferences was as given in Table 9.13. Clearly, the four right-hand columns (Jewish, Muslim, Mormon, Other) would have many cells where f_e is very small (less than 5). In such cases, the standard computation of Chi-square would be inappropriate. We have several ways of handling this difficulty.

Table 9.13. *Religious and Political Preferences (Hypothetical Data)*

Political Preference	Religious Preference						
	Prot.	Cath.	Jewish	Muslim	Mormon	Other	Totals
Democrat	30	40	9	1	0	0	80
Republican	40	20	5	1	3	1	70
Independent	30	10	4	4	1	1	50
Totals	100	70	18	6	4	2	200

For example, we could increase our sample size, especially in the groups with small numbers. If we do not have the resources (of time, money, personnel, and so on), we can consider combining cells. This has the double effects of decreasing the degrees of freedom and building up the value of f_e in the resulting cells.

However, we must be extremely careful that the way the cells are combined makes sense in terms of the research problem. For example, in a study of political preference, it may be statistically helpful to combine Democrats and Republicans (assuming their expected frequencies were small), but to do so would be absolute nonsense in terms of studying a real-world political issue. In such cases the logic of the real world should govern the logic of the statistical world.

In the case of Table 9.13, and assuming that we must collapse cells, it probably makes logical sense to keep the two larger groups distinct and to combine the smaller groups into one category.

Other Measures of Association Based on Chi-Square

The Phi Coefficient

One difficulty with the Chi-square statistic is that it does not lend itself to comparison with other statistics, and unless the values of N are equal, even two Chi-square values cannot meaningfully be compared with each other. In part, this happens because the value of χ^2 is a function of N. Recall that for Table 9.10 we obtained a corrected Chi-square of 1.60. Now let us triple the size of our sample so that N = 120 and let us keep the other cell and marginal values in similar proportion (see Table 9.14). The computed value of Chi-square is 6.55. With df = 1 and α =.05, this value is statistically significant; it leads us to *reject* the null hypothesis. Note that the *proportion* of heads and tails has not changed from Table 9.10. All that has changed is the size of our sample. But notice the effect of this change. In Table 9.10 we conclude that the relationship is due merely to chance, but in Table 9.14 we reject the chance model! From this example, the importance of sample size should be evident.

Because of this difficulty in comparing various Chi-squares, other statistics related to Chi-square have been developed. We shall mention only three such statistics here; discussion of others can be found in other texts (for example, Weiss 1968).

In the special case of a 2 × 2 table, such as Table 9.6, we can define the statistic Phi (Φ) as

(Formula 9.4)

$$\Phi = \frac{(ad - bc)}{\sqrt{klmn}}$$

It can be shown algebraically that Φ is related to χ^2 as follows:

$$\Phi = \sqrt{\frac{\chi^2}{N}} \text{ or } \chi^2 = N\Phi^2 \text{ or } \Phi^2 = \frac{\chi^2}{N}$$

[NOTE: In the immediately preceding equations, Yates's correction has not been applied to Chi-square.] It is in the comparison of Phi for Tables 9.10 and 9.14 that we can see the utility of this statistic. Unlike Chi-square, the computed values of Phi for these two tables are identical. In both cases, Phi = 0.25. The reason for this is that, unlike Chi-square, Phi is unaffected by sample size. [NOTE: Φ^2 is equal to χ^2 divided by sample size, N.] Phi also has the feature of taking on values only between 0.00 and ±1.00. (But with nominal level data, the sign is meaningless.) Consequently, values of Phi may be readily compared. There are other uses of Phi that will be touched on in later chapters. The major disadvantage of Phi in dealing with nominal-level data is that it cannot be applied to tables with dimensions greater than 2 × 2.

Some authors prefer to use the Phi-square statistic, rather than Phi. The advantage of Phi-square is that it is more directly related to

Table 9.14. *Coin Toss (N = 120)*

		Coin		
		Nickel	Dime	Totals
Outcome	Heads	39	24	63
	Tails	21	36	57
	Totals	60	60	120

Chi-square than is Phi. Furthermore, in a 2 × 2 table, Phi-square is equal to Goodman and Kruskal's Tau, a statistic that has a proportional reduction in error (PRE) interpretation. (See further on.)

Quick Quiz
9.4

(A) Compute Phi for Table 9.10.
(B) Compute Phi for Table 9.14.
(C) From the answers to A and B, what can you say about the effect of sample size on Phi?

The Contingency Coefficient

For tables larger than 2 × 2, for which Phi is not appropriate, we may use the contingency coefficient (C), whose formula is

(Formula 9.5)

$$C = \sqrt{\frac{\chi^2}{N + \chi^2}} = \sqrt{\frac{\Phi^2}{1 + \Phi^2}}$$

One difficulty with the contingency coefficient is that its lower limit is zero but its upper limit is always less than 1.00. In a 2 × 2 table, for example, the upper limit of C is 0.707. As the dimensions of the table increase, the upper limit of C also increases, but it never reaches unity. Therefore, two values of C cannot be meaningfully compared unless they are based on two tables possessing identical degrees of freedom. Mendenhall, Ott, and Larson (1974: 351) have described a procedure for computing an adjusted value of C that minimizes the upper limit problem in those cases where the table is "square," that is, where the number of rows equals the number of columns. This adjusted C does have 1.00 as its upper limit.

> *Quick Quiz*
> **9.5**
>
> Compute C from Table 9.4.

Cramer's V

For tables that are larger than 2 × 2 and that are not square, we can use as a measure of association Cramer's V:

(Formula 9.6)

$$V = \sqrt{\chi^2/N \left(\min \begin{matrix}(r-1)\\(c-1)\end{matrix}\right)}$$

where

$\left(\min \begin{matrix}(r-1)\\(c-1)\end{matrix}\right)$ is the smaller of (r - 1) or (c - 1).

Lambda: A "Proportional Reduction in Error" Measure for Nominal-Level Data

In this section we shall discuss a statistic, Lambda (λ), that measures association between two nominal-level variables and that is interpreted according to a proportional reduction in error (PRE) model. The meaning of this phrase will be illustrated shortly. The PRE model, which is a basis for many statistics other than Lambda, is quite different from the model of statistical independence that we used in describing Chi-square. Consider the following example.

Suppose we have a group of fifty adolescent boys and we know that thirty of them have no record of delinquency and that twenty do have a delinquency record. Knowing nothing else, we are asked to predict for each individual whether he has a record of delinquency. Because our information is minimal, our best strategy would be to determine the mode for this group of fifty, and in each individual case, use the mode as our best prediction. Here the mode is nondelinquency and by guessing that each of the fifty boys is nondelinquent, we will be correct thirty times (the modal frequency) and we will be wrong twenty times. Our *prediction rule* ("Guess the mode") has resulted in twenty *errors in prediction*, or an error rate of 20/50 = 40 percent. Given the very limited information we have, we cannot do much better than this. But suppose we add a second variable and, hence, a second piece of information: Twenty-six of the boys have a background of Kids Club membership and twenty-four do not. We can arrange this information in a 2 × 2 cross-classification table (Table 9.15). Again, let us predict delinquency, but this time we shall do so while knowing the club background of each boy. Again our prediction rule will make use of the mode, *but not the overall mode;* rather, we shall predict *within-category modes.* Thus, for the twenty-six boys who do have a club background, the within-category mode is nondelinquent and using this as our predictor results in four errors, or an error rate of 4/26 = 15 percent. Similarly, for the twenty-four boys who do not have a club background, we predict delinquency (because within the category of nonmember the mode is delinquency) and make eight errors in prediction for an error rate of 8/24 = 33 percent. In total we have made 4 + 8 = 12 errors, and our error rate is (4 + 8)/(26 + 24) = 12/50 = 24 percent. We can now easily see the utility of having the additional piece of information (club background): It enables us to reduce our error rate from 40 percent to 24 percent. Stated differently, we have now reduced the number of prediction errors from twenty to twelve, a reduction of eight errors.

We can now define the statistic Lambda as the amount by which we reduce errors in prediction when we move from one prediction scheme (the overall mode) to another (within-category modes), divided by the amount of original error. In general, we can compute a value of Lambda by using the formula

(Formula 9.7)

$$\lambda = \frac{(\Sigma \max f_i) - \max F_d}{N - \max F_d}$$

Table 9.15. *Club Membership and Delinquency (Hypothetical Data), Example 1*

		Club Background		
		Member	Nonmember	Totals
	Delinquent	4	16	20
Record	Nondelinquent	22	8	30
	Totals	26	24	50

where max f_i = the *maximum* frequency *within a subclass of the independent* variable, and max F_d = the modal frequency of the *dependent* variable. For Table 9.15, N is 50; max F_d is 30; and we have two categories of the independent variable. The independent variable is club background and the maximum frequencies within these categories are 22 and 16. Using Formula 9.7, we compute Lambda-r as follows:

$$\lambda_r = \frac{(22 + 16) - 30}{50 - 30} = \frac{8}{20} = 0.40$$

The subscript r indicates that we have designated the *row* variable as *dependent.* We do this because we are predicting delinquency (the row variable) from our knowledge of club background (the column variable). We could similarly compute a value of λ_c by predicting club membership from our information about delinquency. As an exercise, verify that for Table 9.15 the value of $\lambda_c = 0.50$.

Interpretation of Lambda

PRE measures of association generally tell us the proportional (or relative) reduction in error that is achieved when we shift from one prediction rule to another. In the case of Lambda, the prediction rules are as follows.

Prediction Rule 1 (λ): To predict the dependent variable, use its own mode.

> *Prediction Rule 2 (λ):* Within categories of the independent variable, predict the dependent variable by using the within-category modes.

Lambda may vary from 0.0 to 1.0. It cannot be negative. A value of $\lambda = 1.0$ means knowledge of the independent variable enables us to perfectly predict the dependent variable; a value of $\lambda = 0.0$ means that knowledge of the independent variable is of no help in predicting the dependent variable. Intermediate values indicate the proportional reduction in error. A value of $\lambda = 0.40$ means that in shifting from Prediction Rule 1 to Prediction Rule 2, we reduce the amount of prediction error by 40 percent.

It should be noted that a value of $\lambda = 0.0$ does not *necessarily* mean that there is no association between variables. It means that the shift in prediction rules is of no help. To illustrate this point, let us consider Table 9.16. Even a casual examination of this table should convince us that there is a relationship between these variables, because none of the boys with a club background is delinquent and 11/24 = 46 percent of the boys without club backgrounds are delinquent. Yet the computed value of Lambda is zero!

$$\lambda_r = \frac{(26 + 13) - 39}{50 - 39} = \frac{39 - 39}{11} = \frac{0}{11} = 0.0$$

It is zero not because there is no association but because the within-category modes are identical to each other and to the overall mode; hence, *there is no difference in prediction, no difference in error,* and Lambda is zero. In such situations, Lambda is said to be *insensitive* and is clearly an inadequate measure of association. In these specific instances, we must use another measure of association (such as Goodman and Kruskal's Tau, described further on).

Thus far in our discussions we have presented Lambda as an *asymmetric* measure of association. A measure of association is said to be asymmetric if, for a given contingency table, two values of that measure can be computed: one value computed with the row variable conceived of as the independent variable and a second value computed with the column variable conceived of as independent. (We saw an example of Lambda as an asymmetric measure when we computed λ_r

and λ_c for Table 9.16 and obtained two distinct results.) However, a *symmetric* measure yields only a single computed value.

Asymmetric measure always describes *one-way*, as opposed to mutual, association. It should be noted that whether a measure is asymmetric or symmetric is a question of statistical formulation; the question of one-way versus mutual association is a logical question. To paraphrase Weiss (1968: 180), if we want our measure of association to tell us the extent to which all club members are delinquent but we are not interested in the extent to which all of the delinquents are club members, we want a measure of one-way association. But if we want to measure the extent to which both phenomena go together, we need a measure of mutual association. In choosing an appropriate measure, we thus face both a statistical and a logical choice; the question of logic should always be answered before the statistical question. If we wish to measure one-way association, we select, whenever possible, an asymmetric measure. (We say *whenever possible* because we will occasionally encounter situations that are logically one-way but for which we have available only a symmetric measure. An example is the Pearson r discussed in Chapter 11.) If we wish to measure mutual association, we *always* select a symmetric measure.

Table 9.16. *Club Membership and Delinquency (Hypothetical Data), Example 2*

		Club Background		
		Member	Nonmember	Totals
	Delinquent	0	11	11
Record	Nondelinquent	26	13	39
	Totals	26	24	50

Table 9.17. *Parent's and Child's Religious Preferences (Hypothetical Data)*

		Parent's Religion			
		Protestant	Catholic	Other	Totals
	Protestant	10	1	1	12
Child's	Catholic	2	8	1	11
Religion	Other	3	6	13	22
	Totals	15	15	15	45

Table 9.18. *Husbands' and Wives' Religious Preferences (Hypothetical Data)*

		Husband's Religion			
		Protestant	Catholic	Other	Totals
	Protestant	10	1	1	12
Wife's	Catholic	2	8	1	11
Religion	Other	3	6	13	22
	Totals	15	15	15	45

To illustrate the difference between these several types of relationships let us consider Tables 9.17 and 9.18. Table 9.17 presents hypothetical data on parents' and children's religious preferences. Here, logic (or common sense) tells us that the pattern of influence (or cause) should be such that the parents' preferences are independent and the children's preferences are dependent on the fathers'. Thus, we have only a logical relationship and we measure it by using an asymmetric measure of association. Table 9.18 presents hypothetical data on husbands' and wives' religious preferences. But is the relationship between husbands' and wives' preferences one-way or mutual? We might logically argue that men traditionally dominate husband-wife relationships, and therefore, the relationship is one-way, with the wife's religion being dependent. Conversely, we might argue that in religious matters the wife is more influential, and therefore, the wife's religion is the independent variable. Finally, we might suggest that each partner equally influences the other and that the relationship is not one-way but mutual. Which interpretation is correct? To answer this question, the good sociologist would look to the body of relevant theory and previous research and take into account whether the sample has any important features. (For example, one might opt for the first interpretation if the subjects were blue-collar and for the third if the subjects were white-collar.) We will not answer this question here, but for purposes of illustration, let us assume that the relationship is indeed mutual. In that case, we would prefer to have a symmetric statistical measure.

Symmetric Lambda

The symmetric Lambda can be computed by the formula

(Formula 9.8)

$$\frac{(\Sigma \max f_r + \Sigma \max f_c) - (\max F_r + \max F_d)}{2N - (\max F_r + \max F_c)}$$

where r and c are row and column subscripts; max f is the maximum frequency within a row or column; and max F is the maximum *marginal* frequency of a row or column. If we apply this formula to the data from Table 9.18,

$$\lambda_s = \frac{(10 + 8 + 13) + (10 + 8 + 13) - (22 + 15)}{2(45) - (15 + 22)}$$

$$= \frac{(31) + (31) - (37)}{90 - 37} = \frac{25}{53} = 0.47$$

Symmetric Lambda is a PRE measure and can be interpreted as any other PRE measure: It measures the amount of error reduction achieved as we move from one prediction rule to a second prediction rule. Symmetric Lambda differs from asymmetric Lambda in that, with the former, each variable is used to predict the other *simultaneously*.

> *Quick Quiz*
> **9.6**
>
> For Table 9.18, compute λ_r.

The General Logic of PRE: Prediction Rules and Error Rules

Our discussion of Lambda has provided an example of a measure of association based on the PRE model. Let us now examine this model in closer detail.

All PRE statistics depend on two sets of *predictions* that we make about the *dependent variable*. These predictions come from the application of certain well-specified *prediction rules*. However, the prediction rules are subject to error that can be measured.

Every PRE measure has two prediction rules, one that is based on a concept of no association and one that is based on a concept of complete association. If we have two variables, A and B, they are said to be perfectly associated if, knowing the value of variable A we can accurately predict the value of variable B. Tables 9.19 and 9.20 illustrate two instances of perfect association. For Table 9.19, knowing the parent's political preference enables us to predict perfectly the child's preference—it will be the same as the parent's. Table 9.20 also gives us a perfect, but exactly opposite prediction—the child's political preference will be different from the parent's. In examining any square cross-classification table, it is easy to spot perfect association, for in any given row (or column) of the table, all entries will fall in only one cell; all other cells in that row (or column) will have frequencies of zero. In these cases of perfect association, knowledge of one variable enables us to predict the second variable without error.

In this text, the perfect association prediction rule of any PRE statistic will be known as *Rule* 2, and the errors that result from this rule will be identified as E_2. For Lambda, Rule 2 is, in operational terms, "Predict the dependent variable by using the within-category mode of the independent variable." *If* we have perfect association, we

Table 9.19. *Parent-Child Political Preferences, Example 1*

		Parent's Preference	
		Democrat	Republican
Child's Preference	Democrat	10	0
	Republican	0	10

Table 9.20. *Parent-Child Political Preferences, Example 2*

		Parent's Preference	
		Democrat	Republican
Child's Preference	Democrat	0	10
	Republican	10	0

will have no errors, and Lambda will be 1.0. To the extent that the association is less than perfect, as in Table 9.17, we will have some error in prediction and Lambda will be less than 1.0.

The concept of no association and its corresponding rule, *Rule 1*, and the resultant error, E_1, suggest that knowledge of variable A is of no use whatsoever in predicting variable B. In fact, under Rule 1, *we do not use one variable to predict another.* Rather, we predict a variable on the *basis of its own marginal distribution.* Returning to Table 9.19, we can see that the marginal totals for the sons are identical: ten Democrats and ten Republicans. Hence, we could use as our prediction rule, "All children are Democrats" or "All children are Republicans." Because the marginals are identical, each of these rules would be as good as the other. (These are not the only prediction rules possible. Because we know that there is an equal number of Democrats and Republicans, we could base our rule on the toss of a coin—"If heads, Democrat; if tails, Republican." In the long run and on the average, this rule, too, would yield ten errors.) In this particular example, these three prediction rules are equally good; in general, however, this will not be the case, and one of our main tasks is to determine which prediction rules result in the fewest errors.

As we have already indicated, for Lambda, Rule 1 is "Predict the dependent variable by using its own mode."

In general, any PRE statistic can be defined by

(Formula 9.9)

$$PRE = \frac{E_1 - E_2}{E_1}$$

where E_1 and E_2 are the number of errors resulting from the application of Prediction Rule 1 and Prediction Rule 2.

We earlier presented a computational formula for Lambda (Formula 9.7) that used a more direct computational procedure than that indicated in Formula 9.9. However, we can show that the two procedures produce identical results. In our discussion of Table 9.15 we noted that Prediction Rule 1 resulted in twenty errors and that Prediction Rule 2 resulted in twelve errors. Thus, we can compute for Table 9.15 as follows:

$$\lambda_r = \frac{E_1 - E_2}{E_1} = \frac{20 - 12}{20} = \frac{8}{20} = 0.40$$

which is identical to the result obtained from Formula 9.7.

Quick Quiz
9.7

5	8	13
10	11	21
15	9	24
30	28	58

For the above table,
(A) what is λ_r ?
(B) what is λ_c ?
(C) what is λ_s ?

Goodman and Kruskal's Tau

In the previous chapter, we mentioned a situation in which Lambda is not an appropriate statistic because it is insensitive. In this event, we may get a computed value of Lambda = 0.0 even when association is truly present (see Table 9.16). Goodman and Kruskal's Tau (T)* is a PRE measure of asymmetric association for nominal-level data that can help us in such cases. It can do so because its prediction rules are different from those of Lambda.

Whereas the prediction rules for Lambda are based on modes, the prediction rules for Tau are based on the concept of random assignment of subjects within the table, given the set marginal values for the table. Review Table 9.16. Our first prediction rule for Tau, as with all

*Goodman and Kruskal's Tau is a measure of association for nominal-level data. It should not be confused with Kendall's Tau, which will be discussed in Chapter 10, and which is a measure of association for ordinal-level data.

such PRE prediction rules, uses only information about the distribution of the dependent variable. This rule can be stated as

> *Prediction Rule 1 (T)*: All N cases are to be *randomly* assigned to categories of the dependent variable.

If in Table 9.16 we randomly assign eleven of the fifty cases to the delinquency category of the dependent variable, our error rate will be 78 percent (that is, 39/50). Because we are making eleven such assignments, we will make, in the long run and on the average, (11)(39/50) = 8.58 errors. Similarly, the random assignment of thirty-nine cases to the nondelinquency category will yield an error rate of 22 percent (11/50) and we will make (39)(11/50) = 8.58 errors. Taken together, we will make a total of 8.58 + 8.58 = 17.16 errors.

Our second prediction rule, as with all such PRE prediction rules, uses additional information: knowledge of the independent variable. For Goodman and Kruskal's Tau, this rule is

> *Prediction Rule 2 (T)*: Within each category of the independent variable, each case is to be randomly assigned to a category of the dependent variable.

In Table 9.16 we have twenty-six cases within the category of club member. If we randomly assign these twenty-six cases to the delinquency category we shall have an error rate of 100 percent (that is, 26/26) and we will make (0) (26/26) = 0 errors. If we assign the twenty-six cases to the nondelinquency category, we shall have an error rate of 0 percent (that is, 0/26) and will make (26) (0/26) = 0 errors in prediction. In the independent variable category, nonclub member, we have twenty-four cases. If we randomly assign these twenty-four to the delinquency category of the dependent variable we shall have an error rate of 54 percent (13/24) and will make, in the long run and on the average, (11) (13/24) = 5.96 errors. If we assign the twenty-four cases to the nondelinquency category, we shall have an error rate of 46 percent (that is, 11/24) and we will make (13) (11/24) = 5.96 errors. Therefore, E_2, the number of errors made from using Prediction Rule 2, is (0 + 5.96 + 5.96) = 11.92.

Using the general PRE formula (Formula 9.9), we can now determine the value of Tau for Table 9.16.

(Formula 9.10)

$$T_r = \frac{E_1 - E_2}{E_1} = \frac{17.16 - 11.92}{17.16} = \frac{5.24}{17.16} = 0.31$$

If you understand the rationale behind Tau (that is, the use of prediction rules based on the concept of random assignment of cases to categories and cells), we can proceed to a simple formula for computing Tau. However, if you do not understand the underlying rationale for Tau, you should review the previous material.

Although it is very beneficial to think through the logic of random assignment to determine prediction errors, most people will find the following formulas simpler and more direct for purposes of computation.

(Formula 9.11a)

$$E_1 = \Sigma \left(\frac{N - F_d}{N} (F_d)\right)$$

(Formula 9.11b)

$$E_1 = \Sigma \left(F_d - \frac{F^2}{N}\right)$$

(Formula 9.12)

$$E_2 = \Sigma \frac{(F_i - f)f}{F_1} = \Sigma \left(f - \frac{f^2}{F_i}\right)$$

where N is the total number of cases in a table; F is a marginal frequency (that is, a row or a column total); and i and d indicate the independent and dependent variables. Formula 9.11a is derived from the logic of Prediction Rule 1. Formula 9.11b is a more direct, but not as intuitively obvious, computing formula. The same is true with regard to Formula 9.12 and Prediction Rule 2.

With some algebraic manipulation, we can combine the two formulas and develop a direct computing formula for Tau, a formula that allows us to bypass the computation of E_1 and E_2. Again, you should not use these formulas until you fully understand the logic of the Tau statistic. The direct computational formula for Goodman and Kruskal's Tau is

(Formula 9.13)

$$T = \frac{N\Sigma \frac{f^2}{F_i} - \Sigma F_d^2}{N^2 - \Sigma F_d^2}$$

[NOTE: In Formula 9.13 the term f^2/F_i is to be interpreted as follows: Square each cell frequency, then divide the result by the independent variable marginal total associated with that cell.]

We can illustrate the application of these three formulas with the data from Table 9.16.

$$E_1 = (11 - \frac{11^2}{50}) + (39 - \frac{39^2}{50})$$

$$= 8.58 + 8.58 = 17.16$$

$$E_2 = (0 - \frac{0^2}{26}) + (26 - \frac{26^2}{26})$$

$$+ (11 - \frac{11^2}{24}) + (13 - \frac{13^2}{24})$$

$$= 0 + 0 + 5.96 + 5.96$$

$$= 11.92$$

These values for the error terms are identical with those we computed earlier. Finally, T_r can be computed as

$$\frac{50\left(\frac{0^2}{26} + \frac{26^2}{26} + \frac{11^2}{24} + \frac{13^2}{24}\right) - (11^2 + 39^2)}{50^2 - (11^2 + 39^2)} = 0.31$$

A final word: Because Tau is an asymmetric measure of association, we can also compute a value for T_c. For T_c you should verify that E_1 = 24.96, E_2 = 17.33. You may notice that for Table 9.16 T_r will always equal T_c. However, in tables larger than 2 × 2, generally T_r and T_c will *not* be the same.

Tau may range from 0.0 to 1.0. It cannot be negative. A value of Tau = 0.0 indicates that we have no reduction in error in shifting from

Rule 1 to Rule 2, and a value of Tau = 1.0 indicates perfect prediction. Values of Tau between 0.0 and 1.0 indicate the degree to which prediction errors are reduced by substituting random assignment of cases to categories within the independent variable for random assignment of cases to categories of the dependent variable.

An SPSS Example

CROSSTABS is the procedure used in SPSS (1) to set up tables which contain two variables and (2) to generate a wide variety of statistics. In this example, we will use CROSSTABS to generate values of Chi-square, Phi, V, and Lambda.

In the following example, immediately following the command CROSSTABS, are the names of two variables, FEAR and SEX. The variable that is named first will be the row variable in the table, and the second-named variable will be the column variable. (Familiarity with this sequence is a small but important point.) The /CELLS subcommand is used to generate specific information for each cell of the table. Here, I have asked for a COUNT of the cell frequencies and the column (COL) percentages. The /STATISTICS subcommand tells the software to produce certain specific statistics: In this case I have asked for Chi-square, Phi, and Lambda—statistics which are appropriate for the nominal-level variables that I am examining.

SPSS Example: CROSSTABS of FEAR by SEX

```
CROSSTABS FEAR BY SEX   /CELLS = COUNT COL
 /STATISTICS = CHISQ  PHI  LAMBDA
```

FEAR AFRAID TO WALK AT NIGHT IN NEIGHBORHOOD
by SEX RESPONDENTS SEX

(continued)

(continued)

FEAR by SEX

Count / Col Pct	MALE 1	FEMALE 2	Row Total
YES	21 22.3	79 57.7	100 43.3
NO	73 77.7	58 42.3	131 56.7
Column Total	94 40.7	137 59.3	231 100.0

Chi-Square	Value	DF	Significance
Pearson	28.33507	1	.00000
Continuity Correction	26.91446	1	.00000

Statistic	Value	Significance
Phi	.35023	.00000 *1
Cramer's V	.35023	.00000 *1
Lambda :		
symmetric	.18557	
with FEAR dependent	.21000	
with SEX dependent	.15957	

*1 Pearson chi-square probability

When we examine the SPSS output we see first (looking at the columns) that of our 231 respondents, 94 are male and 137 are female. Looking at the rows, we also see that of the 231, 100 are afraid to walk in their neighborhoods at night and 131 are not. When these two variables are cross-tabulated, we can see how SEX and FEAR are associated.

Specifically, of the males, 22 percent are afraid and 78 percent are not afraid; of the females, 43 percent are afraid and 57 percent are not. We thus know that proportionately more women than men are afraid. Chi-square tells us that a difference of this magnitude would occur by chance fewer than once in 100,000 times. The difference is statistically significant. [NOTE: There are two values of Chi-square given. The first is the "uncorrected" value and the second is the corrected (Yates's correction) value.]

The last few statistics give us additional information about our table. Phi is 0.35, and the asymmetric Lambda (with FEAR as the dependent variable) is 0.21.

Important Terms

Association
Statistical independence
Chi-square (χ^2)
Marginal value
Expected cell frequency
Degrees of freedom
Yates's correction
Fisher's exact test
Phi (Φ) and Phi-square
Goodman and Kruskal's Tau (T)
Lambda (λ)
Proportional reduction in error (PRE)
Prediction rule
Error in prediction
Asymmetric measure
Symmetric measure
One-way association
Mutual association

Suggested Readings

Blalock (1979: 279-311); Loether and McTavish (1988: 218-231); Mueller, Schuessler, and Costner (1970: 239-263); Ott et al. (1992: 374-389); and Siegel (1956: 42-47, 96-111, 175-179, 196-202) provide good basic introductions to Chi-square and related measures of association.

Quick Quiz Answers

Quick Quiz 9.1

(A) df = (2 - 1)(3 - 1) = 2

(B) (1) 2 (2) 12
(3) 5 (4) 3
(5) 9

Quick Quiz 9.2

(A) Since $\chi^2 = 5.00$ exceeds the critical value of 3.84, *reject* H_0.
(B) Since $\chi^2 = 5.00$ does not exceed the critical value of 6.64, *accept* H_0.
(C) Since $\chi^2 = 8.14$ exceeds the critical value of 7.82, *reject* H_0.
(D) Since $\chi^2 = 2.96$ does not exceed the critical value of 5.99, *accept* H_0.
(E) Since $\chi^2 = 13.08$ does not exceed the critical value of 13.28, *accept* H_0.
(F) Since $\chi^2 = 13.08$ exceeds the critical value of 12.59, *reject* H_0.

Quick Quiz 9.3

$$\chi_y^2 = \frac{40\left((13)(12) - (7)(8) - \frac{40}{2}\right)^2}{(20)(20)(19)(21)}$$

$$= \frac{40(80)^2}{159{,}600} = 1.60$$

With df = 1, our computed value does not exceed the table value of 3.84; therefore, we *accept* the null hypothesis. The observed "behavior" of the coins does not differ significantly from chance.

Quick Quiz 9.4

$$(A)\quad \Phi = \frac{156 - 56}{\sqrt{(20)(20)(19)(21)}} = \frac{100}{399.5} = 0.25$$

$$(B)\quad \Phi = \frac{1{,}404 - 504}{\sqrt{(60)(60)(63)(57)}} = \frac{900}{3{,}595.5} = 0.25$$

(C) The value of Phi is not affected by sample size.

Quick Quiz 9.5

Because we know that $\chi^2 = 14.57$ (see Table 9.8).

$$C = \sqrt{\frac{14.57}{200 + 14.57}} = 0.26$$

Quick Quiz 9.6

$$\lambda_r = \frac{(10 + 8 + 13) - 22}{45 - 22} = \frac{9}{23} = 0.39$$

Quick Quiz 9.7

$$(A)\quad \lambda_r = \frac{(15 + 11) - 24}{58 - 24} = \frac{2}{34} = 0.06$$

$$(B)\quad \lambda_c = \frac{(8 + 11 + 15) - 30}{58 - 30} = \frac{4}{28} = 0.14$$

$$(C)\quad \lambda_s = \frac{(8 + 11 + 15 + 15 + 11) - (24 + 30)}{58 - 30} = \frac{60 - 54}{116 - 54} = \frac{6}{62} = 0.10$$

10

Measuring the Association Between Two Ordinal Variables

In Chapter 9 we examined several ways of measuring the relationship between two nominal-level variables. In this chapter we shall look at measures of association for ordinal-level variables. Remember that the distinction between nominal and ordinal measurement is that the former is purely qualitative and involves the assignment of data to classes or categories; ordinal measurement introduces the dimension of ranks. When two categories of a variable are nominally different, the only thing that we can say about them is that they are not the same, but when two categories of a variable are ordinally different we can also specify which of the two is larger (or greater, stronger, and so on). This ability to specify differences in rank order gives an added dimension to our measurement capacities.

In this chapter we shall examine four major measures of ordinal association. The computing formulas for these statistics are, for the most part, rather simple. What may not be so simple is the logic that underlies the statistics. In studying this material, pay special attention to the discussions that deal with the why of a statistic. Computing a statistic is easy; understanding why you are doing so may take effort.

Gamma: A Symmetric Measure of One-Way Association

Gamma (G) is a measure of association developed by Goodman and Kruskal (1954; 1959). It measures one-way association; that is, it uses information about one variable to tell us something about a second variable. Gamma is a symmetric measure because any contingency table yields only one value of Gamma, regardless of whether the row variable or column variable is logically dependent or independent. Gamma has a PRE interpretation, but its fundamental meaning is based on the notion of pair-by-pair comparison.

The Logic of Pair-by-Pair Comparison

In the previous chapter we introduced five strategies for measuring association and discussed three of these (percentage differences, departure from independence, and proportional reduction in error) in detail. We now introduce the logic of *pair-by-pair comparison* as the basis for understanding certain of the ordinal measures of association.

If we assign a subject to some rank on each of two ordinal variables, we can think of that subject as being "paired" with any and every other subject in a sample. We can then compare the members of each *pair* to determine whether the relative rankings of the two members on *both* variables are similar or dissimilar. If we summarize all of these paired comparisons and determine whether there is a preponderance of similar or dissimilar pairs, we can derive a measure of association. For example, suppose we have three subjects (A, B, and C) that are ranked on each of two variables (Table 10.1). We can think of these three subjects forming themselves into all possible pairs. In our example, it is easy to see that the possible pairs are AB, AC, and BC. However, if the number of subjects is large, it will not be so easy to list all possible pairs. Fortunately, the statistics we shall be dealing with do not require such a list, but they do require that we know *how many* pairs can be formed. The number of pairs that can be formed for a given value of N is

(Formula 10.1)

$$\text{Number of possible pairs} = \frac{N(N - 1)}{2}$$

We can verify for Table 10.1 that the number of pairs is 3(3 - 1)/2 = 3.

Let us focus our attention on pair AB in Table 10.1. We see that on variable X, A is ranked above B and on variable Y, A is also ranked above B. Therefore, on both variables the rank ordering of the pair members is said to be similar (or the same). It is similar in the sense that one member of the pair is ranked above the other member on *both* variables. Pair AC also shows a *similar* pattern of ranking because subject A is ranked above subject C on *both* variables. If we look at pair

Table 10.1. *An Example of Three Subjects Ranked on Two Variables*

Subject	Rank on Variable X	Rank on Variable Y
A	1	1
B	2	3
C	3	2

BC we see that B is ranked higher than C on variable X but lower than C on variable Y. This pattern of ranked pairs is said to be *dissimilar* (or reversed).

The measures of association discussed in the next three sections are based on the logic of pair-by-pair comparison. These measures involve a determination of the number of similar and dissimilar pairs (symbolized as n_s and n_d), an expression of the differences between such pairs (symbolized as S and equal to $n_s - n_d$), and a ratio of S to some defined quantity.

Gamma: An Example

Suppose we ask two sociology students to rank five occupations. Three possible sets of rankings are given in Table 10.2. We can easily see that in (a) there is perfect positive agreement between the two students. Student X places an architect first; so does Student Y. Both students rank the bank manager second. Their rankings are completely consistent. We should expect any measure of the relationship between the two sets of ranks to have a value of +1.00. In Table 10.2(b) it is equally easy to see that the agreement is also perfect, but negative. The occupation that is ranked first by Student X is ranked last by Student Y. Each student's rank ordering is the perfect opposite of the other student's ranking. However, the situation in Table 10.2(c) is not so clear, for there is both agreement and disagreement in the two sets of ranks. Note, for example, that both students agree that the dentist ranks below the architect. But X and Y disagree about the ranking of the dentist and engineer—Student X places the dentist above the engineer and Y places the engineer above the dentist. In the terms of pair-by-pair comparison, the architect-dentist pair is said to be *similar* and the engineer-dentist pair is said to be *dissimilar*. In like fashion, every possible pair can be similar or dissimilar (or tied).

Table 10.2. *Ranking of Five Occupations by Two Students (Three Hypothetical Examples)*

	Occupation	Student X	Student Y
	Architect	1	1
	Bank Manager	2	2
(a)	Chemist	3	3
	Dentist	4	4
	Engineer	5	5
	Architect	1	5
	Bank Manager	2	4
(b)	Chemist	3	3
	Dentist	4	2
	Engineer	5	1
	Architect	1	1
	Bank Manager	2	2
(c)	Chemist	3	4
	Dentist	4	5
	Engineer	5	3

After counting the number of similar and dissimilar pairs, how shall we determine the level of association between the two sets of ranks? Perhaps the most straightforward procedure is simply to count the number of similar pairs and the number of dissimilar pairs and then find some value which expresses the preponderance of one type of pair over the other. The number of possible pairs is

$$\frac{N(N-1)}{2} = \frac{5(4)}{2} = 10$$

We list these pairs in Table 10.3 and also record, for each of the three hypothetical examples, whether a given pair is similar (s) or dissimilar (d). Of the ten possible pairs in (a), all ten are similar. Of the ten pairs in (b), all ten are dissimilar. And of the ten pairs in (c), eight are similar and two are dissimilar. Let us examine some of the pairs in (c). For pair AB, A is ranked above B by both Student X and Student Y; therefore, this pair is similar (s). For pair CE, Student X

Table 10.3. *List of Pairs from Table 10.2*

Pair	9.2 (a)	9.2 (b)	9.2 (c)
AB	s*	d**	s
AC	s	d	s
AD	s	d	s
AE	s	d	s
BC	s	d	s
BD	s	d	s
BE	s	d	s
CD	s	d	s
CE	s	d	d
DE	s	d	d

For (a): $n_s = 10, n_d = 0$
For (b): $n_s = 0, n_d = 10$
For (c): $n_s = 8, n_d = 2$

* s = Similar Pair   ** d = Dissimilar Pair

ranks C above E but Student Y ranks C below E; this pair is dissimilar (d). Pair DE is also dissimilar.

If we let n_s indicate the number of similar pairs and n_d the number of dissimilar pairs, we can express the differences as $(n_s - n_d)$; we shall indicate this difference by the symbol S. We can also define the total number of similar and dissimilar pairs as $(n_s + n_d)$. Finally, we can define a ratio that expresses the preponderance of similar or dissimilar pairs to the total number of similar and dissimilar pairs; this value is Gamma (G). The simple computing formula for Gamma is

(Formula 10.2)

$$G = \frac{(n_s - n_d)}{(n_s + n_d)} = \frac{S}{(n_s + n_d)}$$

We can now compute a measure of association for the data in Table 10.3.

$$\text{From (a)}, G = \frac{(10 - 0)}{(10 + 0)} = \frac{10}{10} = +1.00$$

$$\text{From (b)}, G = \frac{(0 - 10)}{(0 + 10)} = \frac{-10}{10} = -1.00$$

$$\text{From (c)}, G = \frac{(8 - 2)}{(8 + 2)} = \frac{6}{10} = +0.60$$

In (a), the value of G = +1.00 indicates that the two variables are perfectly and positively ordered in terms of pair-by-pair comparison. In (b), the value of G = -1.00 indicates that the two variables are perfectly and inversely ordered in terms of pair-by-pair comparison. In (c), the value of G = +0.60 indicates the extent to which similar pairs are preponderant over dissimilar pairs relative to the total number of pairs that are similar or dissimilar. Further on we will see that in addition to this explanation of the meaning of G, a more precise interpretation of G can be obtained by using the PRE model.

Before concluding this introductory discussion of Gamma, we must say a word about tied ranks. In the examples cited thus far, we have purposely avoided this problem. But now that you have a basic grasp of Gamma, you should note that it is possible for a judge to be unable to decide how certain ranks should be filled. Suppose Student X was able to assign ranks 1, 2, and 3 to the architect, bank manager, and chemist, but felt that it was really impossible to discriminate between the dentist and engineer; in other words, the dentist and engineer were tied for fourth place. As we shall soon see, different statistics treat tied ranks in different ways. With Gamma, the procedure is to *ignore tied pairs.* Any pair in which a tie exists on either ranking, or both, is excluded from the computation of n_s and n_d. Table 10.4 shows how tied ranks affect the computation of Gamma. It is clear that, because of the tied rank on X, we cannot consider the pair DE as either similar or dissimilar.

Computing Gamma for Grouped Data

Clearly, as the number of cases under analysis becomes large, the number of ranks and the number of possible pairs also become large and attempts to list all similar and dissimilar pairs become quite cumbersome. Also, there are many research situations in which the number of cases is quite large, but the number of ranks in a variable is

Table 10.4. *Computation of Gamma with Tied Ranks (Ungrouped Data)*

Occupation	Student X		Student Y
A	1		1
B	2		2
C	3		4
D	4	} tie	5
E	4		3

Pair	s, d, or t (tie)	
AB	s	
AC	s	$n_s = 8$
AD	s	
AE	s	
BC	s	$n_d = 1$
BD	s	
BE	s	
CD	s	$G = \frac{8 - 1}{8 + 1} = \frac{7}{9} = +0.78$
CE	d	
DE	t	

quite small. In such circumstances, it is usual to group the data into categories. Table 10.5 illustrates such a situation. With N = 40, there are 780 possible pairs to consider in the computation of Gamma; to attempt to list these would be terribly tedious and time-consuming. However, there is an easier and more direct way to determine n_s and n_d and, thereby, to compute Gamma. Consider the six subjects who occupy the upper-left cell of Table 10.5. Each subject, when paired with anyone else in the same *cell,* is a member of a pair that is tied on both variables. When paired with anyone else in the same *row,* each is tied on the ranking of the income variable. And when paired with anyone else in the same column, each is tied in rank on the education variable. Remembering that in the computation of Gamma ties are not counted, we eliminate these pairs from further consideration. We can now see in Figure 10.1(a) that when each of the six members of the upper-left cell is paired with each member of the remaining cells, this results in a *similar* pair. Each member of the upper-left cell is ranked "less than"

Table 10.5. *Income and Education (Hypothetical Data)*

		Level of Education (X)				
		I (=Low)	II	III	IV (= Hi)	Totals
Level of Income (Y)	Low	6	3	3	2	14
	Med.	3	3	7	3	16
	High	1	3	2	4	10
	Totals	10	9	12	9	40

each member of the remaining cells on *both variables*. There are 132 such similar pairs:

$$(6)(3) + (6)(7) + (6)(3) + (6)(3) + (6)(2) + (6)(4) = 132$$

Now consider the cell in the first row, second column. After eliminating its tied pairs, we find that there are forty-eight similar pairs (see Figure 10.1[b]). For the cell in the second row, third column, there are twenty-eight similar pairs (Figure 10.1[c]). In general, *we obtain n_s by multiplying each cell frequency by the sum of the cells below and to the right and summing all such products.* For Table 10.5, the number of similar pairs can be calculated as

$$= 6(3 + 7 + 3 + 3 + 2 + 4) + 3(7 + 3 + 2 + 4) + 3(3 + 4) + 3(3 + 2 + 4) + 3(2 + 4) + 7(4)$$

$$= 132 + 48 + 21 + 27 + 18 + 28$$

$$= 274$$

To find n_d, we must find all pairs in which one member is ranked higher than the other on one variable but lower on the second variable. Consider the cell in the first row, fourth column (Figure 10.1[d]). We first eliminate tied pairs, that is, those formed within the same row and same column. Now each member of the upper-right cell forms a *dissimilar* pair with each member of the six remaining cells; there are thirty-eight such dissimilar pairs. The cell in the first row, third column, yields thirty dissimilar pairs (Figure 10.1[e]) and the cell in the second row, second column, yields three dissimilar pairs (Figure 10.1[f]). In general, *we obtain n_d by multiplying each cell frequency by the sum of the cells below and to the left and summing all such products.* For Table 10.5, this is

$$= 2(3 + 3 + 7 + 1 + 3 + 2) + 3(3 + 3 + 1 + 3) + 3(3 + 1) + 3(1 + 3 + 2) + 7(1 + 3) + 3(1)$$

$$= 38 + 30 + 12 + 18 + 28 + 3$$

$$= 129$$

We can now compute Gamma using Formula 10.2.

$$G = \frac{(n_s - n_d)}{(n_s + n_d)} = \frac{274 - 129}{274 + 129} = \frac{145}{403} = +0.36$$

(a)

6			
	3	7	3
	3	2	4

(b)

	3		
		7	3
		2	4

(c)

		7	
			4

(d)

			2
3	3	7	
1	3	2	

(e)

		3	
3	3		
1	3		

(f)

	3		
1			

For (a): $n_s = 6(3+7+3+3+2+4) = 132$

For (b): $n_s = 3(7+3+2+4) = 48$

For (c): $n_s = 7(4) = 28$

For (d): $n_d = 2(3+3+7+1+3+2) = 38$

For (e): $n_d = 3(3+3+1+3) = 30$

For (f): $n_d = 3(1) = 3$

Figure 10.1. *Calculation of Similar and Dissimilar Pairs for Table 10.5*

This value can be interpreted as follows. If there was perfect association, the preponderance of similar (or dissimilar) pairs would equal the number of possible pairs (excluding ties) and the ratio of the former to the latter would be ±1.00. If there was no association, the number of similar pairs would equal the number of dissimilar pairs, there would be a preponderance of neither, and the ratio would be 0.00. Values between zero and one indicate the extent to which one type of pair is predominant over the other type, divided by the number of possible pairs (ties excluded).

In the previous example, the positive sign tells us that the similar pairs are preponderant and that the pattern of association is, therefore, direct, or positive. If the sign were negative, the dissimilar pairs would be preponderant and the pattern of association would be inverse, or negative.

Quick Quiz
10.1

For the data below, compute Gamma.

		Rank on X		
		1	2	3
	1	10	10	20
Rank on Y	2	10	20	10
	3	20	10	10

Gamma as a PRE Measure

Gamma can also be viewed as a PRE measure. (For a review of the proportional-reduction-in-error concept, see Chapter 9.) To compute a PRE measure we need two prediction rules, one that predicts the dependent variable from knowledge of its own distribution, and one that predicts the dependent variable from knowledge of the independent variable. Each prediction rule results in some error, E_1 and E_2, and the PRE measure is defined as $(E_1 - E_2)/E_1$.

For Gamma, we want to predict whether a *pair* is similar or dissimilar in its rankings on *both* variables. From knowledge of the dependent variable only, we have no reason to predict whether pairs will be similar or dissimilar. The best we can do is to assume that n_s will equal n_d. In simpler terms, we trust to chance, to a flip of a coin, to predict similarity or dissimilarity. To predict rank order on the dependent variable for a pair member, we are just as likely to be correct if we predict the rank to be higher than the rank of the independent variable or if we predict it to be lower than the rank of the independent variable. This logic can be generalized as

> *Prediction Rule 1 (G):* Predict all pairs to be the same, either similar or dissimilar.

Fundamentally, this is a "guessing" rule and results in a theoretically expected error rate of 50 percent. In the long run and on the average, the number of errors, E_1, will be

(Formula 10.3)

$$E_1 = \frac{1}{2}(n_s - n_d)$$

Prediction Rule 2 uses our knowledge of order on the independent variable to predict order on the dependent variable. If we know that there are more similar-order pairs than dissimilar-order pairs, it makes sense to predict "similar" for all pairs. And if the dissimilar-order pairs outnumber the similar-order pairs, we should predict "dissimilar" for all pairs.

> *Prediction Rule 2 (G):* (a) If $n_s > n_d$, predict all pairs to be similar. (b) If $n_s < n_d$, predict all pairs to be dissimilar.

In essence, this rule says, "Go with the majority." (If there is no majority, that is if $n_s = n_d$, then $G = 0$). In situation (a), the number of errors, E_2, will equal n_d, and in (b), the number of errors will equal n_s. In general,

(Formula 10.4)

$$E_2 = \mathit{min}\ \{n_s, n_d\}$$

where *min* $\{n_s, n_d\}$ is the smaller of n_s and n_d. Let us use these rules to compute Gamma for Table 10.5.

$$E_1 = \frac{1}{2}(n_s - n_d) = \frac{1}{2}(274 + 129)$$
$$= \frac{1}{2}(403) = 201.5$$

$$E_2 = min\{n_s, n_d\} = min\{274, 129\} = 129$$

$$G = \frac{E_1}{E_2} = \frac{201.5 - 129}{201.5 + 129} = +0.36$$

This value is identical with that computed from Formula 10.2. It can be interpreted as the amount by which we reduce errors in prediction of similar or dissimilar pairs when we shift from a rule based on "chance" prediction to a rule based on "majority" prediction. When Gamma = $\pm$ 1.00, the reduction in error is total and we have perfect or complete association. When Gamma = 0.00, we have no error reduction and zero association. Intermediate values of Gamma indicate the relative amount of error reduction.

Yule's Q as a Special Case of Gamma

Years before Gamma was developed and became quite prominent in sociological literature, a statistic called Yule's Q was frequently used as a measure of association for a 2 × 2 table. If the four cells of a 2 × 2 table are identified as in Figure 10.2, then it is directly evident that ad = n_s and bc = n_d; Yule's Q is, therefore, a special case of Gamma. (See Formula 10.5.)

(Formula 10.5)

$$Q = \frac{ad - bc}{ad + bc}$$

a	b
c	d

Figure 10.2. *Yule's Q as a Special Case of Gamma*

This point is mentioned here for purposes of information. In reading some of the older research literature, you may come across the Q statistic. Because it is now understood that Q is a special case of Gamma, you should recognize it for what it is and interpret Q not simply as a measure of association with no inherent meaning but as a PRE measure of ordinal association.

Kendall's Tau Statistics: Symmetric Measures of Mutual Association

Kendall (1962) has described a series of three symmetric measures of mutual association for ordinal data, named Tau-a, Tau-b, and Tau-c. All three, like Gamma, are based on the logic of pair-by-pair comparison. Our discussion of these measures will be brief; for a more complete discussion, see Kendall (1962), Blalock (1979), or Weiss (1968).

Let us first compare the three Tau measures and Gamma. All four measures involve the computation of n_s and n_d. All involve the quantity $(n_s - n_d) = S$ in the numerator of the computational formula. However, the four differ in the determination of the maximum possible number of pairs that are to be considered in the computation of the statistic.

For *Gamma*, the maximum number of pairs is $(n_s + n_d)$, that is, the total number of pairs that are either similar or dissimilar. *Ties are excluded.*

Tau-a takes as its maximum number of pairs the total number of pairs, including ties, that can be formed. This value was defined in Formula 10.1 and is equivalent to (1/2)N(N - 1). The computing formula for Tau-a is

(Formula 10.6)

$$\text{Tau-a} = S/(1/2)\,N\,(N-1)$$

Tau-b takes as its maximum value the number of pairs, *excluding ties,* that could be formed *if* there were complete mutual association between both variables. Figure 10.3 illustrates two cases of complete mutual association. Complete mutual association exists when both variables have the same number of ranks and all nondiagonal cell

(a)

4	0	0	4
0	6	0	6
0	0	5	5
4	6	5	15

(b)

0	0	65	65
0	70	0	70
48	0	0	48
48	70	65	183

Figure 10.3. *Illustration of Complete Mutual Association*

values are zero. If we have complete mutual association, knowledge of a subject's rank in either variable enables us to perfectly predict that subject's rank on the other variable. For Figure 10.3(a), the maximum number of pairs is not (1/2)N(N - 1) = 105 (as it would be for Tau-a) because in the upper-left cell there are (1/2)(4)(3) = 6 pairs that are tied on both variables; these pairs must be excluded. In the middle cell there are (1/2)(6)(5) = 15 tied pairs that must be excluded. In the lower-right cell there are (1/2)(5)(4) = 10 ties that must be excluded. In this case of complete mutual association, the maximum number of untied pairs is, therefore, 105 - (6 + 15 + 10) = 74.

In the computing formula for Tau-b we use S in the numerator; in the denominator we use an estimate of the maximum number of untied pairs, assuming complete mutual association (Weiss 1968).

(Formula 10.7)

$$\text{Tau-b} = S/(1/2)\sqrt{(N^2 - \Sigma F_r^2)(N^2 - \Sigma F_c^2)}$$

where F_r and F_c are, respectively, the row totals and column *totals*.

A limitation of Tau-b is that it is applicable only to tables in which the number of rows is the same as the number of columns. *Tau-c* incorporates a correction that enables us to compute a measure of association for any r × c table. The computing formula for Tau-c is

(Formula 10.8)

$$\text{Tau-c} = S/(1/2)N^2\,[(m - 1)/m]$$

where m is the *smaller* of the number of rows or number of columns.

For Table 10.5 we computed a value of Gamma = +0.36. For that same table, let us now compute and compare values of Tau-a, Tau-b, and Tau-c.

$$\text{Tau-a} = S/(1/2)\,N(N-1)$$
$$= 145/(1/2)\,40(39) = 145/780$$
$$= +0.19$$

$$\text{Tau-b} = S/(1/2)\,\sqrt{(N^2 - \Sigma F_r^2)\,(N^2 - \Sigma F_c^2)}$$

$$= 145/(1/2)\sqrt{[40^2 - (14^2 + 16^2 + 10^2)][40^2(10^2 + 9^2 + 10^2 + 12^2)]}$$

$$= 145/(1/2)\sqrt{(1{,}600 - 377)(1{,}600 - 406)}$$
$$= 145/(1/2)\sqrt{(1{,}223)(1{,}194)}$$
$$= 145/(1/2)\sqrt{1{,}251{,}312} = 145/559.31$$
$$= +0.26$$

$$\text{Tau-c} = S/(1/2)N^2[(m-1)/m]$$
$$= \frac{145}{(1/2)40^2\,[(3-1)/3]}$$
$$= \frac{145}{533.33} = +0.27$$

[NOTE: Although the values of Tau-b and Tau-c are very close to each other in this particular example, values for the various Tau measures will not necessarily be similar.]

Quick Quiz
10.2

What is the number of tied pairs in Figure 10.3(b)?

Which Measure to Use?

All four measures described thus far in this chapter are *symmetric* measures of association. Gamma differs from the Tau measures in that Gamma measures *one-way* association and Tau measures *mutual* association. Tau-a has a fairly limited application in sociological research. It is preferred to Tau-b or Tau-c "only when the investigator has some reason to believe that ties are relevant cases against the interpretation of association" (Weiss 1968: 204). In other words, we use Tau-a only in those circumstances where ties do not, or in theory should not, exist. As for Tau-b and Tau-c, there is little difference between them except that Tau-b applies to those tables where the number of rows equals the number of columns and Tau-c applies to cases where the number of rows is different from the number of columns. Tau-c is easier to compute, but its interpretation is not as clear as that of Tau-b. Finally, note that Kendall's Tau measures do not have a PRE interpretation, except for a special case of Tau-b (Wilson 1969).

Somers's d: An Asymmetric Measure of Association

Somers (1962) has introduced an asymmetric measure of association for ordinal data that enjoys some popularity in the sociological literature. Like Gamma and Kendall's Tau, Somers's d is based on the logic of pair-by-pair comparison. Unlike Gamma and the Taus, d is an asymmetric measure. This means that, as for asymmetric Lambda (see Chapter 9), there are *two* values for d that can be computed for any contingency table—one that assumes the row variable to be the predictor, and another that assumes the column variable to be the predictor. We shall follow common usage and refer to these two values as d_{YX} and d_{XY}. (That is, if we have two variables, X and Y, and we wish to predict Y from our knowledge of X, the resulting statistic is noted as d_{YX}. Similarly, d_{XY} measures the extent to which the X variable can be predicted from the Y variable.)

Somers's d is logically very similar to Gamma, with one notable exception: *The denominator includes those variables which are tied on the dependent variable only* but excludes those which are tied on the independent variable only and those tied on both variables. The numerator of d is the now familiar quantity S. The computing formulas for d are

(Formula 10.9)

$$d_{YX} = S/(1/2)\,(N^2 - \Sigma F_X^2)$$

(Formula 10.10)

$$d_{XY} = S/(1/2)\,(N^2 - \Sigma F_Y^2)$$

where F_X and F_Y are the marginal (that is, column or row) totals of the X and Y variables. Let us compute the two values of d for the data from Table 10.5:

$$\begin{aligned} d_{YX} &= (274 - 129)/(1/2)\,[40^2 - (10^2 + 9^2 + 12^2 + 9^2)] \\ &= 145/(1/2)\,(1{,}600 - 406) = 145/597 \\ &= +0.24 \end{aligned}$$

$$\begin{aligned} d_{XY} &= (274 - 129)/(1/2)\,[40^2 - (14^2 + 16^2 + 10^2)] \\ &= 145/(1/2)\,(1{,}600 - 552) = 145/524 \\ &= +0.28 \end{aligned}$$

Somers's d does not have a distinct PRE interpretation. Otherwise, the interpretation of d is analogous to that of Gamma. Indeed, the interpretations of all six measures discussed thus far are similar in that all are based on the logic of pair-by-pair comparison. The six measures differ in the manner in which tied pairs are treated. *Gamma completely eliminates all tied pairs,* whether tied on the independent variable, the dependent variable, or both. *Tau-a includes all tied pairs. Tau-b* (and, by modification, *Tau-c)* treats all pairs as if there were complete mutual association and *excludes all tied pairs.* Somers's d treats all pairs as does Gamma but *excludes all pairs that are tied on the independent variable.* A summary of these six measures is presented in Table 10.6.

The decision as to which measure should be used is not an easy one to make. Costner (1965) has argued that, because of its clear PRE interpretation, Gamma is always the preferred measure. But Gamma does not measure mutual association, nor does it statistically distinguish between the independent and dependent variables. If we wish to measure mutual association, we may prefer one of the Tau measures, but the interpretation of Tau (except in limited circumstances) is not as clear as that of Gamma. Somers's d does give us an asymmetric measure, but one that lacks a clear conceptual interpretation (except in a 2 × 2 table, where d is analogous to the percentage difference. See Somers 1962).

Testing for the Significance of Gamma, Tau, and d

All of the measures previously described are subject to tests of statistical significance. More properly, it is not the measures themselves that are subject to test, but the value of S. Whether we are ultimately interested in Gamma, Tau, or d, it is essential that we first compute the value of S, and because every cross-classification table has only one value of S, we need concern ourselves with only a single test of significance. A test for the significance of S is, indirectly, a test for the significance of Gamma, Tau, and d.

The logic of this test involves the determination of the sampling distribution of S. From this, we compute the probability that we will observe any given value of S. If the number of cases involved is small (if $N \leq 10$), the procedure is very simple. When N is above 10, the procedure becomes a bit complicated.

Determining Significance When N < 10

Kendall (1962) has prepared a table that enables us to determine directly the probability of observing a given value of S when $N \leq 10$. This table is reproduced in Appendix Table E. To use this table, simply compute S and enter the table for the given values of S and N. The table value is the exact probability of obtaining the observed value (or a greater value) of S under a one-tail test. (For a two-tail test, proceed in the same way but *double* the probability values in the table.) For example, in Table 10.2(c), we computed a value of S = 6. With N = 5, the one-tailed probability of observing a value of $S \geq 6$ is 0.117. If we had specified a level of α = .05, the result of this test would lead us to accept (or more accurately, we would fail to reject)

> *Quick Quiz*
> **10.3**
>
> With N = 8, what is the probability (one-tail test) of observing a value of S = 8? What is the probability for a two-tail test?

Table 10.6. *Summary of Characteristics of Measures of Ordinal Association*

STATISTIC	COMPUTING FORMULA	TYPE OF ASSOCIATION	PRE INTERPRETATION	OTHER INTERPRETATION	MAJOR ADVANTAGE	MAJOR DISADVANTAGE
G	$\frac{S}{n_s + n_d}$	One-way and symmetric	Yes	Excess of similar (or dissimilar) pairs relative to the total number of similar and dissimilar pairs. Ties are excluded.	Can be interpreted as a PRE measure.	Insensitive to asymmetry
τ_a	$\frac{S}{\frac{1}{2}N(N-1)}$	Mutual and symmetric	No	Excess of similar (or dissimilar) pairs relative to number of all possible pairs. Ties are included.	Useful when presence of ties is an argument against association.	Lacks PRE interpretation
τ_b	$\frac{S}{\frac{1}{2}\sqrt{(N^2 - \Sigma F_x^2)(N^2 - \Sigma F_y^2)}}$	Mutual and symmetric	In limited circumstances	Excess of similar (or dissimilar) pairs relative to all possible pairs, assuming complete mutual association. Ties are excluded.	Best measure of mutual associaton.	Limited PRE interpretation
τ_c	$\frac{S}{\left(\frac{1}{2}N^2 \frac{m-1}{m}\right)}$	Mutual and symmetric	No	As τ_b, but modified for tables of any dimensions.	As τ_b	As τ_b
d_{yx}	$\frac{S}{\frac{1}{2}(N^2 - \Sigma F_x^2)}$	One-way and asymmetric	No	As G, except pairs tied on the independent variable are excluded. Also analogous to the percentage difference.	Statistically distinguishes between independent and dependent variables.	Lacks PRE interpretation
d_{xy}	$\frac{\Sigma}{\frac{1}{2}(N2 - \Sigma Fy2)}$	One-way and asymmetric	No	As d_{yx}	As d_{yx}	As d_{yx}

the null hypothesis. We would conclude that the pattern of association observed in Table 10.2(c) is a pattern that could occur "by chance." (For a two-tail test, the probability of observing a value of $S \geq 6$ is 0.234.)

Testing for the Significance of S When N ≥ 10

Kendall (1962) has shown that when $N \geq 10$ the sampling distribution of S is approximately normal with a mean $\bar{S} = 0$ and a standard deviation of

$$\sigma_s = \sqrt{(1/18)N(N - 1)(2N + 5)}$$

(This last value, whose derivation need not concern us, is technically correct only when no ties exist. Because such a situation rarely occurs, a necessary correction, described next, must be made for whenever the number of ties is not negligible.) Because we have a close approximation to the normal curve, we can test for the significance of S by using z-scores.

$$z = \frac{S - \bar{S}}{\sigma_s} = \frac{S - 0}{\sigma_s} = \frac{S}{\sigma_s}$$

This statistic tests the null hypothesis that $S = 0$; in other words, we are testing a hypothesis of no association.

Because the distribution of S is finite and discrete, and the normal distribution is infinite and continuous, it is necessary to correct S and σ_S. (This is analogous to Yates's correction for Chi-square.) Freeman (1965) has provided us with the following procedures for estimating the corrected values of S (called $\hat{S}$) and σ_s (called $\sigma_{\hat{s}}$). These are

(Formula 10.11)

$$\hat{S} = |S| - \frac{N}{2(r - 1)(c - 1)}$$

where $|S|$ is the absolute value of S, N is the number of cases, and r and c are the number of rows and columns.

(Formula 10.12)

$$\sigma_{\hat{s}} = \sqrt{\frac{R_2 C_2}{N-1} - \frac{R_2 C_3}{N(N-1)} + \frac{R_3 C_3}{N(N-1)(N-2)}}$$

where R_2 (and C_2) *is the sum of the products of the row (column)* totals taken two at a time, and R_3 (and C_3) *is the sum of the products of the row (column)* totals taken three at a time. To test the significance of S, we compute a z-score using the corrected values $\hat{S}$ and $\sigma_{\hat{s}}$.

(Formula 10.13)

$$z = \frac{\hat{S}}{\sigma_{\hat{s}}}$$

Let us return to the data from Table 10.5 as an example.

1. *Null hypothesis:* S = 0. Stated differently, there is no association between the two variables.
2. Let $\alpha = .05$, one-tail test.
3. *Decision rules:* Reject H_0 if $z \geq 1.64$; do not reject H_0 if $z < 1.64$.

The computation of $\hat{S}$ and $\sigma_{\hat{s}}$ is as follows. (See Table 10.7 for calculations.)

$$\hat{S} = 145 - \frac{40}{2(2)(3)} = 145 - \frac{40}{12}$$

$$= 145 - 3.33 = 141.67$$

and

$$\sigma_{\hat{s}} = \sqrt{\frac{(524)(597)}{39} - \frac{(524)(3,924) + (597)(2,240)}{40(39)} + \frac{(2,240)(3,942)}{40(39)(38)}}$$

and

$$z = \frac{141.67}{77.39} = 1.83$$

Because our computed value of z exceeds the critical value from the table (1.83 > 1.64), we reject the null hypothesis (which states that

Table 10.7. *Values Needed for Testing the Significance of S from Table 10.5*

6	3	3	2	14
3	3	7	3	16
1	3	2	4	10
10	9	12	9	40

$S = n_s - n_d = 274 - 129 = 145$
$N = 40$
$r = 3$
$c = 4$

$$\begin{aligned} R_2 &= 14(16) + 14(10) + 16(10) \\ &= 224 + 140 + 160 \\ &= 524 \end{aligned}$$

$$\begin{aligned} R_3 &= 14(16)(10) \\ &= 2{,}240 \end{aligned}$$

$$\begin{aligned} C_2 &= 10(9) + 10(12) + 10(9) + 9(12) + 9(9) + 12(9) \\ &= 90 + 120 + 90 + 180 + 81 + .108 \\ &= 597 \end{aligned}$$

$$\begin{aligned} C_3 &= 10(9)(12) + 10(9)(9) + 10(12)(9) + 9(12)(9) \\ &= 1{,}080 + 810 + 1{,}080 + 972 \\ &= 3{,}942 \end{aligned}$$

there is no association). By extension, we can conclude that the two variables are related.

Spearman's Rank-Order Correlation Coefficient, Rho

In the final section of this chapter, we focus on the oldest of the frequently used measures of ordinal association, Spearman's rank-order correlation coefficient, Rho (ρ), and its associated value, Rho-square. Rho is a measure of the extent to which two sets of ranks are in agreement or disagreement with each other. Rho may take on values between 0.00 (indicating no rank-order correlation) and ± 1.00 (indicating perfect association of ranks).

The underlying logic of Rho centers on the differences between ranks. Suppose we have the rankings as described in Table 10.2. Clearly, for (a) we want a measure that yields a coefficient of +1.00; for (b) we want a measure that yields a coefficient of -1.00; and for (c) we want a measure that yields an intermediate value, one that expresses the amount of agreement or disagreement between the two sets of ranks. Spearman's Rho gives us such a value. For computation purposes, Rho is defined as

(Formula 10.14)

$$\rho = 1 - \left(\frac{6\Sigma D^2}{N(N^2 - 1)} \right)$$

where D is the difference between the ranks assigned to each object. For the first two examples given previously in Table 10.2,

(a)

X Rank	Y Rank	D	D^2
1	1	0	0
2	2	0	0
3	3	0	0
4	4	0	0
5	5	0	0
			$\Sigma D^2 = 0$

$$\rho = 1 - \frac{6(0)}{5(24)} = 1 - 0 = +1.00$$

(b)

X Rank	Y Rank	D	D^2
1	5	-4	16
2	4	-2	4
3	3	0	0
4	2	2	4
5	1	4	16
			$\Sigma D^2 = 40$

$$\rho = 1 - \frac{6(40)}{5(24)} = 1 - \frac{240}{120}$$

$$= 1 - 2 = -1.00$$

Quick Quiz
10.4

For the data in Table 10.2(c), what is the value of Rho?

Table 10.8. *Computing ρ with Tied Ranks*

Object	Judge X	Judge Y	D	D^2
I	1	1	0	0
II	2	3	-1	1
III	3	5	-2	4
IV	4	7	-3	9
V	5	3	2	4
VI	6.5	6	0.5	0.25
VII	6.5	3	3.5	12.25
VIII	8	8	0	0
			0	$30.50 = \Sigma D^2$

$$\rho = 1 - \frac{6(30.5)}{8(8^2 - 1)} = 1 - \frac{183}{504} = 1 - 0.36 = +0.64$$

Tied Ranks

It occasionally happens that a judge cannot distinguish between two objects and declares that the objects are tied at some rank. In such cases, the common procedure is to assign to each object the mean value of the tied ranks. Suppose eight objects are ranked by two judges. Judge A cannot decide which two objects belong in the sixth and seventh places; Judge B cannot decide which three belong in the second, third, and fourth places. Table 10.8 shows these rankings. For Judge X, objects VI and VII are assigned the mean of ranks 6 and 7; for Judge Y, objects II, V, and VII are assigned the mean of ranks 2, 3, and 4 (2 + 3 + 4)/3 = 3. Rho is then computed in the usual fashion and yields a value of +0.64. [NOTE: When the number of ties is relatively large, the value of Rho becomes inflated. Kendall (1962: 32) has described a procedure to correct this.]

Interpretation: Rho-Square as a PRE Measure

Rho is like Chi-square in that it has no inherently logical meaning except to say that as the value of Rho moves from zero to unity, there is evidence of increasing association. However, if we square the value of Rho and obtain Rho-square, we have a measure that has a PRE interpretation.

Rho-square is a symmetric measure of one-way association for ranked data. Because it can fit the general PRE formula,

$$PRE = \frac{E_1 - E_2}{E_1}$$

it is a PRE measure. We have already seen that every PRE measure is derived from the errors associated with two prediction rules. For Rho-square, the first prediction rule, which yields E_1, uses only knowledge of the dependent variable.

> *Prediction Rule 1 (ρ^2):* For Rho-square, to predict the Y-rank for a given object, use the mean of all ranks on Y. In symbols, predict $\widehat{R}_Y = \overline{R}_Y$.

If N items are being ranked, the mean rank, $\overline{R}_Y$, is defined as the sum of all ranks divided by N, and can be easily computed as

(Formula 10.15)

$$\overline{R}_Y = \frac{N+1}{2}$$

If we apply Rule 1 to Table 10.9 we shall predict a value of $\overline{R}_Y$ = (5 + 1)/2 = 3 for each object being ranked on Y.

The second prediction rule, which yields E_2, uses knowledge of the X ranks (R_X) to predict the Y ranks. We obtain the predicted value of rank Y (R_Y) from a formula that incorporates the computed value of Rho.

> *Prediction Rule 2 (ρ^2):* Predict a value for Y, $\widehat{R}_Y$, such that

$$\widehat{R}_Y = (R_X)(\rho) + \frac{N+1}{2}(1 - \rho)$$

For Rho-square, the definition of error is slightly different from other error definitions we have already seen. *Error is defined in terms of square deviations:*

Table 10.9. *Computation of E_1 and E_2 for ρ^2*

Rank of $X = (R_X)$	Rank of $Y = (R_Y)$	$\bar{R}_Y^*$	$(R_Y - \bar{R}_Y)$	$(R_Y - \bar{R}_Y)^2$	$\hat{R}_Y^{**}$	$(R_Y - \hat{R}_Y)$	$(R_Y - \hat{R}_Y)^2$
1	1	3	-2	4	1.6	-0.6	0.36
2	2	3	-1	1	2.3	-0.3	0.09
3	4	3	1	1	3.0	1.0	1.00
4	5	3	2	4	3.7	1.3	1.69
5	3	3	0	0	4.4	-1.4	1.96
			0	$E_1 = 10$		0.0	$E_2 = 5.10$

$$\rho^2 = \frac{E_1 - E_2}{E_1} = \frac{10 - 5.10}{10} = \frac{4.90}{10} = 0.49$$

$^*\bar{R}_Y \quad = (N + 1)/2 = 6/2 = 3$

$^{**}\hat{R}_Y \quad = (R_X)(r) + (N + 1)/2(1 - r) = (R_X)(0.7) + (3)(0.3) = 0.7R_X + 0.9$

$$E_1 = \Sigma\,(R_Y - \bar{R}_Y)^2 \text{ and } E_2 = \Sigma\,(R_Y - \hat{R}_Y)^2$$

The computing formulas for E_1 and E_2 are

(Formula 10.16)

$$E_1 = \frac{N(N^2 - 1)}{12}$$

and

(Formula 10.17)

$$E_2 = \frac{N(N^2 - 1)}{12}(1 - \rho^2)$$

Note that the sum of the deviations, $(R_Y - \bar{R}_Y)$ and $(R_Y - \hat{R}_Y)$, will always be zero because some deviations are positive and others are negative, and the two cancel each other. To eliminate this difficulty, we must use the squared deviations; we must square each error value before summing. (This procedure is analogous to that used in computing the standard deviation, in which deviations from the mean were squared, then summed. [See Chapter 4.])

The computing formulas for E_1 and E_2 should be used in preference to the "logical" formulas for two reasons: (1) the computing formulas are far easier to use, and (2) the logical formulas do not adequately handle tied ranks.

While Rho-square has a PRE interpretation, it is not an adequate measure of the *direction of* association; that is, it does not tell us whether a pattern of association is direct (or positive) or inverse (or negative). However, we can get such information for Rho, which can be positive, zero, or negative.

Finally we note that it is possible to determine Rho-square not through the PRE procedures just described, but by simply computing the value of Rho and squaring. There is no reason you should not use the simpler computing procedure as long as you understand that Rho and Rho-square are two different statistics with two different interpretations.

Testing for the Significance of Rho

Appendix Table F contains critical values for testing the significance of Rho. Let us use the data from Table 10.9 as an example of its use. We first state our null hypothesis and decision rules. (For Rho, df = [N - 2], where N is the number of pairs.)

1. *Null hypothesis (H_0):* $\rho = 0$. Or there is no association between the two sets of ranks.
2. Let $\alpha = .05$, one-tail test.
3. *Decision rules:* If the observed value of Rho equals or exceeds the table value (.900), reject H_0; if the observed value is less than the table value, do not reject H_0.

Our computed value of Rho is 0.70, which is less than the critical value from the table. Therefore, we do not reject H_0. A reasonable conclusion is that this pattern of association could occur "by chance" (where the level of chance is defined by $\alpha = .05$).

Quick Quiz
10.5

For Table 10.8, test for the significance of Rho. Let α = .01, one-tail test.

An SPSS Example

To generate most of the ordinal measures described in this chapter, CROSSTABS—which was introduced in the previous chapter—is also used. The procedure is virtually the same, with the only notable exception being the specification of the particular statistics requested.

In this example, I have chosen to look at the relationship between a measure of satisfaction with one's health (the dependent, or criterion, variable) and one's educational level (the independent, or predictor, variable). Both of these NORC variables have been RECODED into three categories for simplicity of presentation. The statistics asked for are Gamma, Tau-b, and Somers's d.

Example: CROSSTABS of Health and Education

```
CROSSTABS NEWHEALT BY NEWEDUC
 /CELLS = COUNT COL   /STATISTICS = GAMMA BTAU D
```

File: GENERAL SOCIAL SURVEY (NORC) 1990

NEWHEALT THREE CATEGORY MEASURE OF HEALTH
by NEWEDUC EDUCATION: LOW/MEDIUM/HIGH

(continued)

(continued)

NEWEDUC

Count / Col Pct / NSATHLTH	LOW: NO H.S.DIP 1.00	MED: HS SOME COL 2.00	HI: 3+ YRS COLL 3.00	Row Total
1.00 LOW	19 37.3	22 19.1	11 16.4	52 22.3
2.00 MED	9 17.6	21 18.3	14 20.9	44 18.9
3.00 HIGH	23 45.1	72 62.6	42 62.7	137 58.8
Column Total	51 21.9	115 49.4	67 28.8	233 100.0

Statistic	Value	Approx. T-value
Kendall's Tau-b	.12837	2.11520
Gamma	.21079	2.11520
Somers' D :		
symmetric	.12823	2.11520
with NSATHLTH dependent	12239	2.11520
with NEWEDUC dependent	.13465	2.11520

Number of Missing Observations: 120

The results are presented in a straightforward manner. The value of Gamma is +0.14; Tau-b is +0.21; symmetric d is +0.12 and d with NSATHLTH dependent is also +0.12.

Unfortunately, SPSS does not provide a straightforward test of significance for these statistics. What SPSS does provide is an "approximate" t-value, which I interpret by using the Appendix Table B for the t-test (see Chapter 7).

Important Terms

Pair-by-pair comparison	Tau-a (Tau-b, Tau-c)
Similar pair	Somers's d
Dissimilar pair	Spearman's Rho
Tied pair	Rho-square
Yule's Q	

Suggested Readings

Costner (1965); Goodman and Kruskal (1954; 1959; 1963); Kendall (1962); Loether and McTavish (1988: 231-242); Mueller, Schuessler, and Costner (1970: 267-292); Ott et al. (1992: 389-411); Somers (1962).

Quick Quiz Answers

Quick Quiz 10.1

$n_s = 1{,}100$ and $n_d = 2{,}200$

$S = n_s - n_d = 1{,}100 - 2{,}200 = -1{,}100$

$$G = \frac{S}{n_s + n_d} = \frac{-1{,}100}{3{,}300} = -0.33$$

Quick Quiz 10.2

We first determine the total number of possible pairs as (1/2)N(N - 1) = (1/2)(183)(182) = 16,653, and we then eliminate the tied pairs. The number of tied pairs is thus (1/2)(48)(47) + (1/2)(70)(69) + (1/2)(65) = 1,128 + 2,415 + 2,080 = 5,623. Our solution, therefore, is 16,653 - 5,623 = 11,030.

Quick Quiz 10.3

For a one-tail test, p = 0.199; for a two-tail test, p = 0.398.

Quick Quiz 10.4

$$\Sigma D^2 = 6; r = 1 - \left(\frac{6(6)}{5(24)}\right) = +0.70$$

Quick Quiz 10.5

With α =.01, one-tail test, and N = 8, the critical value of Rho is 0.833. Because our observed value is less than the critical value, we do not reject H_0.

11

Measuring the Association Between Two Interval Variables

In this chapter we will devote our attention almost exclusively to two statistical measures of association, the Pearson product-moment correlation coefficient, r, and its associated value, r^2, the coefficient of determination. In Chapters 9 and 10 we encountered several statistics, each of which is, in the proper circumstances, an appropriate measure of association for nominal- or ordinal-level data. However, this diversity of available measures means that one of our data-analysis problems will be to select the "best" statistic to use. When working with interval-level (or ratio-level) data, our problem is greatly minimized by the fact that the Pearson r, or r^2, is the almost universal choice as the measure of association. (An exception to this statement will be made at the end of this chapter.) The Pearson r is also of great importance because it is the basis of many advanced statistical techniques that are used in sociological analysis. We will not discuss these techniques, such as path analysis, in this book, but an understanding of r will at least enable you to read more advanced research literature with increased comprehension.

One of the important distinctions between interval-level measurement and measurement at lower levels (nominal and ordinal) concerns the nature of prediction errors. With the lower levels of measurement, an error is simply an error: We cannot determine the magnitude of error. If we recall the hypothetical example used in describing Lambda, our prediction of delinquency based on club background resulted in either a correct prediction or an incorrect prediction (error); for any given case, we were either right or wrong. We could not measure the magnitude of error because of the nature of nominal-level measurement. Similarly, with ordinal measures such as

Gamma, we predicted pairs of data to be either similar or dissimilar; again, such predictions were either right or wrong with no information as to *how* wrong an error might be. We could not determine the magnitude of error because of the nature of ordinal measurement. But because of the properties of interval-level measurement, the Pearson r can be used to tell how much change in one variable can be expected given a set amount of change in the other variable. It is in this sense that r provides us with an example of the fifth way of viewing association, as described in Chapter 9. The Pearson r describes the extent to which an increase or decrease in one variable is accompanied by an increase or decrease in the other. In the history of statistics, this notion is usually referred to not as association but as *correlation* or as *linear regression.*

The Pearson r and r^2 are two very useful and versatile statistics. Each has several important interpretations, and each interpretation focuses on a different aspect of the data. We shall begin our discussion with a PRE interpretation of r^2.

The Pearson r^2 as a PRE Measure

Following the general logic of PRE measures of association, we wish to develop two measures of error, one based on a prediction rule that uses only information about the dependent variable, and one based on a prediction rule that uses information about the independent variable. We shall use an overly simplified example to illustrate the PRE interpretation of r^2. Suppose five students are to take a quiz in their statistics course. Each spends the amount of time studying and receives the quiz grade indicated in Table 11.1. Because both variables are interval or ratio measures, the Pearson r, or r^2, is an appropriate measure of association. Upon simple inspection of the data we can see that as study time increases, the quiz grade also tends to increase. We also note that this tendency is not perfect: Student D, who studied three hours, received a lower grade than Student C, who studied only two hours.

It is reasonably clear that the dependent variable is the Y-variable, the quiz grade. If we know nothing about these data except the distribution of grades, what would be our best guess of the grade received by any individual? It should be clear by now that with interval data, the best guess for any individual score in a distribution is the mean of the distribution. The mean is the best guess in the sense

Table 11.1. *Hours Studied and Quiz Scores*

Student	Hours Studied (X)	Quiz Score (Y)
A	0	4
B	1	6
C	2	8
D	3	7
E	4	10

that it is the mean that minimizes the sum of squared deviations. (See Chapter 4 for a review of this concept.) This line of thought leads us to our first PRE prediction rule for r^2.

> *Prediction Rule 1 (r^2):* To predict a value of the dependent variable, use its mean.

With our data we are interested in predicting the quiz scores. The quiz score variable has been designated as the Y-variable, so we must find the value of $\overline{Y}$, the mean of Y. In Table 11.2, we see that $\overline{Y} = 7$. We measure E_1, the error resulting from the application of Prediction Rule 1, by finding the deviation of observed Y-scores; this value is the *deviation score*, y, or $Y - \overline{Y}$. But because the sum of deviation scores about a mean will always equal zero, we must *square* the deviation scores, and sum these squared deviations, thus obtaining y^2.

(Formula 11.1)

$$E_1 = \Sigma(Y - \overline{Y})^2 = \Sigma y^2$$

From Table 11.2 we see that $E_1 = 20$.

Prediction Rule 2 and computation of E_2 are more complex. Let us approach this rule slowly, visually. In Figure 11.1, we have plotted the X and Y scores as a coordinate system. If we look at this graph we can see that there is a crude pattern of positive association. We can also see how E_1 was determined, for we can see that there is a certain amount of distance, or deviation, which is equal to $(Y - \overline{Y}) = y$, between any value of Y and $\overline{Y}$. The mean of Y is indicated by the dashed line, and the deviations are indicated by brackets. When these distances (that is, deviations from the mean) are squared and summed, we have

Table 11.2. *Calculation of E_1*

Y	$\overline{Y}$	$y = Y - \overline{Y}$	y^2	
4	7	-3	9	
6	7	-1	1	
8	7	1	1	
7	7	0	0	
10	7	3	9	
35	35	0	20	$= E_1$

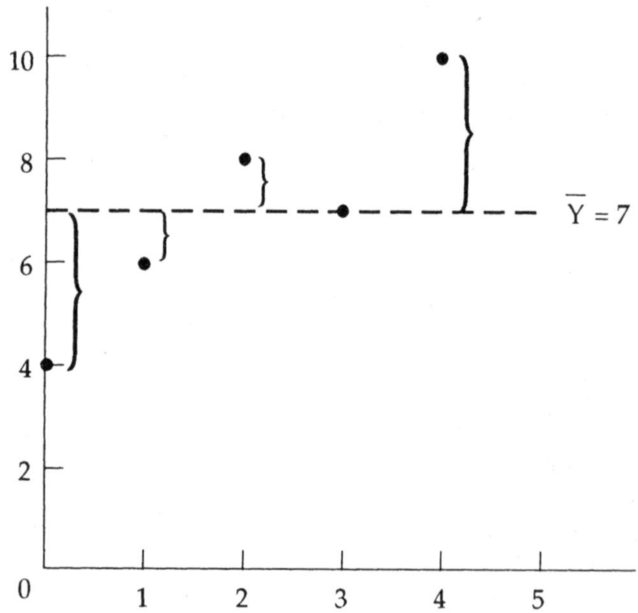

● indicates an observed value.

– – indicates the mean of Y, a predicted value.

} indicates the difference between the observed and predicted values $(Y - \overline{Y})$. The sum of these distances squared, $\Sigma (Y - \overline{Y})^2$, is E_1.

Figure 11.1. *Prediction Error as Deviation from the Mean*

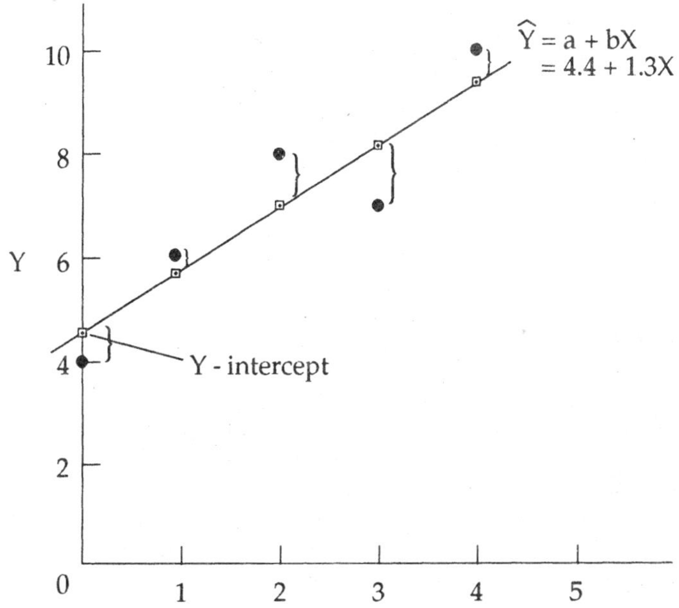

● indicates an observed value.

⊡ indicates a predicted value derived from the "best-fitting straight line."

} indicates the difference between the observed and predicted values $(Y - \hat{Y})$. The sum of these distances squared, $\Sigma\,(Y - \hat{Y})^2$, is E_2.

Figure 11.2. *Prediction Error as Deviation from the Regression Line*

E_1. We might now ask: Is there some line other than Y that would result in even *less* error than that in Figure 11.1?

If we can now introduce information about the independent (X) variable, we will be able to define a "best fitting" straight line (sometimes called a *regression* line), a line that minimizes the sum of squared deviations. Figure 11.2 anticipates part of the discussion yet to come and illustrates the best-fitting straight line for our data. Where does this line come from?

Any straight line can be defined by Formula 11.2,

(Formula 11.2)

$$\hat{Y} = a_{YX} + b_{YX}X$$

Table 11.3. *Calculation of a_{YX} and b_{YX}*

X	Y	X^2	Y^2	XY
0	4	0	16	0
1	6	1	36	6
2	8	4	64	16
3	7	9	49	21
4	10	16	100	40
10	35	30	265	83

$\bar{X} = 2$ $\quad\quad$ $\bar{Y} = 7$

$$b_{YX} = \frac{5\ (83) - 10\ (35)}{5\ (30\ ) - 10^2}$$

$$= \frac{415 - 350}{150 - 100} = \frac{65}{50}$$

$$= 1.3$$

$$a_{YX} = 7 - (1.3)\ (2)$$

$$= 7 - 2.6$$

$$= 4.4$$

where $\hat{Y}$ is the predicted value of Y; a_{YX} is the *Y-intercept*, or point where the line crosses the Y-axis; and b_{YX} is the *slope* of the line. It is the slope of the line that tells us how much of a change in Y will occur as a result of change in X. To be more specific, for every unit of change in X, there will be bX change in Y. Formula 11.3 defines the slope of the regression line. (The derivation of this formula is beyond the scope of the present discussion.)

(Formula 11.3)

$$b_{YX} = \frac{\Sigma(X - \bar{X})(Y - \bar{Y})}{(X - \bar{X})^2} = \frac{N(\Sigma XY) - (\Sigma X)(\Sigma Y)}{N(\Sigma X^2) - (\Sigma X)^2}$$

From Table 11.3 we see that for our data, $b_{YX} = 1.3$. We can now define the Y-intercept as

(Formula 11.4)

$$a_{YX} = \overline{Y} - b\overline{X}$$

For our data, $a_{YX} = 4.4$.

Quick Quiz
11.1

For the following data, determine the values of a_{YX} and b_{YX}.

X	Y
2	6
3	8
4	7

Now that we have the values of a and b we can solve the straight line equation for any value of X. We use the formula

$$\hat{Y} = 4.4 + 1.3X$$

to obtain the $\hat{Y}$ values found in Table 11.4, and by using these values, we plotted the straight line in Figure 11.2.

> *Prediction Rule 2 (r^2):* To predict any value of Y, use the straight-line equation from Formula 11.2.

As with E_1, E_2 is defined in terms of squared deviations of the observed scores of Y from the predicted values of $\hat{Y}$.

(Formula 11.5)

$$E_2 = \Sigma(Y - \hat{Y})^2$$

From Table 11.4 we see that E_2 is 3.10. We can now compute r^2 as a PRE measure of association.

$$r^2 = \frac{E_1 - E_2}{E_1} = \frac{20 - 3.10}{20} = \frac{16.90}{20} = 0.84$$

Table 11.4. *Calculation of* $\hat{Y}$ *and* E_2

X	Y	Y = 4.4 + 1.3X	$(Y - \bar{Y})$	$(Y - \hat{Y})$
0	4	4.4	-0.4	0.16
1	6	5.7	0.3	0.09
2	8	7.0	1.0	1.00
3	7	8.3	-1.3	1.69
4	10	9.6	0.4	0.16
10	35	35	0.0	3.10 = E_2

For computational purposes, it is usually more convenient to think of data not in terms of raw scores but in terms of deviation scores. Figure 11.3 presents our data in deviation format. Note that the general configuration of Figure 11.3 is identical with that of Figure 11.2 except that the X axis has shifted to $\bar{Y}$ and the Y axis is now $\bar{X}$.

One notable consequence of expressing the data as deviation scores is that the y-intercept becomes 0; as a result, the straight-line equation for deviation scores is

(Formula 11.6)

$$\hat{y} = b_{yx}$$

The computing formula for b_{yx} can be expressed as

(Formula 11.7)

$$b_{yx} = \frac{\Sigma xy}{\Sigma y^2}$$

From Table 11.5 we see that b_{YX} = 1.3, which is, of course, identical to the value computed from raw scores (Table 11.3). With our scores now expressed in deviation form, we can calculate values for y and $\hat{y}$, and, thereby, utilize a more direct computing formula for r^2

$$r^2_{yx} = \frac{\Sigma \hat{y}^2}{\Sigma y^2}$$

Again, using Table 11.5, we first see that $\Sigma y^2 = 20$ and $\Sigma \hat{y}^2 = 16.90$. This value is identical with the value of r^2 computed earlier. It represents the proportional amount by which we reduce error when we shift from using the mean of Y to predict Y to using the best-fitting straight line as a predictor of Y when error is defined in terms of squared deviations.

Let us now consider $E_1 = (Y - \bar{Y})^2 = \Sigma y^2$ as the total variation in Y; that is, let E_1 represent the sum (or total) of the squared deviations (or variation) from the mean of Y. Then the quantity

$$E_2 = \Sigma(Y - \hat{Y})^2 = \Sigma\hat{y}^2$$

is the amount of *un*explained variation in Y; it is the amount that is not explained by our information concerning the independent variable, X.

This conceptualization of r^2 as a *ratio of explained to total variation* is important for an understanding of many advanced statistical techniques that will not be examined in this book. However, make a mental note of this interpretation, for you will surely encounter it as you read through the sociological literature; you will then have at least a simple intuitive idea of what is being discussed.

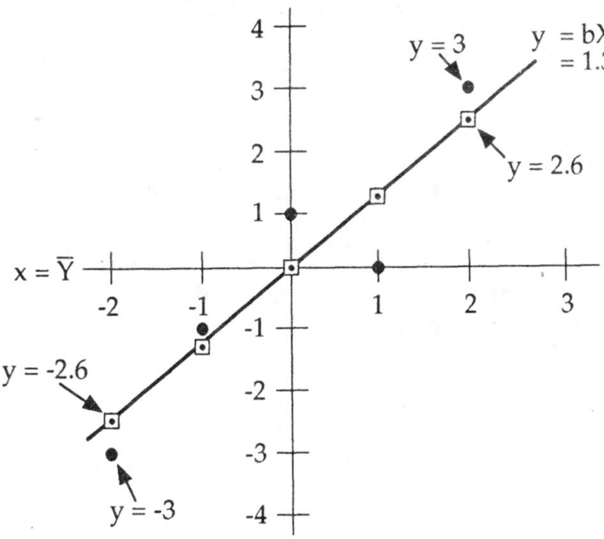

Figure 11.3. *Using Deviation Scores*

Table 11.5. *Deviation Scores*

X	Y	x	y	x^2	y^2	xy	y = bx	y^2
0	4	-2	-3	4	9	3	-2.6	6.76
1	6	-1	-1	1	1	1	-1.3	1.69
2	8	0	1	0	1	0	0.0	0.00
3	7	1	0	1	0	0	1.3	1.69
4	10	2	3	4	9	6	2.6	6.76
10	35	0	0	10	20	13	0.0	16.90

$$a_{yx} = 0$$

$$b_{yx} = \frac{13}{10} = 1.3$$

Viewed in this light,

$$r^2 = \frac{\text{Total Variation - Unexplained Variation}}{\text{Total Variation}}$$

$$= \frac{\text{Explained Variation}}{\text{Total Variation}}$$

The Pearson r

Despite the logical PRE interpretation and the logical "explained variation" interpretation of r^2, r is the more frequently used measure of association. One reason for this is the purely historical fact that early statisticians worked with r, not with r^2. Another reason is that r^2 varies between 0 and + 1 and, therefore, does not indicate the *direction* of any relationship; from r^2 we cannot determine whether a relationship is positive or negative.

To understand the meaning of r, let us use the same set of data with which we have been working. But let us transform these data into *standard scores* (that is, z-scores, as described on pp. 72-75). To do this, we first express each raw score as a deviation score, then divide the deviation score by the standard deviation. For our data, these computations are presented in Table 11.6. Next we compute the cross-products of the z-scores and sum. If we divide this sum by N, the

Table 11.6. *Standard Scores as a Basis of Calculating the Pearson r*

x	y	x^2	y^2	$z_x = x/s_x$	$z_y = y/s_y$	$z_x z_y$
-2	-3	4	9	-1.42	-1.50	2.13
-1	-1	1	1	-0.71	-0.50	0.36
0	1	0	1	0.00	0.50	0.00
1	0	1	0	0.71	0.00	0.00
2	3	4	9	1.42	1.50	2.13
0	0	10	20	0.00	0.00	4.62

$$s_x = \sqrt{\Sigma x^2/N} = \sqrt{10/5} = \sqrt{2} = 1.41 \qquad s_y = \sqrt{\Sigma y^2/N} = \sqrt{20/5} = \sqrt{4} = 2.00$$

number of cases, we will have computed the *mean* of the z-score cross-products. *This value is the Pearson r; it is also the slope of the best-fitting straight line **when data are recorded as standard scores.*** The computing formula for this value is given by Formula 11.8.

(Formula 11.8)

$$r_{YX} = \frac{\Sigma(z_X z_Y)}{N}$$

From the previous discussion you can perhaps see why the full technical designation of r is "the Pearson product-moment correlation coefficient." (In mathematics, a *moment* can be a mean and the *product* refers to the multiplication of z-scores; it was Karl Pearson who pioneered the development of this correlation coefficient.) With this understanding we can offer the following interpretation of r: *It is the mean change in Y for every unit of change in X **when data are expressed as standard scores.*** Let us apply this interpretation to our data. The value of r = .92 means that for every *standard* unit (z-score unit) of increase or decrease in Y, there is a .92 standard unit of increase or decrease in X. If X increases by $1\sigma_X$, Y increases by $.92\sigma_Y$; if X decreases by $2\sigma_X$, Y decreases by $2(.92)\sigma_Y$. Consequently, if we can express any X score as a standard score of z-score, we should be able to predict a Y score expressed in its standard form. Just as we earlier were able to

Table 11.7. *Calculation of* $\hat{z}_y$

z_x	$\hat{z}_y = rz_x$	z_x	$\hat{z}_y = rz_x$
-1.42	-1.31	1.00	0.92
-0.71	-0.65	-2.00	-1.84
0.00	0.00	2.50	2.30
0.71	0.65	-1.08	-0.99
1.42	1.31		

compute Y (or y) on the basis of our knowledge of X (or x), we can now predict a value of $\hat{z}_Y$ given knowledge of z_X. We do this by the formula

(Formula 11.9)

$$\hat{z}_Y = r(z_X)$$

For our data, Table 11.7 provides the computational details, and the results are presented graphically in Figure 11.4.

Computing Formulas

The previous discussion of r and r^2 was not presented for the purpose of actually computing these statistics. Rather, it was intended to demonstrate logically the meanings of r and r^2. Once these meanings are understood, we can move on to simpler and more direct procedures for computing this measure of association. Specifically, we offer the following formulas for computing r from ungrouped data.

(Formula 11.10)

$$r_{yx} = \frac{\Sigma xy}{\sqrt{\Sigma x^2 \Sigma y^2}}$$

(Formula 11.11)

$$r_{YX} = \frac{N\Sigma XY - \Sigma X \Sigma Y}{\sqrt{[N\Sigma X^2 - (\Sigma X^2)][N\Sigma Y^2 - (\Sigma Y^2)]}}$$

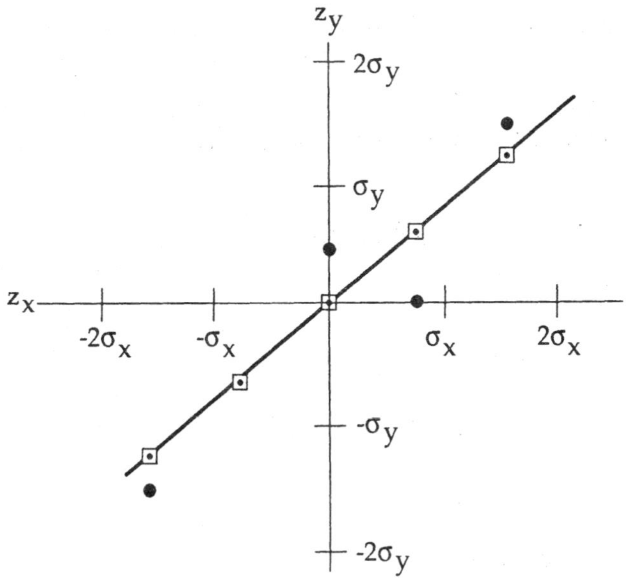

Figure 11.4. *Using z-Scores*

Table 11.5 contains the necessary information to compute r using Formula 11.10.

$$r_{yx} = \frac{13}{\sqrt{(10)(20)}} = \frac{13}{\sqrt{200}}$$

$$= \frac{13}{14.14} = +0.92$$

And Table 11.3 provides the necessary information to compute r using Formula 11.11.

$$r_{YX} = \frac{5(83) - 10(35)}{\sqrt{[5(30) - 10^2][5(265) - 35^2]}}$$

$$= \frac{415 - 350}{\sqrt{(150 - 100)(1325 - 1225)}}$$

$$= \frac{65}{\sqrt{50(100)}} = \frac{65}{70.71} = +0.92$$

As is evident, both computing formulas yield values of r that are identical to each other and to the value computed using z-score cross-products.

It should be pointed out that although Formula 11.11 *looks* forbidding, it actually provides probably the easiest method of computing r for ungrouped data. All it requires is the computation of five sums. In using this formula, do not worry about deviations, standard scores, cross-products, and the like; the raw data quickly and accurately yield the value of r.

We should also note that there is no similar simple, direct computing formula for r^2. We may, however, easily determine r^2 by computing r (using any of the previous methods) and squaring. For our data, $.92^2 = .8467 = r^2$. Within rounding error, this value is identical to the value of r^2 computed earlier.

Quick Quiz
11.2

For the data below, compute r and r^2.

X	Y
2	5
3	2
4	3
7	-2

Testing for the Significance of r

The null hypothesis that r = 0 may be tested directly by using Appendix Table G. To use the table, first calculate the degrees of freedom associated with r. For r,

(Formula 11.13)

$$df = N - 2$$

Table 11.8. *Hypothetical Homicide and Suicide Rates*

Homicide Rate	Suicide Rate	Homicide Rate	Suicide Rate
3	6	4	8
0	5	9	15
6	12	14	20
3	7	10	18
8	16	10	23
5	19	5	9
1	4	13	22
4	12	4	10
9	20	11	16
6	11	1	2
1	1	6	13
2	3	7	13
8	23	7	17
7	18	5	11
2	24	8	14

$r = +0.88$

If the observed value of r equals or exceeds the table value, reject H_0; if the observed value is less than the table value, do not reject H_0.

As an example, we can test the hypothesis that $r = 0$ for the data found in Table 11.8.

1. *Null hypothesis:* There is no correlation between the homicide rates and suicide rates in the thirty cities. Or the correlation between homicide rates and suicide rates is zero.
2. Let $\alpha = .01$; one-tail; df = 28.
3. *Decision rules:* Reject H_0 if $r \geq .423$. Do not reject if $r < .423$.

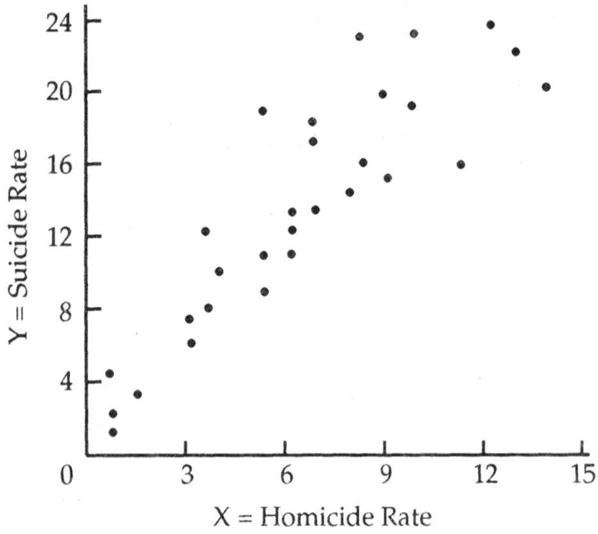

Figure 11.5. *Homicide and Suicide Rates*

Because our observed value of r = .88 is larger than the critical value found in Appendix Table G, we can safely reject the hypothesis of no association. A reasonable further inference is that the homicide rates and suicide rates are associated.

Additional Notes

Assumptions

The application of the Pearson r requires certain assumptions. Suppose we tabulate the homicide rates and suicide rates for thirty medium-sized cities. These data are presented in a scatterplot of the X and Y values (Figure 11.5). On a plot we find the (X,Y) coordinate points. That is, for each of the thirty cities, we plot the homicide rate and the suicide rate as a single point. Most researchers will agree that a scatterplot is a useful device when preparing to assess correlation. A glance at Figure 11.5 immediately tells us that (1) the relationship between homicide rate (X) and suicide rate (Y) is *linear* (or rectilinear), that is, there is a tendency for the scatter points to fall along a straight line as opposed to a curved line (Figure 11.6 illustrates other linear and *curvilinear* plots); and (2) the

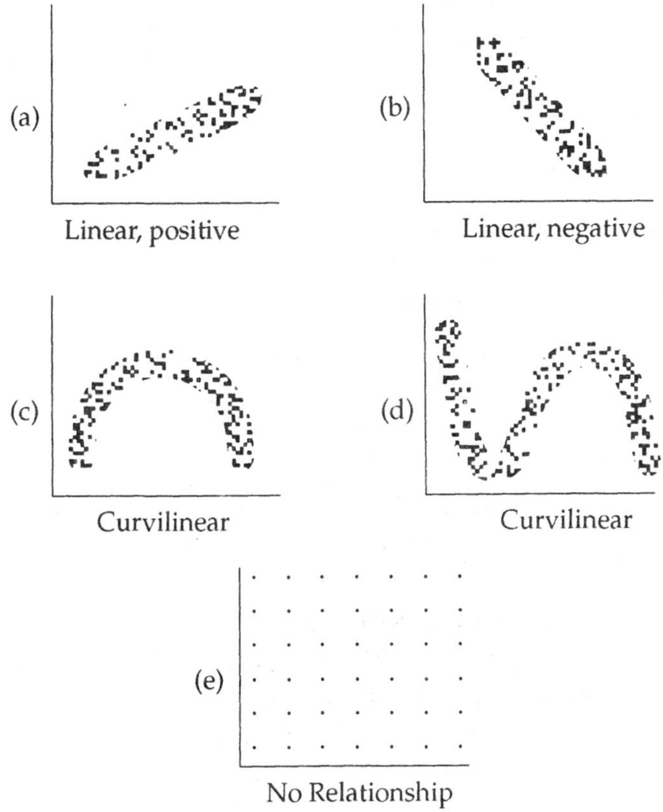

Figure 11.6. *Types of Relationships*

relationship is positive, that is, as the homicide rate increases, the suicide rate also increases. The first piece of information, that the relationship is linear, is vital, for the Pearson r is applicable only to data that are linear or reasonably close to being linear. If the data markedly depart from linearity, as in Figure 11.6(c) and 11.6(d), the Pearson r is not an appropriate measure of association. (Instead, Eta-square is used; see further on.)

There is one other assumption that must be met before r can be properly and fully utilized: If we compute the variance (the standard deviation squared) for each of the class intervals within each variable, the variances for each variable should be similar in value. This property of equal class variances bears the technical label of homoscedasticity. A scatterplot can be used to give us a rough visual estimate of whether our data are homoscedastic (Figure 11.7). If data are homoscedastic, the points will fall within a cigar shape in 11.7(a) and 11.7(b); marked deviations from such a shape indicate heteroscedasticity as in 11.7(c), (d), and (e).

We have now established three critical assumptions that must be met in order to properly use the Pearson r: (1) the data must be at the interval level of measurement; (2) the pattern of the relationship must be linear, that is, it must fall along a straight line; and (3) the data must be homoscedastic.

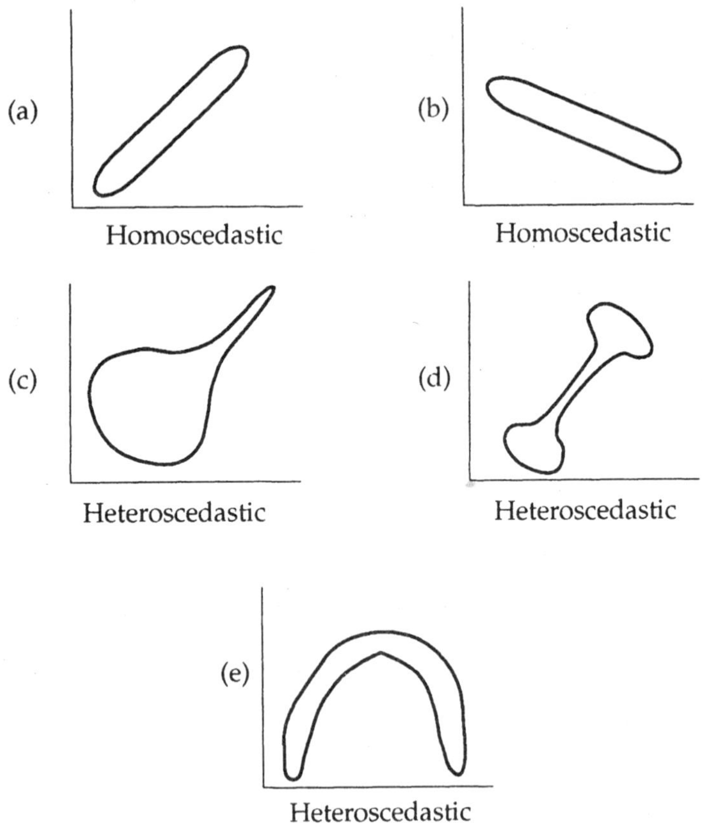

Figure 11.7. *Homo- and Heteroscedasticity*

Interpretation

Pearson's r^2 is a PRE measure of association for interval-level data. It measures the relative reduction in error achieved when we shift from a prediction rule that states that any Y-value is equal to the mean of Y to a prediction rule that uses the formula for a straight line, $Y = a + bX$. The Pearson r^2 may also be interpreted as a ratio of explained to total variation.

The product-moment correlation coefficient, r, is a measure of the extent to which a change in one variable is associated with a change in a second variable. Specifically, for every standard deviation unit of change in the independent variable, we predict that the dependent variable will change by $(r)(\sigma)$ units. The Pearson r may also be viewed as the slope of the regression line when data are presented as standard scores.

Type of Measure

Both r and r^2 are *symmetric* measures of *one-way* association. They differ, however, in that r indicates direction and r^2 does not.

Mathematical Relationship Between r and r^2

It is too easy and possibly misleading to simply say that $r = \sqrt{r^2}$, for although this is arithmetically correct, it has no logical meaning. The Pearson r is not the square root of explained variation and r^2 is not the squared slope of the regression line. For computational purposes we can, of course, use one value to derive the other (except that when we extract the square root of r^2, we do not know which sign to use for r, but we should be careful not to confuse the meanings of the two. Furthermore, because r will always be larger than r^2 (except when both are zero or one), we should be certain that the appropriate value, r or r^2, is chosen so that we deal properly with the aspect of the data being discussed.

Reversibility

Because r and r^2 are symmetric measures of association, $r_{YX} = r_{XY}$, and $r^2_{YX} = r^2_{XY}$. Given two variables, X and Y, the measure of association will have the same value whether X or Y is designated as the independent, or predictor, variable. However, this observation should not mask the fact that for any set of raw (or unstandardized) data there can be *two* regression lines: (1) Y = a + bX, and (2) X = a + bY. Two regression lines can be plotted for any set of data expressed as raw scores or as deviation scores. However, note that if r = 1.00 the two lines will be identical and that if r = 0, there is no best-fitting line.

Finally, in computing r^2_{XY} rather than r^2_{YX}, care must be taken to adjust computing formulas. For example, Formula 11.3,

$$b_{YX} = \frac{N(\Sigma XY) - \Sigma X \Sigma Y}{N(\Sigma X^2) - (\Sigma X)^2}$$

becomes

$$b_{XY} = \frac{N(\Sigma XY) - \Sigma X \Sigma Y}{N(\Sigma Y^2) - (\Sigma Y)^2}$$

and

$$r^2_{YX} = \frac{\Sigma \hat{y}^2}{\Sigma y^2} \text{ becomes } r^2_{XY} = \frac{\Sigma \hat{x}^2}{\Sigma x^2}$$

That is, there is a different slope, or rate of change, in predicting Y from X, compared to predicting X from Y.

Measuring Curvilinear Correlation: Eta-Square

We mentioned previously that one of the necessary preconditions for calculation of the Pearson r or r^2 is that the data must tend to fall along a straight line. When there are marked departures from the assumption of rectilinearity, the Pearson r is inappropriate as a measure of association. Figure 11.6(c) and (d) showed two instances where a strong relationship exists between two variables but for which the computed value of r would not accurately reflect the strength of the relationship. For these data, it is obvious that a *curved* line would offer a better prediction model than would any straight line.

Eta-square (η^2) is an asymmetric measure of one-way association for curvilinear data. Because it is asymmetric, we can compute two values, η^2_{YX} and η^2_{XY}, for any set of two variables. In most respects η^2 is interpreted as r^2.

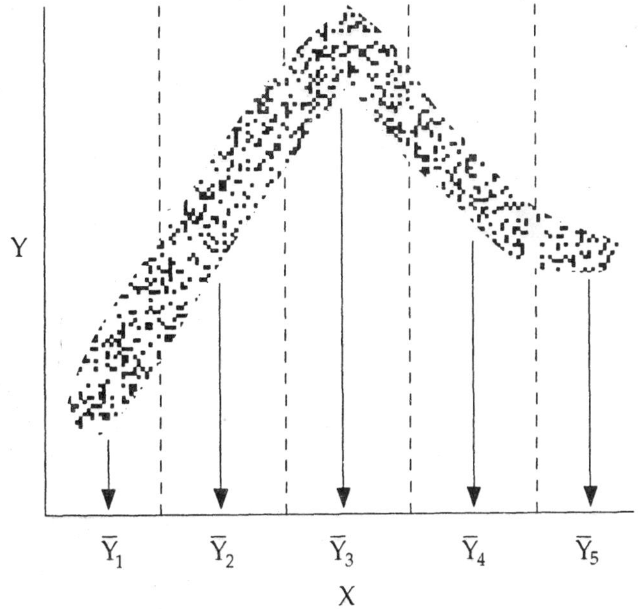

Figure 11.8. *Within-Category Means as a Prediction Rule for Eta-Square*

A noteworthy distinction between η^2 and r^2 is that the former requires only that the dependent variable be measured at the interval level; the independent variable may be at the interval level, but it may also be at the ordinal or nominal level of measurement.

Mathematically, η^2 differs from r^2 in that the calculation of η^2 involves "breaking up the data" into segments (Figure 11.8) and, for each segment, predicting a Y-value on the basis of the mean of Y *within* each segment rather than on the basis of the regression line (as in the case with r^2). The segments, or class intervals, are somewhat arbitrarily selected, so care should be taken to ensure that they accurately reflect the nature of the distribution.

Eta-square has a PRE interpretation. In terms of the PRE logic, the first prediction rule for η^2 is the same as for r^2.

Prediction Rule 1 (η^2): To predict Y, use the mean of Y.

E_1 is defined similarly as for r^2. Prediction Rule 2, however, differs from that for r^2.

Prediction Rule 2 (η^2): To predict Y, in any given category of X use the within-category mean of Y.

E_2 is defined as the sum of squared deviations of the within-category means from the grand mean.

Procedures for calculating Eta-square will not be described here. The interested student can consult Freeman (1965) for a simple procedure for ungrouped data and Meuller, Schuessler, and Costner (1970) for a procedure for grouped data.

An SPSS Example: The Pearson r

To produce a set of CORRELATIONS using SPSS, one need only specify the variables that are to be correlated. In the following example, the /FORMAT command is used to simplify the output.

CORRELATIONS Example:

```
CORRELATIONS VARIABLES = CHILDS AGEWED EDUC
 /FORMAT = SERIAL

File:   GENERAL SOCIAL SURVEY (NORC) 1990

             - - - Correlation Coefficients - - -
Variable               Variable               Variable
Pair                   Pair                   Pair
--------               --------               --------
CHILDS   -.3279        CHILDS  -.2426         AGEWED  .2352
with     N( 276)       with    N( 353)        with    N( 276)
AGEWED   Sig .000      EDUC    Sig .000       EDUC    Sig .000

Sig is 2-tailed. "." is printed if a coefficient cannot be computed.
```

The results from this output tell us that the number of children one has (CHILDS) is negatively correlated ($r = -.33$) with one's age at marriage (AGEWED), that CHILDS is negatively correlated with EDUC ($r = -.24$), and that AGEWED is positively correlated with EDUC ($r = +.24$). What this means is that if one marries at a later age, one has fewer children; that people with more years of education have fewer children; and that people who marry later have more education. The significance of all three measures is reported as .000, which means that there is less than one chance in a thousand that such a relationship could have occurred "by chance." None of this tells us anything about cause and effect.

Important Terms

Pearson product-moment correlation coefficient (r)
The coefficient determination (r^2)
Regression line
Three assumptions for r
Eta-square (η^2)

Suggested Readings

Blalock (1979, Chap. 17); Levin and Fox (1991: 314-329); Mueller, Schuessler, and Costner (1970: 195-341).

Quick Quiz Answers

Quick Quiz 11.1

$$\Sigma X = 9 \qquad \Sigma Y = 21 \qquad \Sigma XY = 64$$
$$\Sigma X^2 = 29 \qquad \overline{X} = 3 \qquad \overline{Y} = 7$$

$$b_{YX} = \frac{3(64) - 9(21)}{3(29) - 9^2} = \frac{192 - 189}{87 - 81}$$
$$= \frac{3}{6} = 0.5$$

$$a_{YX} = 7 - 0.5(3) = 7 - 1.5 = 5.5$$

Quick Quiz 11.2

X	Y	X^2	Y^2	XY	x	y	x^2	y^2	xy
2	5	4	25	10	-2	3	4	9	-6
3	2	9	4	6	-1	0	1	0	0
4	3	16	9	12	0	1	0	1	0
7	-2	49	4	-14	3	-4	9	16	-12
16	8	78	42	14	0	0	14	26	-18

$$\overline{X} = 4 \qquad \overline{Y} = 2$$

Using Formula 11.10,

$$r = \frac{-18}{\sqrt{14(26)}} = \frac{-18}{\sqrt{364}}$$

$$= \frac{-18}{19.08} = -.94$$

And using Formula 11.11,

$$r = \frac{4(14) - 16(8)}{\sqrt{[4(78) - 16^2][4(42) - 8^2]}}$$

$$= \frac{56 - 128}{\sqrt{(56)(104)}} = \frac{-72}{\sqrt{5,824}}$$

$$= \frac{-72}{76.32} = -.94$$

12

Multivariate Analysis: Three or More Variables

In Chapters 2, 3, and 4 we examined some common statistical techniques that are used to describe a single variable, and in Chapters 9, 10, and 11 we described techniques that are used to analyze the relationship between two variables. Although one- and two-variable analyses are undeniably common and valuable in sociological research, the inescapable fact remains that most problems with which we deal are not univariate or even bivariate but multivariate in nature. We may describe suicide rates (a single variable), and we might show that married persons have lower suicide rates than do single persons (two variables); but we also should be able to say something about the suicide rates of married persons who are Catholic as opposed to those who are Protestant (three variables: suicide, marital status, and religion). And, of course, we could add a fourth variable, a fifth, and so on until we reach the point where adding another variable brings nothing more to our explanation of suicide.

In this chapter we shall examine four ways of analyzing multivariate data sets: elaboration, multiple correlation, partial correlation, and analysis of variance. We will focus on three-variable problems, but you should note that the principles involved in the analysis of three variables can readily be extended to the analysis of four or more variables.

Elaboration: Tabular Analysis of Percentage Differences

One of the simplest ways of mathematically analyzing more than two variables at a time is *elaboration*. Simply put, the logic of elaboration is as follows. We begin by noting a relationship between two variables. We then select a third variable, called a *control variable* or test factor, and examine the original relationship as it exists under different control or test conditions. In some instances, an originally strong relationship will weaken or disappear; in others, a relationship that originally seemed virtually nonexistent will emerge; or a strong relationship may be shown to exist under one test condition but not under another. Let us illustrate this point with several examples.

Suppose we examine two hundred geographical areas. In each area we obtain a measure of the human birthrate and of the number of storks. We are interested in determining whether a relationship exists between the number of storks in an area and the human birthrate. Our simple research hypothesis is that as the number of storks increases, the birthrate increases. The null hypothesis is that there is no association between storks and babies. After collecting our data, we arrange the findings in a conventional 2 × 2 table (and perhaps compute some measure of association). The data of Table 12.1 appear to confirm the research hypothesis, and the statistical test leads to a rejection of the null hypothesis. But now common sense enters the scene. Someone points out that there is no plausible reason for associating storks and babies and also notes that both storks and babies might be a function of whether the geographical area under scrutiny is rural or urban. Therefore, we decide to introduce as a test factor the variable rural-urban. In so doing we organize the original data into a *conditional table* (Table 12.2). In this elaborated table we see that under the rural condition, the original relationship is greatly changed. We see this in two ways. (1) In Table 12.1, the original percentage difference across columns was thirty (the difference between seventy and forty, or between thirty and sixty). In the conditional table, the rural percentage difference is two (the difference between forty and forty-two or between sixty and fifty-eight). (2) Even more striking, the zero-order Gamma, which was +0.56 ($p < .01$), has now become, under the rural condition, -0.04. The original strong and positive relationship has become, with the introduction of the control variable, weaker, and is now negative. Under the urban condition we do not observe this dramatic change of direction, but we do see that the originally strong relationship is considerably weakened; the value of Gamma has dropped from 0.56 to 0.20.

Table 12.1. *Number of Storks and Human Birthrate*

		Number of Storks in Area			
		Few		Many	
		%	(N)	%	(N)
	Low	70	(70)	40	(40)
Birthrate	High	30	(30)	60	(60)
	Totals	100	(100)	100	(100)

$G = +0.56$

$p < 0.01$

What shall we make of this? (1) We can first note that the original relationship is spurious. That is, a relationship does exist between storks and babies, but this relationship is not direct and not causal. The relationship exists because both of the variables, storks and babies, are related to a third variable. Stated differently, a relationship is said to be spurious if the introduction of a test factor reduces the original relationship to zero (or near zero). (2) The example illustrates the importance of models and theory. In the first instance we had a very simple two-variable model:

Model A:

Storks ⟶ Babies
(Independent Variable, X) (Dependent Variable, Y)

This model was supported by our original examination of the data. But then someone questioned the model, perhaps because of previous research, a theoretical proposition, or common sense, or perhaps on a hunch. The questioner wondered if the relationship might not be better explained by an alternative model, a three-variable model. (See next page.) The new model, by introducing the test variable, T, postulated that X and Y were not related in any causal sequence. Examination of the conditional table (Table 12.2) confirmed this.

Model B:

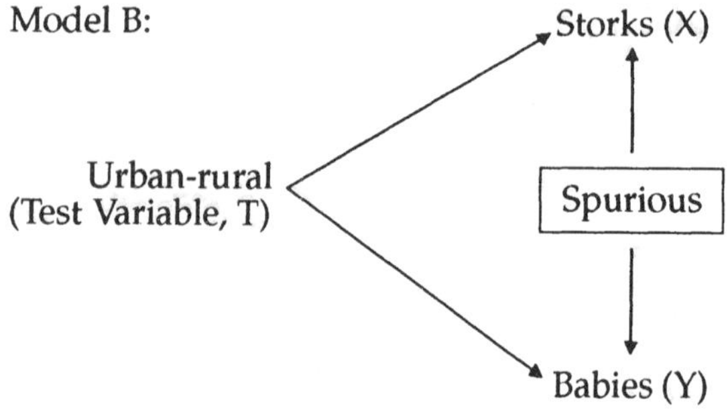

The pattern of spuriousness is not the only pattern that can be detected by elaboration. Introduction of a control variable may reveal a pattern of *specification*. For example, suppose that in a study of political behavior a researcher found that a greater proportion of Republicans voted in a certain election (Table 12.3). The researcher then recalled studies showing that Republicans tended to come from higher socioeconomic classes than did Democrats and, therefore, decided to develop conditional tables using social class as a test factor. The results obtained might be similar to those in Table 12.4. This table specifies the condition under which the original relationship holds. In this case, the original finding that Republicans vote in greater

Table 12.2. *Storks and Babies by Type of Area*

		Type of Area							
		Rural				Urban			
		Number of Storks							
		Few		Many		Few		Many	
		%	(N)	%	(N)	%	(N)	%	(N)
Birth-rate	Low	40	(6)	42	(36)	69	(59)	60	(9)
	High	30	(9)	58	(49)	31	(26)	40	(6)
	Totals	100	(15)	100	(85)	100	(85)	100	(15)
		G = -0.04				G = 0.20			
		p = NS				p = NS			

Table 12.3. *Party and Voting*

	Party Affiliation			
	Democrat		Republican	
	%	(N)	%	(N)
Voted	60	(36)	72	(36)
Did Not Vote	40	(24)	28	(14)
Totals	100	(60)	100	(50)

Table 12.4. *Party and Voting by Social Class*

	Social Class							
	Lower				Higher			
	Party Affiliation							
	Democrat		Republican		Democrat		Republican	
	%	(N)	%	(N)	%	(N)	%	(N)
Voted	50	(15)	72	(18)	70	(21)	72	(18)
Did Not Vote	50	(15)	28	(7)	30	(9)	28	(7)
Totals	100	(30)	100	(25)	100	(10)	100	(25)

numbers than do Democrats is found to hold under the condition of relatively lower social class. However, under the condition of high social class, there is virtually no difference in the proportion of Republicans and Democrats who vote.

In some instances, the zero-order association may be at or near zero, but when a test factor is introduced, a relationship may suddenly appear. Such a pattern is called *suppression* because, until identified, the test factor suppresses the underlying relationship. To construct an example, suppose we begin with the data of Table 12.5, which suggest that there is no relationship between social class and attitudes toward abortion. Then, because attitudes toward abortion are theoretically linked to religious beliefs, we introduce as a test variable a measure of religious liberalism-conservatism. We then obtain results as in Table

Table 12.5. *Social Class and Attitude Toward Abortion (Hypothetical Data)*

	Social Class					
	Low		Middle		High	
	%	(N)	%	(N)	%	(N)
Less Tolerant	52	(26)	54	(54)	55	(22)
More Tolerant	48	(24)	46	(46)	45	(18)
Totals	100	(50)	100	(100)	100	(40)

Table 12.6. *Social Class and Attitude Toward Abortion by Religious Liberalism (Hypothetical Data)*

	Religious Type											
	Liberal						Conservative					
	Social Class											
	Low		Middle		High		Low		Middle		High	
	%	(N)	%	(N)	%	(N)	%	(N)	%	(N)	%	(N)
LT	40	8	50	25	60	9	67	20	56	28	48	12
MT	60	12	50	25	40	6	33	10	44	22	52	13
Tot	100	20	100	50	100	15	100	30	100	50	100	25
	G = -0.23						G = +0.23					

LT = Less Tolerant MT = More Tolerant Tot = Total

12.6. The conditional tables reveal two opposite patterns. For persons who are religiously liberal, there is a tendency to become less tolerant as social class is elevated. For persons who are religiously conservative, the pattern is just the opposite.

In sum, the process of elaboration involves the reanalysis of a two-variable relationship by the introduction of a third variable, called a test factor or a control variable. This process breaks an original pattern of association called zero-order association into two or more conditional associations. In other words, the original relationship is analyzed under various conditions of the test factor. The purpose of elaboration is to determine whether the zero-order association is as it seems to be. A more complete discussion of the techniques of elaboration can be found in Rosenberg (1968) or Zeisel (1957).

Partial Correlation

Elaboration of tabular differences involves a considerable exercise in analyzing the logical relationships among variables. It requires that we look at a relationship between two variables under different conditions of a third variable. In this section we take a slightly different approach to the problem of analyzing three variables. Using diagrams to illustrate what is involved, we can visualize the relationship between the number of storks and the number of babies as a pair of overlapping circles (Figure 12.1). The area of overlap (shaded area) represents the statistical relationship between the two variables. If a relationship is perfect, the two circles will be congruent as in Figure 12.2(a); a zero relationship will be illustrated by two circles that do not overlap at all, as in Figure 12.2(b). These diagrams, of course, give an oversimplified view of reality, for two variables rarely coexist in total isolation from other variables. For example, we earlier saw that some rural-urban dimension might be related to both storks and babies. Thus Figure 12.3 gives a more accurate picture of the "real world." But this picture also shows us that a measurement of the relationship between X (storks) and Y (babies) is "contaminated" by Z (rural-urban factor). We might ask, What will happen if we pull (or,

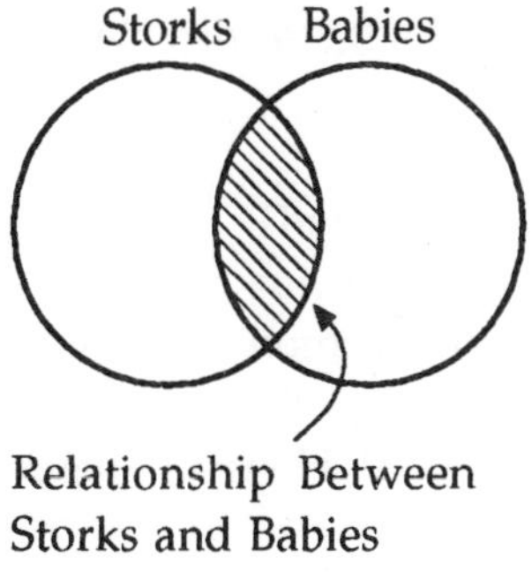

Figure 12.1. *Storks and Babies*

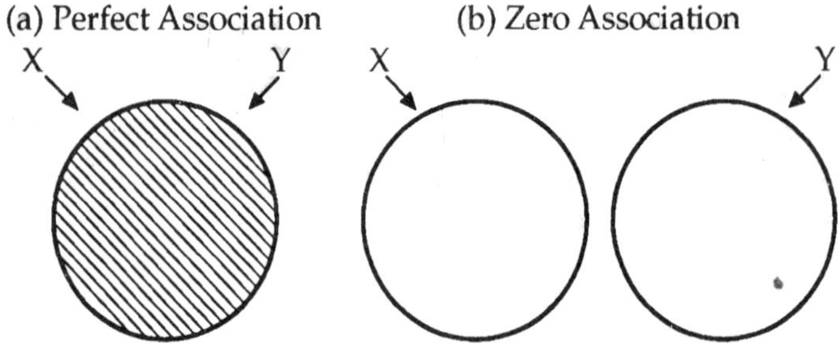

Figure 12.2. *Perfect and Zero Association*

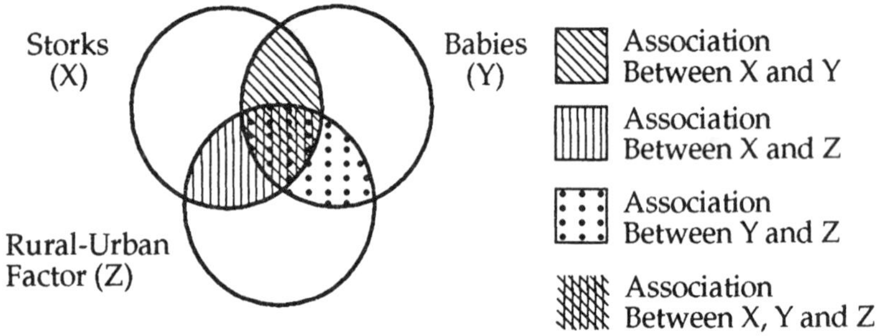

Figure 12.3. *Storks, Babies, and Rural-Urban Areas*

technically, if we partial) Z out of the relationship between X and Y? Will X and Y remain as strongly associated as they originally appeared to be in Figure 12.1? Or is Z so involved with X and with Y that partialling out Z will eliminate some or even all of the overlap between X and Y?

The Partial Correlation Coefficient

The partial correlation coefficient provides us with answers to these questions. (Actually, there are several different partial coefficients, as we shall see. But unless one of the others is directly specified, a reference to a partial coefficient will usually mean a reference to the partial r.) If we have three variables, X, Y, and Z, we can compute a Pearson r for the relationship between X and Y, between

X and Z, and between Y and Z. These zero-order coefficients can then be statistically manipulated to reveal the "true" relationship between any two variables with the effect of the third variable "partialled out." Without going into the complex mathematics underlying this procedure, we present a simple formula for computing partial r.

(Formula 12.1)

$$r_{XY.Z} = \frac{r_{XY} - r_{XZ}\, r_{YZ}}{\sqrt{(1 - r_{XZ}^2)(1 - r_{YZ}^2)}}$$

The notation $r_{XY.Z}$ indicates that we are interested in the relationship between X and Y with Z partialled out. We could also compute $r_{XZ.Y}$ or $r_{YZ.X}$ by simply rearranging the values of Formula 12.1. [NOTE: The variable being partialled appears in every subscript except the first term of the numerator.]

We can illustrate the application of this formula with a simple example. Suppose we obtained interval-level measures on the age (X), weight (Y), and some test score (Z) for a group of schoolchildren. We then calculate the Pearson r for each pair of variables and obtain

$$r_{XY} = .80 \qquad r_{XZ} = .60 \qquad r_{YZ} = .50$$

Looking at these data, we might be puzzled by the moderately strong relationship between weight and test score r_{YZ}. Why should a person's weight be related to test score? Is this relationship at all meaningful, or is it perhaps spurious? We have data on a third variable, age, which might be related to both weight and test score (older children weigh more than younger children, and older children may do better on the test than younger children), so we can reexamine the original weight-test score relationship by statistically removing the effect of age:

$$r_{YZ.X} = \frac{.50 - (.80)(.60)}{\sqrt{(1 - .80)^2(1 - .60)^2}}$$

$$= \frac{.50 - .48}{\sqrt{(.36)(.64)}}$$

$$= \frac{.02}{.48} = .04$$

The partial correlation coefficient, $r_{YZ.X}$, reveals that the association between Y and Z "shrinks" from .50 to .04 when X is partialled out. Stated differently, the YZ relationship is shown to be spurious when X is removed.

It is a simple matter to extend Formula 12.1 so that we can partial out yet another, and another, variable. For example, if we have four variables, we can determine the relationship between any two of them with the effects of the remaining two variables partialled out by using Formula 12.2:

(Formula 12.2)

$$r_{12.34} = \frac{r_{12.3} - r_{14.3}\, r_{24.3}}{\sqrt{(1 - r_{14.3}^2)(1 - r_{24.3}^2)}}$$

Quick Quiz
12.1

Using the data from the previous page, compute $r_{XY.Z}$.

We can do the same with five variables (three being partialled out):

(Formula 12.3)

$$r_{12.345} = \frac{r_{12.34} - r_{15.34}\, r_{25.34}}{\sqrt{(1 - r_{15.34}^2)(1 - r_{25.34}^2)}}$$

We could, in principle, add variables indefinitely, but there is usually little to be gained by going beyond a four- or five-variable partialling.

The partial r is similar in meaning and interpretation to the simple Pearson r. It varies in magnitude from +1.00 to -1.00. The partial r may be squared and given an interpretation analogous to that of r-square.

Partial Tau

The ordinal-level measure of association, Kendall's Tau, is subject to the same partialling procedure as is r. When we use a different set of subscripts (not because they have any inherent meaning but because you should get used to seeing different notations), the computing formula for partial Tau is exactly as the formula for partial r, except for replacing r with T.

(Formula 12.4)

$$T_{ab.c} = \frac{T_{ab} - T_{ac}T_{bc}}{\sqrt{(1 - T_{ac}^2)(1 - T_{bc}^2)}}$$

Because the formula and procedures for partial Tau are the same as for partial r, we will not discuss this statistic in detail.

Partial Gamma

The procedures involved in computing a partial Gamma can be extended to any of the measures of association based on pair-by-pair comparison. The procedure calls for the categorization of any two-variable relationship under different conditions of the control variable. The values of n_s and n_d are then computed for each of the two or more conditional tables; these values are then summed across tables, and the partial Gamma is defined as

(Formula 12.5)

$$G_p = \frac{\Sigma(n_s - n_d)}{\Sigma(n_s + n_d)}$$

For example, consider again the data from Tables 12.1 and 12.2. In 12.1 the value of Gamma is +0.56, indicating a strong relationship between the number of storks (X) and babies (Y). In 12.2 the original two variable relationship has been categorized into two conditions of a rural-urban factor (Z). For each of these conditional tables we then compute n_s and n_d:

	n_s	n_d	$(n_s - n_d)$	$(n_s + n_d)$
Rural:	294	324	-30	678
Urban:	354	234	120	588
Sum			90	1,206

With the sums of the last two columns we can compute the partial Gamma:

$$G_{XY.Z} = \frac{90}{1,206} = .07$$

Thus we see that when the rural-urban factor is partialled out of the relationship between storks and babies, the value of Gamma shrinks from +.56 to +.07. The partial Gamma has statistically removed the effects of the test variable and given us a more refined measure of the true relationship between the number of storks and babies.

The value of a partial Gamma is an overall measure of association; as such, it has certain advantages and disadvantages when compared to simple tabular differences. An obvious advantage is simplicity: A single figure conveys accurate information about a relatively complex set of variables. The disadvantage is that the partial coefficient does not have the capacity to point out some of the more interesting patterns of elaboration that can be revealed in tabular analysis.

Quick Quiz
12.2

Using the data from Table 12.6, compute a partial Gamma that shows the relationship between social class and attitudes toward abortion with the effects of religious liberalism/conservatism removed.

Multiple Correlation

In a certain sense, multiple correlation is the opposite of partial correlation. Whereas the partial r tells us the relationship between two variables with the effect of a third variable removed, multiple-R (the capital R is frequently used to distinguish multiple correlation from other types of correlation) tells us the relationship between one variable, the dependent variable, and the combined effects of two or more variables.

Let us use circle diagrams to illustrate this basic concept. A dependent variable, X, may be related to two independent variables, Y and Z, as in Figure 12.4. Furthermore, Y and Z may also be related to each other. In each case, the shaded area represents the simple correlation between two variables. But what kind of picture will we

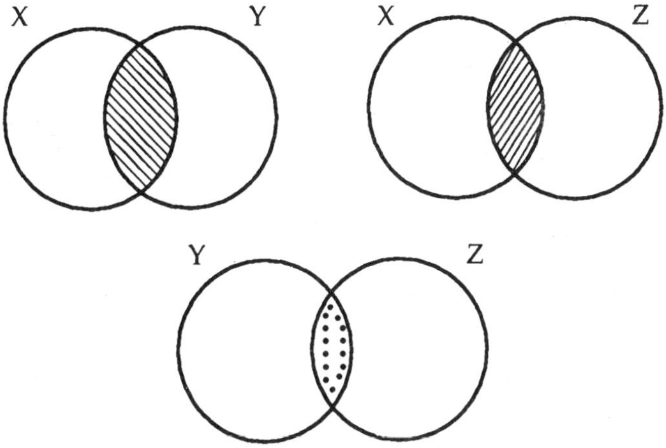

Figure 12.4. *Simple Relationships Among Three Variables*

get if we recognize the fact that all three variables are interrelated? This "real world" probably looks something like Figure 12.5. In visual terms, how can we assess this multiple relationship? We can see the relationship between X and Y (Figure 12.4), and we can statistically measure this relationship by using the Pearson r. But if we now try to add the X-Z relationship to the X-Y relationship, we will be adding in a portion (the crosshatched area) that has already been accounted for by X-Y. So to add the effects of Z to X-Y we must first partial out the Y variable from the X-Z relationship. But this is further complicated by the fact that some of Z's influence on X is inextricably bound up with Y, and partialling Y does not give us a completely accurate picture of Z's influence. (The reasons for this are complicated and will not be discussed here.) This means that we cannot simply add the XY value and the XZ.Y value to obtain the multiple correlation coefficient. The actual mathematical relationship is

(Formula 12.6)

$$R_{X.YZ} = \sqrt{r_{XY}^2 + (r_{XZ.Y}^2)(1 - r_{XY}^2)}$$

(This formula also permits us to calculate $R_{X.YZ}{}^2$ by simply removing the square root sign from the right-hand side of the equation.)

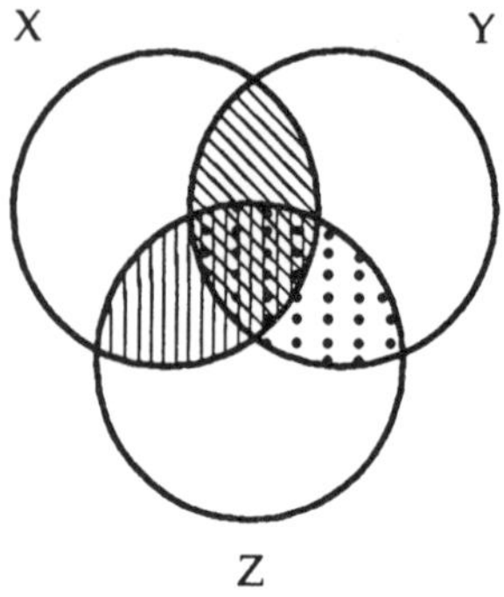

Figure 12.5. *Relationships Among Three Variables*

Let us look at another way of conceptualizing multiple correlation. In Chapter 10 we began our discussion of the Pearson r with the straight line equation

$$Y = a + bX$$

Now, if we have not one independent variable but two, this equation can be simply extended to

$$Y = a + b_1 X_1 + b_2 X_2$$

and for n independent variables

$$Y = a + b_1 X_1 + b_2 X_2 + b_3 X_3 + \ldots + b_n X_n$$

This process can be extended indefinitely, depending only on the number of independent variables. The mathematical solution of these multivariate equations is beyond the scope of this book, but the logic of the approach should be easily grasped.

The most frequently used computational formula for determining multiple-R for two independent variables uses the zero-order correlation coefficients. The formula may appear a bit awesome, but it is actually quite easy to use.

(Formula 12.7)

$$R_{X.YZ} = \sqrt{\frac{r_{XY}^2 + r_{XZ}^2 - 2r_{XY}\,r_{XZ}\,r_{YZ}}{1 - r_{YZ}^2}}$$

To illustrate the application of this formula, we will suppose we have three interval level variables, age (X), income (Y), and education (Z). These variables are related to each other as follows:

$$r_{XY} = 0.70 \qquad r_{XZ} = -0.20 \qquad r_{YZ} = 0.50$$

If we wish to examine the effect on income, as dependent variable, of the combined effects of age and education, we can use Formula 12.7.

$$R_{Y.XZ} = \sqrt{\frac{.70^2 + .50^2 - 2(.70)(.50)(-.20)}{1 - (-.20^2)}}$$

$$= \sqrt{\frac{.49 + .25 - (-.14)}{1 - .04}} = \sqrt{\frac{.88}{.96}}$$

$$= \sqrt{.9167} = .96$$

The logical interpretation of the multiple-R is complicated, but the interpretation of the multiple-R^2 is straightforward: It is the same as that given to the simple r-square in Chapter 11. In the previous example, 92 percent of the variance in income (Y) can be explained by age *and* education combined. Whereas age alone explains 49 percent of the variance in income, and education alone explains 25 percent of the variance in income, the two together combine to give a much more powerful explanation of the dependent variable. The interpretation of the multiple-R^2 is also similar to the interpretation of r^2 in that both may vary from 0.00 to +1.00, with a value of one indicating that the independent variables perfectly predict the dependent variable and a value of zero indicating that the dependent variable bears no linear relationship to the combined independent variables.

Three or More Independent Variables

The extension of multiple correlations to three or more independent variables is accomplished by a manipulation of Formula 12.6. With three independent variables, the formula becomes

Quick Quiz
12.3.

As a check on the above computations, find $R_{Y.XZ}$ by using a variant of Formula 12.6.

$$R_{1.234} = \sqrt{R^2_{1.23} + (r^2_{14.23})(1 - R^2_{1.23})}$$

and for the general case of k independent variables

(Formula 12.8)

$$R_{1.23...k} = \sqrt{R^2_{1.23...k} + (r^2_{1k.23...(k-1)})(1 - R^2_{1.23...(k-1)})}$$

To put Formula 12.8 into words, if we have k variables, we first compute a multiple-R for (k - l) variables; we then compute a partial r, which gives the relationship between the dependent variable and the k-th variable (this is then multiplied by $[1 - R^2]$); finally, we extract the square root.

Correction for Sampling Error

If formulas 12.6, 12.7, or 12.8 are used on population data, the computed values of R will be accurate. However, if *sample* data are used, the computed values of R will be an overestimate. This bias can be corrected by the following formula:

(Formula 12.9)

$$R_c = \sqrt{1 - \frac{n-1}{n-k}(1 - R^2)}$$

where R_c is the corrected value; n is the sample size; and k is the number of independent variables. In most instances, the corrected value will not differ greatly from the original value, unless n is relatively small or k is relatively large.

An SPSS Example: Partial Correlation

SPSS uses the PARTIAL CORR command to generate both the "zero order" coefficients (i.e., without the partialling-out effect) and the "first order" partials (i.e., with the effect of education statistically removed). In the following example, we look first at the relationship between SIBS (the number of siblings one has) and CHILDS (the number of children one has).

Partial Correlation Example:

```
PARTIAL CORR SIBS CHILDS BY EDUC (1)
 /STATISTICS = ALL   /FORMAT = SERIAL

VARIABLE    MEAN       STD DEV    CASES
SIBS        4.1460     3.1736     226
CHILDS      2.2743     1.7088     226
EDUC        13.0265    3.0709     226

---- P A R T I A L   C O R R E L A T I O N   C O E F F I C I E N T S ----

ZERO ORDER PARTIALS
VARIABLE  PAIR       VARIABLE PAIR          VARIABLE PAIR
------------------   -----------------      --------

SIBS    .1540        SIBS         -.3675    CHILDS         -.2665
WITH   DF = 224      WITH   DF =  224       WITH   DF =  224
CHILDS SIG .010      EDUC      SIG. 000     EDUC    SIG   .000

" . " IS PRINTED IF A COEFFICIENT CANNOT BE COMPUTED.

---P A R T I A L   C O R R E L A T I O N   C O E F F I C I E N T S---
CONTROLLING FOR..  EDUC

VARIABLE PAIR
-------------------------
SIBS          .0626
WITH                       DF =  223
CHILDS        SIG .175
" . " IS PRINTED IF A COEFFICIENT CANNOT BE COMPUTED.
```

PARTIAL CORR first provides us with the mean and standard deviation for each named variable. For example, our subjects have an average of 4.1 siblings and 2.3 children; they also have an average of 13.0 years of education. Next, and not surprisingly, we find that these two variables are positively correlated and that this correlation is one that could not have occurred by chance. We reject the null hypothesis (that the two variables are not associated).

Important Terms

Control variable	Zero-order association
Test factor	Partial correlation
Spurious relationship	Multiple correlation

Suggested Readings

Loether and McTavish (1988: 340-350); Rosenberg (1968); Zeisel (1985).

Quick Quiz Answers

Quick Quiz 12.1

$$r_{XY.Z} = \frac{.80 - (.60)(.50)}{\sqrt{(1 - .60^2)(1 - .50^2)}}$$

$$= \frac{.80 - .30}{\sqrt{(.51)(.96)}} = \frac{.50}{.69} = .72$$

Quick Quiz 12.2

	n_s	n_d	$(n_s - n_d)$	$(n_s + n_d)$
Liberal:	398	633	-235	1,031
Conservative:	1,064	664	400	1,728
Total			165	2,759

$$G_p = \frac{165}{2,759} = +0.06$$

Quick Quiz 12.3

First, compute the partial r:

$$r_{YZ.X} = \frac{.50 - (.70)(-.20)}{\sqrt{(1 - .70^2)(1 - (-.20^2))}}$$

$$= \frac{.64}{\sqrt{(.51)(.96)}} = .91$$

Then, using Formula 12.6,

$$R_{Y.XZ} = \sqrt{.70^2 + (.91^2)(1 - .70^2)}$$

$$= \sqrt{.49 + (.83)(.51)}$$

$$= \sqrt{.9133} = .96$$

Appendix

Proportions of Area Under the Normal Curve: Table A

How to use this table. The values in Table A represent proportions of the area under the standard normal curve. The curve has a mean of 0.00, a standard deviation of 1.00 and a total area of 1.00. Because the normal curve is symmetrical, the areas corresponding to negative z-scores are identical to the areas corresponding to positive z-scores. Thus, areas corresponding to -z are the same as those of +z.

Values of z are given in column (A). Column (B) contains the corresponding area between the mean and z.

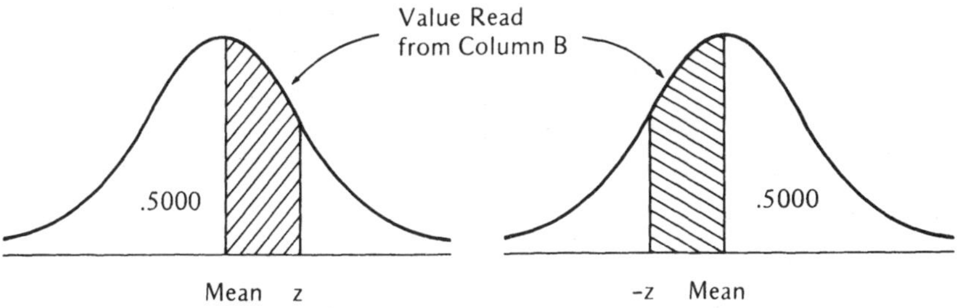

Column (C) describes the area beyond the given value of z.

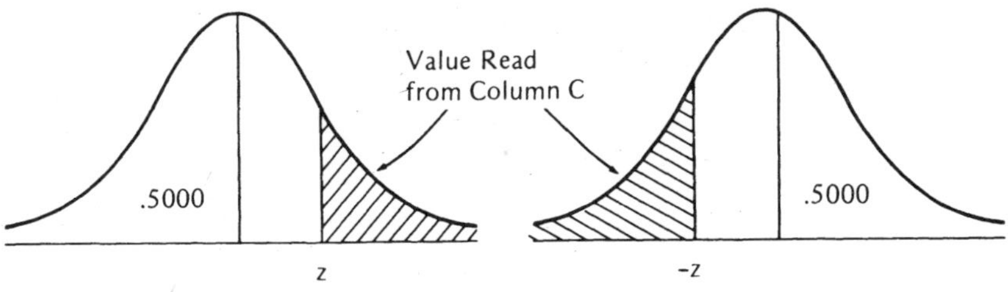

Because the curve is symmetric, each half of the curve contains .5000 of the total area. This fact, plus the values from the table, enables us to calculate any area under the curve in terms of a z-score or z-scores.

Table A: Proportions of the Area Under the Normal Curve

(A) z	(B) area between mean and z	(C) area beyond z	(A) z	(B) area between mean and z	(C) area beyond z	(A) z	(B) area between mean and z	(C) area beyond z
0.00	.0000	.5000	0.55	.2088	.2912	1.10	.3643	.1357
0.01	.0040	.4960	0.56	.2123	.2877	1.11	.3665	.1335
0.02	.0080	.4920	0.57	.2157	.2843	1.12	.3686	.1314
0.03	.0120	.4880	0.58	.2190	.2810	1.13	.3708	.1292
0.04	.0160	.4840	0.59	.2224	.2776	1.14	.3729	.1271
0.05	.0199	.4801	0.60	.2257	.2743	1.15	.3749	.1251
0.06	.0239	.4761	0.61	.2291	.2709	1.16	.3770	.1230
0.07	.0279	.4721	0.62	.2324	.2676	1.17	.3790	.1210
0.08	.0319	.4681	0.63	.2357	.2643	1.18	.3810	.1190
0.09	.0359	.4641	0.64	.2389	.2611	1.19	.3830	.1170
0.10	.0398	.4602	0.65	.2422	.2578	1.20	.3849	.1151
0.11	.0438	.4562	0.66	.2454	.2546	1.21	.3869	.1131
0.12	.0478	.4522	0.67	.2486	.2514	1.22	.3888	.1112
0.13	.0517	.4483	0.68	.2517	.2483	1.23	.3907	.1093
0.14	.0557	.4443	0.69	.2549	.2451	1.24	.3925	.1075
0.15	.0596	.4404	0.70	.2580	.2420	1.25	.3944	.1056
0.16	.0636	.4364	0.71	.2611	.2389	1.26	.3962	.1038
0.17	.0675	.4325	0.72	.2642	.2358	1.27	.3980	.1020
0.18	.0714	.4286	0.73	.2673	.2327	1.28	.3997	.1003
0.19	.0753	.4247	0.74	.2704	.2296	1.29	.4015	.0985
0.20	.0793	.4207	0.75	.2734	.2266	1.30	.4032	.0968
0.21	.0832	.4168	0.76	.2764	.2236	1.31	.4049	.0951
0.22	.0871	.4129	0.77	.2794	.2206	1.32	.4066	.0934
0.23	.0910	.4090	0.78	.2823	.2177	1.33	.4082	.0918
0.24	.0948	.4052	0.79	.2852	.2148	1.34	.4099	.0901
0.25	.0987	.4013	0.80	.2881	.2119	1.35	.4115	.0885
0.26	.1026	.3974	0.81	.2910	.2090	1.36	.4131	.0869
0.27	.1064	.3936	0.82	.2939	.2061	1.37	.4147	.0853
0.28	.1103	.3897	0.83	.2967	.2033	1.38	.4162	.0838
0.29	.1141	.3859	0.84	.2995	.2005	1.39	.4177	.0823
0.30	.1179	.3821	0.85	.3023	.1977	1.40	.4192	.0808
0.31	.1217	.3783	0.86	.3051	.1949	1.41	.4207	.0793
0.32	.1255	.3745	0.87	.3078	.1922	1.42	.4222	.0778
0.33	.1293	.3707	0.88	.3106	.1894	1.43	.4236	.0764
0.34	.1331	.3669	0.89	.3133	.1867	1.44	.4251	.0749
0.35	.1368	.3632	0.90	.3159	.1841	1.45	.4265	.0735
0.36	.1406	.3594	0.91	.3186	.1814	1.46	.4279	.0721
0.37	.1443	.3557	0.92	.3212	.1788	1.47	.4292	.0708
0.38	.1480	.3520	0.93	.3238	.1762	1.48	.4306	.0694
0.39	.1517	.3483	0.94	.3264	.1736	1.49	.4319	.0681
0.40	.1554	.3446	0.95	.3289	.1711	1.50	.4332	.0668
0.41	.1591	.3409	0.96	.3315	.1685	1.51	.4345	.0655
0.42	.1628	.3372	0.97	.3340	.1660	1.52	.4357	.0643
0.43	.1664	.3336	0.98	.3365	.1635	1.53	.4370	.0630
0.44	.1700	.3300	0.99	.3389	.1611	1.54	.4382	.0618
0.45	.1736	.3264	1.00	.3413	.1587	1.55	.4394	.0606
0.46	.1772	.3228	1.01	.3438	.1562	1.56	.4406	.0594
0.47	.1808	.3192	1.02	.3461	.1539	1.57	.4418	.0582
0.48	.1844	.3156	1.03	.3485	.1515	1.58	.4429	.0571
0.49	.1879	.3121	1.04	.3508	.1492	1.59	.4441	.0559
0.50	.1915	.3085	1.05	.3531	.1469	1.60	.4452	.0548
0.51	.1950	.3050	1.06	.3554	.1446	1.61	.4463	.0537
0.52	.1985	.3015	1.07	.3577	.1423	1.62	.4474	.0526
0.53	.2019	.2981	1.08	.3599	.1401	1.63	.4484	.0516
0.54	.2054	.2946	1.09	.3621	.1379	1.64	.4495	.0505

Table A: Proportions of the Area Under the Normal Curve (continued)

(A) z	(B) area between mean and z	(C) area beyond z	(A) z	(B) area between mean and z	(C) area beyond z	(A) z	(B) area between mean and z	(C) area beyond z
1.65	.4505	.0495	2.22	.4868	.0132	2.79	.4974	.0026
1.66	.4515	.0485	2.23	.4871	.0129	2.80	.4974	.0026
1.67	.4525	.0475	2.24	.4875	.0125	2.81	.4975	.0025
1.68	.4535	.0465	2.25	.4878	.0122	2.82	.4976	.0024
1.69	.4545	.0455	2.26	.4881	.0119	2.83	.4977	.0023
1.70	.4554	.0446	2.27	.4884	.0116	2.84	.4977	.0023
1.71	.4564	.0436	2.28	.4887	.0113	2.85	.4978	.0022
1.72	.4573	.0427	2.29	.4890	.0110	2.86	.4979	.0021
1.73	.4582	.0418	2.30	.4893	.0107	2.87	.4979	.0021
1.74	.4591	.0409	2.31	.4896	.0104	2.88	.4980	.0020
1.75	.4599	.0401	2.32	.4898	.0102	2.89	.4981	.0019
1.76	.4608	.0392	2.33	.4901	.0099	2.90	.4981	.0019
1.77	.4616	.0384	2.34	.4904	.0096	2.91	.4982	.0018
1.78	.4625	.0375	2.35	.4906	.0094	2.92	.4982	.0018
1.79	.4633	.0367	2.36	.4909	.0091	2.93	.4983	.0017
1.80	.4641	.0359	2.37	.4911	.0089	2.94	.4984	.0016
1.81	.4649	.0351	2.38	.4913	.0087	2.95	.4984	.0016
1.82	.4656	.0344	2.39	.4916	.0084	2.96	.4985	.0015
1.83	.4664	.0336	2.40	.4918	.0082	2.97	.4985	.0015
1.84	.4671	.0329	2.41	.4920	.0080	2.98	.4986	.0014
1.85	.4678	.0322	2.42	.4922	.0078	2.99	.4986	.0014
1.86	.4686	.0314	2.43	.4925	.0075	3.00	.4987	.0013
1.87	.4693	.0307	2.44	.4927	.0073	3.01	.4987	.0013
1.88	.4699	.0301	2.45	.4929	.0071	3.02	.4987	.0013
1.89	.4706	.0294	2.46	.4931	.0069	3.03	.4988	.0012
1.90	.4713	.0287	2.47	.4932	.0068	3.04	.4988	.0012
1.91	.4719	.0281	2.48	.4934	.0066	3.05	.4989	.0011
1.92	.4726	.0274	2.49	.4936	.0064	3.06	.4989	.0011
1.93	.4732	.0268	2.50	.4938	.0062	3.07	.4989	.0011
1.94	.4738	.0262	2.51	.4940	.0060	3.08	.4990	.0010
1.95	.4744	.0256	2.52	.4941	.0059	3.09	.4990	.0010
1.96	.4750	.0250	2.53	.4943	.0057	3.10	.4990	.0010
1.97	.4756	.0244	2.54	.4945	.0055	3.11	.4991	.0009
1.98	.4761	.0239	2.55	.4946	.0054	3.12	.4991	.0009
1.99	.4767	.0233	2.56	.4948	.0052	3.13	.4991	.0009
2.00	.4772	.0228	2.57	.4949	.0051	3.14	.4992	.0008
2.01	.4778	.0222	2.58	.4951	.0049	3.15	.4992	.0008
2.02	.4783	.0217	2.59	.4952	.0048	3.16	.4992	.0008
2.03	.4788	.0212	2.60	.4953	.0047	3.17	.4992	.0008
2.04	.4793	.0207	2.61	.4955	.0045	3.18	.4993	.0007
2.05	.4798	.0202	2.62	.4956	.0044	3.19	.4993	.0007
2.06	.4803	.0197	2.63	.4957	.0043	3.20	.4993	.0007
2.07	.4808	.0192	2.64	.4959	.0041	3.21	.4993	.0007
2.08	.4812	.0188	2.65	.4960	.0040	3.22	.4994	.0006
2.09	.4817	.0183	2.66	.4961	.0039	3.23	.4994	.0006
2.10	.4821	.0179	2.67	.4962	.0038	3.24	.4994	.0006
2.11	.4826	.0174	2.68	.4963	.0037	3.25	.4994	.0006
2.12	.4830	.0170	2.69	.4964	.0036	3.30	.4995	.0005
2.13	.4834	.0166	2.70	.4965	.0035	3.35	.4996	.0004
2.14	.4838	.0162	2.71	.4966	.0034	3.40	.4997	.0003
2.15	.4842	.0158	2.72	.4967	.0033	3.45	.4997	.0003
2.16	.4846	.0154	2.73	.4968	.0032	3.50	.4998	.0002
2.17	.4850	.0150	2.74	.4969	.0031	3.60	.4998	.0002
2.18	.4854	.0146	2.75	.4970	.0030	3.70	.4999	.0001
2.19	.4857	.0143	2.76	.4971	.0029	3.80	.4999	.0001
2.20	.4861	.0139	2.77	.4972	.0028	3.90	.49995	.00005
2.21	.4864	.0136	2.78	.4973	.0027	4.00	.49997	.00003

From Richard P. Runyon and Audrey Haber, *Fundamentals of Behavioral Statistics*, 2nd edition. Reading, Mass.: Addison-Wesley, 1971, pp. 290–291. Reprinted by permission of the authors and the publisher.

Critical Values of Student's t: Table B

How to use this table. The first two rows of figures in the table indicate the level of significance (a) for one- and two-tail tests, respectively. The first column of figures indicates the degrees of freedom for the test. Remember: (1) When the data are not matched (that is, for the large-sample and the small-sample t-test), df = $n_1 + n_2 - 2$. For all practical purposes, however, the df for the large sample t-test may be assumed to be infinite. (2) When the data are correlated, or matched, df = n - 1, where n is the number of pairs.

Once df has been determined and the level of significance has been chosen, simply locate the critical value of t from the corresponding row and column. If the computed value of t equals or exceeds the critical value obtained from the table, reject the null hypothesis. If the observed value of t is less than the critical value, do not reject the null hypothesis.

Example: For a set of uncorrelated data, where $n_1 = 20$ and $n_2 = 16$, a value of t = 1.92 was computed. For a one-tail test with = .05, this observed value exceeds the critical value (which is 1.697); therefore, reject the null hypothesis.

One-tail Test, $\alpha = .05$
df = 30

t = 1.697

Two-tail Test, $\alpha = .01$
df = ∞

t = -2.326 t = 2.326

Table B: Critical Values of Student's t

df	Level of significance for one-tailed test					
	.10	.05	.025	.01	.005	.0005
	Level of significance for two-tailed test					
	.20	.10	.05	.02	.01	.001
1	3.078	6.314	12.706	31.821	63.657	636.619
2	1.886	2.920	4.303	6.965	9.925	31.598
3	1.638	2.353	3.182	4.541	5.841	12.941
4	1.533	2.132	2.776	3.747	4.604	8.610
5	1.476	2.015	2.571	3.365	4.032	6.859
6	1.440	1.943	2.447	3.143	3.707	5.959
7	1.415	1.895	2.365	2.998	3.499	5.405
8	1.397	1.860	2.306	2.896	3.355	5.041
9	1.383	1.833	2.262	2.821	3.250	4.781
10	1.372	1.812	2.228	2.764	3.169	4.587
11	1.363	1.796	2.201	2.718	3.106	4.437
12	1.356	1.782	2.179	2.681	3.055	4.318
13	1.350	1.771	2.160	2.650	3.012	4.221
14	1.345	1.761	2.145	2.624	2.977	4.140
15	1.341	1.753	2.131	2.602	2.947	4.073
16	1.337	1.746	2.120	2.583	2.921	4.015
17	1.333	1.740	2.110	2.567	2.898	3.965
18	1.330	1.734	2.101	2.552	2.878	3.922
19	1.328	1.729	2.093	2.539	2.861	3.883
20	1.325	1.725	2.086	2.528	2.845	3.850
21	1.323	1.721	2.080	2.518	2.831	3.819
22	1.321	1.717	2.074	2.508	2.819	3.792
23	1.319	1.714	2.069	2.500	2.807	3.767
24	1.318	1.711	2.064	2.492	2.797	3.745
25	1.316	1.708	2.060	2.485	2.787	3.725
26	1.315	1.706	2.056	2.479	2.779	3.707
27	1.314	1.703	2.052	2.473	2.771	3.690
28	1.313	1.701	2.048	2.467	2.763	3.674
29	1.311	1.699	2.045	2.462	2.756	3.659
30	1.310	1.697	2.042	2.457	2.750	3.646
40	1.303	1.684	2.021	2.423	2.704	3.551
60	1.296	1.671	2.000	2.390	2.660	3.460
120	1.289	1.658	1.980	2.358	2.617	3.373
∞	1.282	1.645	1.960	2.326	2.576	3.291

Abridged from R. A. Fisher and F. Yates, *Statistical Tables for Biological, Agricultural and Medical Research*, 6th edition. London: Longman Group Ltd., 1974, Table III, p. 46. (Previously published by Oliver & Boyd, Edinburgh.) Reprinted by permission of the authors and publishers.

Critical Values of F (for ANOVA): Table C

How to use this table. The first two pages of this table are used when α = .05; the second two pages are used when α = .01.

The first row of figures indicates the degrees of freedom associated with the *larger* mean square; the first column indicates the degrees of freedom associated with the *lesser* mean square. The body of the table contains the critical values of F. If a computed value of F equals or exceeds the critical value, reject the null hypothesis. If the computed value is less than the critical value, do not reject the null hypothesis.

The F-test is nondirectional, so no distinction is made between one- and two-tail tests.

Example. A value of F = 3.26 is computed; with df(1) = 6 and df(2) = 16, this value is significant at the .05 level because it exceeds the critical value of 2.74. F = 3.26 is not significant at the .01 level, however, because it does not exceed the critical value of 4.20.

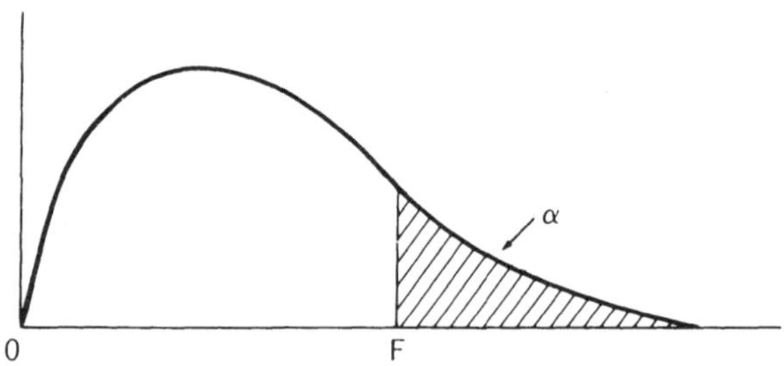

Table C: Critical Values of F ($\alpha = .05$)

df_1 / df_2	1	2	3	4	5	6	8	10
1	161.4	199.5	215.7	224.6	230.2	234.0	238.9	241.9
2	18.51	19.00	19.16	19.25	19.30	19.33	19.37	19.40
3	10.13	9.55	9.28	9.12	9.01	8.94	8.85	8.79
4	7.71	6.94	6.59	6.39	6.26	6.16	6.04	5.96
5	6.61	5.79	5.41	5.19	5.05	4.95	4.82	4.74
6	5.99	5.14	4.76	4.53	4.39	4.28	4.15	4.06
7	5.59	4.74	4.35	4.12	3.97	3.87	3.73	3.64
8	5.32	4.46	4.07	3.84	3.69	3.58	3.44	3.35
9	5.12	4.26	3.86	3.63	3.48	3.37	3.23	3.14
10	4.96	4.10	3.71	3.48	3.33	3.22	3.07	2.98
11	4.84	3.98	3.59	3.36	3.20	3.09	2.95	2.85
12	4.75	3.89	3.49	3.26	3.11	3.00	2.85	2.75
13	4.67	3.81	3.41	3.18	3.03	2.92	2.77	2.67
14	4.60	3.74	3.34	3.11	2.96	2.85	2.70	2.60
15	4.54	3.68	3.29	3.06	2.90	2.79	2.64	2.54
16	4.49	3.63	3.24	3.01	2.85	2.74	2.59	2.49
17	4.45	3.59	3.20	2.96	2.81	2.70	2.55	2.45
18	4.41	3.55	3.16	2.93	2.77	2.66	2.51	2.41
19	4.38	3.52	3.13	2.90	2.74	2.63	2.48	2.38
20	4.35	3.49	3.10	2.87	2.71	2.60	2.45	2.35
21	4.32	3.47	3.07	2.84	2.68	2.57	2.42	2.32
22	4.30	3.44	3.05	2.82	2.66	2.55	2.40	2.30
23	4.28	3.42	3.03	2.80	2.64	2.53	2.37	2.27
24	4.26	3.40	3.01	2.78	2.62	2.51	2.36	2.25
25	4.24	3.39	2.99	2.76	2.60	2.49	2.34	2.24
26	4.23	3.37	2.98	2.74	2.59	2.47	2.32	2.22
27	4.21	3.35	2.96	2.73	2.57	2.46	2.31	2.20
28	4.20	3.34	2.95	2.71	2.56	2.45	2.29	2.19
29	4.18	3.33	2.93	2.70	2.55	2.43	2.28	2.18
30	4.17	3.32	2.92	2.69	2.53	2.42	2.27	2.16
40	4.08	3.23	2.84	2.61	2.45	2.34	2.18	2.08
60	4.00	3.15	2.76	2.53	2.37	2.25	2.10	1.99
80	3.96	3.11	2.72	2.48	2.33	2.21	2.05	1.95
120	3.92	3.07	2.68	2.45	2.29	2.17	2.02	1.91
∞	3.84	3.00	2.60	2.37	2.21	2.10	1.94	1.83

Table C: Critical Values of F (α = .05) (continued)

df_1 / df_2	12	15	20	30	40	60	120	∞
1	243.9	245.9	248.0	250.1	251.1	252.2	253.3	254.3
2	19.41	19.43	19.45	19.46	19.47	19.48	19.49	19.50
3	8.74	8.70	8.66	8.62	8.59	8.57	8.55	8.53
4	5.91	5.86	5.80	5.75	5.72	5.69	5.66	5.63
5	4.68	4.62	4.56	4.50	4.46	4.43	4.40	4.36
6	4.00	3.94	3.87	3.81	3.77	3.74	3.70	3.67
7	3.57	3.51	3.44	3.38	3.34	3.30	3.27	3.23
8	3.28	3.22	3.15	3.08	3.04	3.01	2.97	2.93
9	3.07	3.01	2.94	2.86	2.83	2.79	2.75	2.71
10	2.91	2.85	2.77	2.70	2.66	2.62	2.58	2.54
11	2.79	2.72	2.65	2.57	2.53	2.49	2.45	2.40
12	2.69	2.62	2.54	2.47	2.43	2.38	2.34	2.30
13	2.60	2.53	2.46	2.38	2.34	2.30	2.25	2.21
14	2.53	2.46	2.39	2.31	2.27	2.22	2.18	2.13
15	2.48	2.40	2.33	2.25	2.20	2.16	2.11	2.07
16	2.42	2.35	2.28	2.19	2.15	2.11	2.06	2.01
17	2.38	2.31	2.23	2.15	2.10	2.06	2.01	1.96
18	2.34	2.27	2.19	2.11	2.06	2.02	1.97	1.92
19	2.31	2.23	2.16	2.07	2.03	1.98	1.93	1.88
20	2.28	2.20	2.12	2.04	1.99	1.95	1.90	1.84
21	2.25	2.18	2.10	2.01	1.96	1.92	1.87	1.81
22	2.23	2.15	2.07	1.98	1.94	1.89	1.84	1.78
23	2.20	2.13	2.05	1.96	1.91	1.86	1.81	1.76
24	2.18	2.11	2.03	1.94	1.89	1.84	1.79	1.73
25	2.16	2.09	2.01	1.92	1.87	1.82	1.77	1.71
26	2.15	2.07	1.99	1.90	1.85	1.80	1.75	1.69
27	2.13	2.06	1.97	1.88	1.84	1.79	1.73	1.67
28	2.12	2.04	1.96	1.87	1.82	1.77	1.71	1.65
29	2.10	2.03	1.94	1.85	1.81	1.75	1.70	1.64
30	2.09	2.01	1.93	1.84	1.79	1.74	1.68	1.62
40	2.00	1.92	1.84	1.74	1.69	1.64	1.58	1.51
60	1.92	1.84	1.75	1.65	1.59	1.53	1.47	1.39
80	1.88	1.80	1.70	1.60	1.54	1.49	1.41	1.32
120	1.83	1.75	1.66	1.55	1.50	1.43	1.35	1.25
∞	1.75	1.67	1.57	1.46	1.39	1.32	1.22	1.00

Table C: Critical Values of F (α = .01) (continued)

df_2 \ df_1	1	2	3	4	5	6	8	10
1	4052	4999.5	5403	5625	5764	5859	5982	6056
2	98.50	99.00	99.17	99.25	99.30	99.33	99.37	99.40
3	34.12	30.82	29.46	28.71	28.24	27.91	27.49	27.23
4	21.20	18.00	16.69	15.98	15.52	15.21	14.80	14.55
5	16.26	13.27	12.06	11.39	10.97	10.67	10.29	10.05
6	13.75	10.92	9.78	9.15	8.75	8.47	8.10	7.87
7	12.25	9.55	8.45	7.85	7.46	7.19	6.84	6.62
8	11.26	8.65	7.59	7.01	6.63	6.37	6.03	5.81
9	10.56	8.02	6.99	6.42	6.06	5.80	5.47	5.26
10	10.04	7.56	6.55	5.99	5.64	5.39	5.06	4.85
11	9.65	7.21	6.22	5.67	5.32	5.07	4.74	4.54
12	9.33	6.93	5.95	5.41	5.06	4.82	4.50	4.30
13	9.07	6.70	5.74	5.21	4.86	4.62	4.30	4.10
14	8.86	6.51	5.56	5.04	4.69	4.46	4.14	3.94
15	8.68	6.36	5.42	4.89	4.56	4.32	4.00	3.80
16	8.53	6.23	5.29	4.77	4.44	4.20	3.89	3.69
17	8.40	6.11	5.18	4.67	4.34	4.10	3.79	3.59
18	8.29	6.01	5.09	4.58	4.25	4.01	3.71	3.51
19	8.18	5.93	5.01	4.50	4.17	3.94	3.63	3.43
20	8.10	5.85	4.94	4.43	4.10	3.87	3.56	3.37
21	8.02	5.78	4.87	4.37	4.04	3.81	3.51	3.31
22	7.95	5.72	4.82	4.31	3.99	3.76	3.45	3.26
23	7.88	5.66	4.76	4.26	3.94	3.71	3.41	3.21
24	7.82	5.61	4.72	4.22	3.90	3.67	3.36	3.17
25	7.77	5.57	4.68	4.18	3.85	3.63	3.32	3.13
26	7.72	5.53	4.64	4.14	3.82	3.59	3.29	3.09
27	7.68	5.49	4.60	4.11	3.78	3.56	3.26	3.06
28	7.64	5.45	4.57	4.07	3.75	3.53	3.23	3.03
29	7.60	5.42	4.54	4.04	3.73	3.50	3.20	3.00
30	7.56	5.39	4.51	4.02	3.70	3.47	3.17	2.98
40	7.31	5.18	4.31	3.83	3.51	3.29	2.99	2.80
60	7.08	4.98	4.13	3.65	3.34	3.12	2.82	2.63
80	6.96	4.88	4.04	3.56	3.25	3.04	2.74	2.55
120	6.85	4.79	3.95	3.48	3.17	2.96	2.66	2.47
∞	6.63	4.61	3.78	3.32	3.02	2.80	2.51	2.32

Abridged from R. A. Fisher and F. Yates, *Statistical Tables for Biological, Agricultural and Medical Research*, 6th Edition. London: Longman Group Ltd., 1974, Table V, p. 57. (Previously published by Oliver & Boyd, Edinburgh.) Reprinted by permission of the authors and publishers.

Table C: Critical Values of F ($\alpha = .01$) (continued)

df_2 \ df_1	12	15	20	30	40	60	120	∞
1	6106	6157	6209	6261	6287	6313	6339	6366
2	99.42	99.43	99.45	99.47	99.47	99.48	99.49	99.50
3	27.05	26.87	26.69	26.50	26.41	26.32	26.22	26.13
4	14.37	14.20	14.02	13.84	13.75	13.65	13.56	13.46
5	9.89	9.72	9.55	9.38	9.29	9.20	9.11	9.02
6	7.72	7.56	7.40	7.23	7.14	7.06	6.97	6.88
7	6.47	6.31	6.16	5.99	5.91	5.82	5.74	5.65
8	5.67	5.52	5.36	5.20	5.12	5.03	4.95	4.86
9	5.11	4.96	4.81	4.65	4.57	4.48	4.40	4.31
10	4.71	4.56	4.41	4.25	4.17	4.08	4.00	3.91
11	4.40	4.25	4.10	3.94	3.86	3.78	3.69	3.60
12	4.16	4.01	3.86	3.70	3.62	3.54	3.45	3.36
13	3.96	3.82	3.66	3.51	3.43	3.34	3.25	3.17
14	3.80	3.66	3.51	3.35	3.27	3.18	3.09	3.00
15	3.67	3.52	3.37	3.21	3.13	3.05	2.96	2.87
16	3.55	3.41	3.26	3.10	3.02	2.93	2.84	2.75
17	3.46	3.31	3.16	3.00	2.92	2.83	2.75	2.65
18	3.37	3.23	3.08	2.92	2.84	2.75	2.66	2.57
19	3.30	3.15	3.00	2.84	2.76	2.67	2.58	2.49
20	3.23	3.09	2.94	2.78	2.69	2.61	2.52	2.42
21	3.17	3.03	2.88	2.72	2.64	2.55	2.46	2.36
22	3.12	2.98	2.83	2.67	2.58	2.50	2.40	2.31
23	3.07	2.93	2.78	2.62	2.54	2.45	2.35	2.26
24	3.03	2.89	2.74	2.58	2.49	2.40	2.31	2.21
25	2.99	2.85	2.70	2.54	2.45	2.36	2.27	2.17
26	2.96	2.81	2.66	2.50	2.42	2.33	2.23	2.13
27	2.93	2.78	2.63	2.47	2.38	2.29	2.20	2.10
28	2.90	2.75	2.60	2.44	2.35	2.26	2.17	2.06
29	2.87	2.73	2.57	2.41	2.33	2.23	2.14	2.03
30	2.84	2.70	2.55	2.39	2.30	2.21	2.11	2.01
40	2.66	2.52	2.37	2.20	2.11	2.02	1.92	1.80
60	2.50	2.35	2.20	2.03	1.94	1.84	1.73	1.60
80	2.41	2.28	2.11	1.94	1.84	1.75	1.63	1.49
120	2.34	2.19	2.03	1.86	1.76	1.66	1.53	1.38
∞	2.18	2.04	1.88	1.70	1.59	1.47	1.32	1.00

Critical Values of Chi-Square: Table D

How to use this table. The first row of this table lists the probabilities, or levels of significance, of observing given values of Chi-square. The first column of figures indicates the degrees of freedom. For the Chi-square statistic,

$$df = (r - 1)(c - 1)$$

where r and c are the number of rows and columns, respectively, in the data table. A computed value of Chi-square is significant at a given level if it is equal to or greater than the critical value in the table.

Example. If df = 4, a computed value of Chi-square = 10.03 is significant at the .05 level because the computed value exceeds the table value of 9.488. This observation would lead us to reject the null hypothesis; in other words, we would reject the model of statistical independence. If the observed value was less than the table value, we would not reject the null hypothesis, and we could assume that the model of statistical independence was valid.

[NOTE: With Chi-square, all tests of significance are essentially one-tail tests. This is because the Chi-square test is nondirectional. The test simply determines whether there is any departure from the chance model.]

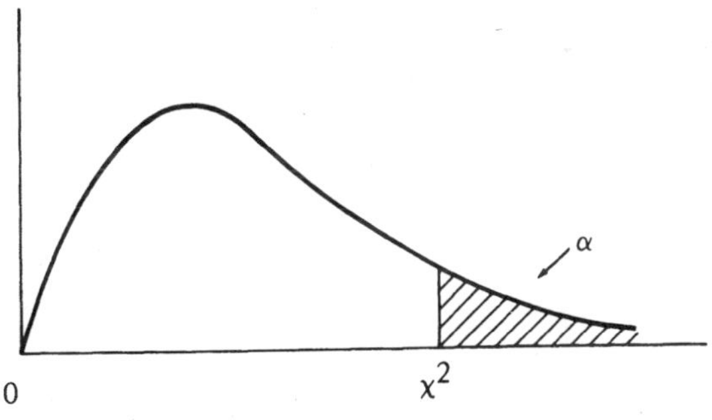

Table D: Critical Values of Chi-Square

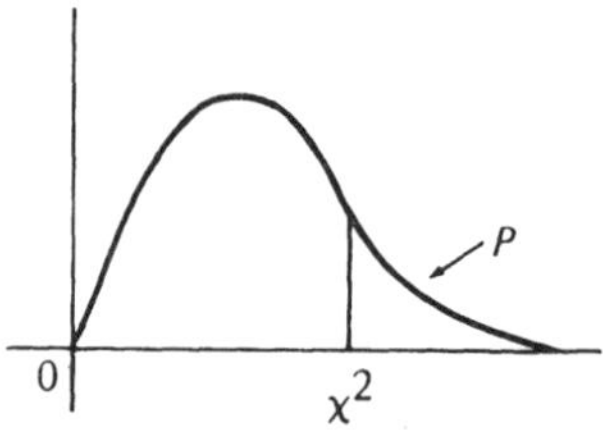

VALUES OF χ^2 FOR VARIOUS VALUES OF P^* AND DEGREES OF FREEDOM n

	P^*			
Degrees of Freedom n	0.10	0.05	0.02	0.01
1	2.706	3.841	5.412	6.635
2	4.605	5.991	7.824	9.210
3	6.251	7.815	9.837	11.341
4	7.779	9.488	11.668	13.277
5	9.236	11.070	13.388	15.086
6	10.645	12.592	15.033	16.812
7	12.017	14.067	16.622	18.475
8	13.362	15.507	18.168	20.090
9	14.684	16.919	19.679	21.666
10	15.987	18.307	21.161	23.209
11	17.275	19.675	22.618	24.725
12	18.549	21.026	24.054	26.217
13	19.812	22.362	25.472	27.688
14	21.064	23.685	26.873	29.141
15	22.307	24.996	28.259	30.578
16	23.542	26.296	29.633	32.000
17	24.769	27.587	30.995	33.409
18	25.989	28.869	32.346	34.805
19	27.204	30.144	33.687	36.191
20	28.412	31.410	35.020	37.566
21	29.615	32.671	36.343	38.932
22	30.813	33.924	37.659	40.289
23	32.007	35.172	38.968	41.638
24	33.196	36.415	40.270	42.980
25	34.382	37.652	41.566	44.314
26	35.563	36.885	42.856	45.642
27	36.741	40.113	44.140	46.963
28	37.916	41.337	45.419	48.278
29	39.087	42.557	46.693	49.588
30	40.256	43.773	47.962	50.892

Abridged from R. A. Fisher and F. Yates, *Statistical Tables for Biological, Agricultural and Medical Research*, 6th edition. London: Longman Group Ltd., 1974, Table IV, p. 47. (Previously published by Oliver & Boyd, Edinburgh.) Reprinted by permission of the authors and publishers.

*"P" refers to the level of significance, or alpha.

Probability That S (for Kendall's Tau, Goodman and Kruskal's Gamma, and Somers's d) Attains or Exceeds a Specific Value: Table E

How to use this table. This table is used when $n < 11$. After S is computed as $n_s - n_d$, enter the table for the corresponding values of S and n. The table value is the exact probability of observing a given value of S under sample size n.

The table is constructed for a one-tail test. For a two-tail test, simply double the values in the body of the table. For example, for a two-tail test with $n = 7$, suppose a value of $S = 15$ was computed. The table value for these data is 0.015; doubling this gives us a probability of 0.03. In other words, under a two-tail test there is only a 3 percent chance of observing values of S equal to or greater than 15.

The table lists only positive values of S. However, because the distribution of S is symmetric, the probabilities of negative values of S are the same as the corresponding positive values.

Table E: Probability that S Attains or Exceeds a Specific Value. (Shown only for Positive Values. Negative Values Obtainable by Symmetry.)

S	VALUES OF *n*				*S*	VALUES OF *n*		
	4	5	8	9		6	7	10
0	0·625	0·592	0·548	0·540	1	0·500	0·500	0·500
2	0·375	0·408	0·452	0·460	3	0·360	0·386	0·431
4	0·167	0·242	0·360	0·381	5	0·235	0·281	0·364
6	0·042	0·117	0·274	0·306	7	0·136	0·191	0·300
8		0·042	0·199	0·238	9	0·068	0·119	0·242
10		$0\cdot0^{2}83$	0·138	0·179	11	0·028	0·068	0·190
12			0·089	0·130	13	$0\cdot0^{2}83$	0·035	0·146
14			0·054	0·090	15	$0\cdot0^{2}14$	0·015	0·108
16			0·031	0·060	17		$0\cdot0^{2}54$	0·078
18			0·016	0·038	19		$0\cdot0^{2}14$	0·054
20			$0\cdot0^{2}71$	0·022	21		$0\cdot0^{3}20$	0·036
22			$0\cdot0^{2}28$	0·012	23			0·023
24			$0\cdot0^{3}87$	$0\cdot0^{2}63$	25			0·014
26			$0\cdot0^{3}19$	$0\cdot0^{2}29$	27			$0\cdot0^{2}83$
28			$0\cdot0^{4}25$	$0\cdot0^{2}12$	29			$0\cdot0^{2}46$
30				$0\cdot0^{3}43$	31			$0\cdot0^{2}23$
32				$0\cdot0^{3}12$	33			$0\cdot0^{2}11$
34				$0\cdot0^{4}25$	35			$0\cdot0^{3}47$
36				$0\cdot0^{5}28$	37			$0\cdot0^{3}18$
					39			$0\cdot0^{4}58$
					41			$0\cdot0^{4}15$
					43			$0\cdot0^{5}28$
					45			$0\cdot0^{6}28$

Note.—Repeated zeros are indicated by powers, *e.g.* $0\cdot0^{3}47$ stands for 0·00047.

Critical Values of Rho (Spearman's Rank-Order Correlation Coefficient): Table F

How to use this table. The first two rows give the levels of significance (α) for one- and two-tail tests. In the first column is the number of pairs (n) that are ranked. The body of the table contains the critical values. If a computed value of Rho equals or exceeds the table value, reject the null hypothesis. If the computed value of Rho is less than the table value, do not reject the null hypothesis.

Example. A value of Rho = .66 was computed from a set of data; with n = 20, α = .01, and a one-tail test, we would reject the null hypothesis because the computed value is greater than the table value of .534. (If the computed value was less than .534, we would not reject the null hypothesis.)

For Rho, df = n - 2, where n is the number of pairs. Table F, however, does not require the use of degrees of freedom.

	Level of significance for one-tailed test			
	.05	.025	.01	.005
	Level of significance for two-tailed test			
n*	.10	.05	.02	.01
5	.900	1.000	1.000	--
6	.829	.886	.943	1.000
7	.714	.786	.893	.929
8	.643	.738	.833	.881
9	.600	.683	.783	.833
10	.564	.648	.746	.794
12	.506	.591	.712	.777
14	.456	.544	.645	.715
16	.425	.506	.601	.665
18	.399	.475	.564	.625
20	.377	.450	.534	.591
22	.359	.428	.508	.562
24	.343	.409	.485	.537
26	.329	.392	.465	.515
28	.317	.377	.448	.496
30	.306	.364	.432	.478

*n = number of pairs

Adapted from E. G. Olds, *Annals of Mathematical Statistics,* Vol. 9 (1938), pp. 133–148 and Vol. 20 (1949), pp. 117–118. Reprinted by permission.

Critical Values of the Pearson r: Table G

How to use this table. For r, df = N - 2. The critical value of r is determined by df, the level of α, and the use of a one- or two-tail test. If a computed value of r equals or exceeds the table value, the null hypothesis r = 0.0 is rejected. If the computed value is less than the table value, the null hypothesis is not rejected.

Example. With df = 15, α = .01, and a two-tail test, any value of r equal to or greater than .606 would not enable us to reject the null hypothesis. In other words, with df = 15 and a two-tail test, a computed value of r as large or larger than .606 would occur by chance only one time in a hundred.

Table G: Critical Values of the Pearson r.

	Two-Tailed Test		One-Tailed Test	
	$\alpha = .05$	$\alpha = .01$	$\alpha = .05$	$\alpha = .01$
df				
1	.997	.9999	.988	.9995
2	.950	.990	.900	.980
3	.878	.959	.805	.934
4	.811	.917	.729	.882
5	.754	.874	.669	.833
6	.707	.834	.622	.789
7	.666	.798	.582	.750
8	.632	.765	.549	.716
9	.602	.735	.521	.685
10	.576	.708	.497	.658
11	.553	.684	.476	.634
12	.532	.661	.458	.612
13	.514	.641	.441	.592
14	.497	.623	.426	.574
15	.482	.606	.412	.558
16	.468	.590	.400	.542
17	.456	.575	.389	.528
18	.444	.561	.378	.516
19	.433	.549	.369	.503
20	.423	.537	.360	.492
21	.413	.526	.352	.482
22	.404	.515	.344	.472
23	.396	.505	.337	.462
24	.388	.496	.330	.453
25	.381	.487	.323	.445
26	.374	.479	.317	.437
27	.367	.471	.311	.430
28	.361	.463	.306	.423
29	.355	.456	.301	.416
30	.349	.449	.296	.409
35	.325	.418	.275	.381
40	.304	.393	.257	.358
45	.288	.372	.243	.338
50	.273	.354	.231	.322
60	.250	.325	.211	.295
70	.232	.303	.195	.274
80	.217	.283	.183	.256
90	.205	.267	.173	.242
100	.195	.254	.164	.230

R. A. Fisher and F. Yates, *Statistical Tables for Biological, Agricultural and Medical Research*, 6th edition. London: Longman Group Ltd., 1974, Table VII, p. 61. (Previously published by Oliver & Boyd, Edinburgh.) Reprinted by permission of the authors and publishers.

References

Anderson, Theodore R., and Morris Zelditch, Jr. 1975. *A Basic Course in Statistics.* Third edition. New York: Holt, Rinehart and Winston.

Arney, William Ray. 1990. *Understanding Statistics in the Social Sciences.* New York: W. H. Freeman.

Bainbridge, William Sims. *Social Research Methods: A Computer-Assisted Introduction.* Belmont, CA: Wadsworth.

Blalock, Hubert M., Jr. 1979. *Social Statistics.* Second edition. New York: McGraw-Hill.

Campbell, Stephen K. 1974. *Flaws and Fallacies in Statistical Thinking.* Englewood Cliffs, NJ: Prentice-Hall.

Costner, Herbert L. 1965. Criteria for measures of association. *American Sociological Review.* 30: 341-353.

Darlington, Richard B., and Patricia M. Carlson. 1987. *Behavioral Statistics.* New York: Free Press.

Davis, James A. 1967. A partial coefficient for Goodman and Kruskal's Gamma. *Journal of the American Statistical Association.* 62: 189-193.

Davis, James Allan, and Smith, Tom W. 1990. *General Social Surveys, 1972-1990: Cumulative Codebook.* Chicago: National Opinion Research Center.

Dometrius, Nelson C. 1992. *Social Statistics Using SPSS.* New York: Harper Collins.

Edward, Allen L. 1974 *Statistical Analysis.* Fourth edition. New York: Holt, Rinehart and Winston.

Federer, Walter T. 1991. *Statistics and Society: Data Collection and Interpretation.* New York: Marcel Dekker.

Fisher, Sir Ronald A., and Frank Yates. 1963. *Statistical Tables for Biological, Agricultural and Medical Research.* New York: Hafner Press.

Freeman, Linton C. 1965. *Elementary Applied Statistics.* New York: John Wiley.

Freund, John E. 1988. *Modern Elementary Statistics.* Seventh edition. Englewood Cliffs, NJ: Prentice-Hall.

Goodman, Leo A., and William H. Kruskal. 1954. Measures of association for cross classifications. *Journal of the American Statistical Association.* 49: 732-764.

_______. 1959. Measures of association for cross classifications. II: Further discussion and references. *Journal of the American Statistical Association.* 54: 123-163.

_______. 1963. Measures of association for cross classifications. III: Approximate sampling theory. *Journal of the American Statistical Association.* 58: 310-364.

_______. 1979. *Measures of Association for Cross Classifications.* New York: Springer-Verlag.

Gravetter, Frederick J., and Larry B. Wallnau. 1991. *Essentials of Statistics for the Behavioral Sciences.* St. Paul, MN: West Publishing.

Hamilton, Lawrence C. 1990. *Modern Data Analysis.* Pacific Grove, CA: Brooks/Cole.

Henry, Gary T. 1990. *Practical Sampling.* Newbury Park, CA: Sage.

Hickey, Anthony A. 1986. *An Introduction to Statistical Techniques for Social Research.* New York: Random House.

Hildebrand, David K. 1986. *Statistical Thinking for Behavioral Scientists.* Boston: Duxbury.

Hildebrand, David K., James D. Laing, and Howard Rosenthal. 1977. *Analysis of Ordinal Data.* Beverly Hills, CA: Sage.

Horowitz, Gideon. 1979. *Sadistic Statistics.* Wayne, NJ: Avery.

Horowitz, Lucy, and Lou Ferleger. 1980. *Statistics for Social Change.* Boston: South End Press.

Huff, Darrel. 1954. *How to Lie with Statistics.* New York: Norton.

Jaccard, James, and Michael A. Becker. 1990. *Statistics for the Behavioral Sciences.* Belmont, CA: Wadsworth.

Jaeger, Richard M. 1990. *Statistics: A Spectator Sport.* Newbury Park, CA: Sage.

Kachigan, Sam Kash. 1986. *Statistical Analysis.* New York: Radius Press.

Kendall, Maurice G. 1962. *Rank Correlation Methods.* Third edition. London: Charles Griffin.

Kendall, Maurice G., and A. Stuart. 1961, 1963. *The Advanced Theory of Statistics.* (Volumes One and Two). London: Charles Griffin.

Kimble, Gregory R. 1978. *How to Use (and Misuse) Statistics.* Englewood Cliffs, NJ: Prentice-Hall.

Kolstoe, Ralph H. 1973. *Introduction to Statistics for the Behavioral Sciences* . Revised edition. Homewood, IL: Dorsey Press.

Knoke, David, and George W. Bohrnstedt. 1991. *Basic Social Statistics.* Itasca, IL: F. E. Peacock.

Levin, Jack, and James Alan Fox. 1988. *Elementary Statistics in Social Research.* Fourth edition. New York: Harper Collins.

______. 1991. *Elementary Statistics in Social Research.* Fifth edition. New York: Harper Collins.

Loether, Herman J., and Donald G. McTavish. 1988. *Descriptive and Inferential Statistics.* Third edition. Boston: Allyn and Bacon.

MacKenzie, Donald A. 1981. *Statistics in Britain: 1865-1930.* Edinburgh: Edinburgh University Press.

Mendenhall, William, Lyman Ott, and Richard F. Larson. 1974. *Inferential Statistics for Sociologists.* North Scituate, MA: Duxbury Press.

Moore, David S. 1991. *Statistics: Concepts and Controversies.* Third edition. New York: W. H. Freeman.

Mueller, John H., Karl F. Schuessler, and Herbert L. Costner. 1970. *Statistical Reasoning in Sociology.* Second edition. Boston: Houghton Mifflin.

Norusis, Marija J. 1990. *SPSS Introductory Statistics Student Guide.* Chicago: SPSS.

Ott, R. Lyman, Richard Larson, Cynthia Rexroat, and William Mendenhall. 1992. *Statistics: A Tool for the Social Sciences.* Fifth edition. Boston: PWS-Kent.

Paulos, John Allen. 1988. *Innumeracy.* New York: Hill and Wang.

Phillips, John L., Jr. 1988. *How to Think about Statistics.* New York: W. H. Freeman.

Reynolds, H. T. 1984. *Analysis of Nominal Data.* Second edition. Newbury Park, CA: Sage.

Rosenberg, Morris. 1968. *The Logic of Survey Analysis.* New York: Basic Books.

Runyon, Richard P., and Audrey Haber. 1984. *Fundamentals of Behavioral Statistics.* Fifth edition. Reading, MA.: Addison-Wesley.

Schutte, Jerald G. 1977. *Everything You Always Wanted to Know About Elementary Statistics (but Were Afraid to Ask).* Englewood Cliffs, NJ: Prentice-Hall.

Siegel, Sidney. 1956. *Nonparametric Statistics.* New York: McGraw-Hill.

Siegel, Sidney, and N. John Castellan, Jr. 1988. *Nonparametric Statistics for the Behavioral Sciences.* Second edition. New York: McGraw-Hill.

Slonim, Morris J. 1960. *Sampling.* New York: Simon and Schuster.

Somers, Robert H. 1962. A new asymmetric measure of association for ordinal variables. *American Sociological Review.* 27 (December): 799-811.

Spence, Janet T., John W. Cotton, Benton J. Underwood, and Carl P. Duncan. 1992. *Elementary Statistics.* Englewood Cliffs, NJ: Prentice-Hall.

Steven, S. S. 1946. On the theory of scales of measurement. *Science.* 103 (June 7): 677- 680.

Weisberg, Herbert F. 1992. *Central Tendency and Variability.* Newbury Park, CA: Sage.

Weiss, Robert S. 1968. *Statistics in Social Research.* New York: John Wiley.

Wilson, T. P. 1969. A proportional-reduction-in-error interpretation for Kendall's tau-b. *Social Forces.* 47 (March): 340-342.

Winer, B. J., Donald R. Brown, and Kenneth M. Michels. 1991. *Statistical Principles in Experimental Design.* Third edition. New York: McGraw-Hill.

Zeisel, Hans. 1985. *Say It with Figures.* Sixth edition. New York: Harper & Row.

Zeller, Richard A. 1974. On teaching correlation and regression. *Teaching Sociology.* 1 (April): 224-241.

Index

Absolute value, 65
Alpha, 94
Analysis of variance (ANOVA), Chapter 8
  between-groups sum of squares in, 133
  degrees of freedom for, 139
  F-ratio in, 138
  total sum of squares in, 133, 140
  within-groups sum of squares in, 133–134
Association. *See also* Correlation
  defined, 147–148
  direction of, 149
  interval measures of, Chapter 11
  nominal measures of, Chapter 9
  ordinal measures of, Chapter 10
  and PRE logic, 150, 172–175
  types of, 169–171
Asymmetric measure, 169
Average. *See also* Mean; Median; Mode
  comparison of, 54–56
Average deviation, 65–66

Between-groups sum of squares, 133, 140
Binomial distribution, 88–89
Boundaries, 20–22

C. *See* Contingency coefficient
Causation, 148–149
Centile, 39
Central tendency, Chapter 3. *See also* Mean; Median; Mode
Chance, 83–84
Chi-square, 151–161
  cell collapsing, 162–163
  computation of, 155–156
  degrees of freedom for, 157
  expected frequencies for, 154–155
  Fisher's exact test for, 161–162
  related measures and, 163–166
  Yates's correction for, 161
Class boundaries. *See* Boundaries
Conditional association, 246–247
Conditional table, 242–244
Confidence interval, 110–113
Contingency coefficient (C), 165–166
Continuous distribution, 91
Control variable, 246
Correlated samples, 125–126

Correlation. *See Also* Association
  curvilinear, 232–233
  linear, 232–233
  multiple, 233–236
  partial, 247–251
  rank-order (Rho), 206–211
Cramer's V, 166
Criterion variable, 18

d (Somers's). *See* Somers's d
Decile, 39
Degrees of freedom
  for Chi-square, 157
  discussed, 123–124
  for F-test, 139
  for r, 230–231
  for Rho, 209
  for t-test, 123–124, 127
Descriptive statistics, 4
Deviation
  mean, 47
  measures of, 65–70
Discrete distribution, 91
Dispersion, 6; Chapter 4
Dissimilar pairs, 186–187

Elaboration, 241–246
Empirical probability, 83
Error, proportional reduction in
  for Eta-square, 237–238
  for Gamma, 194–196
  for Lambda, 168–169
  for r^2, 218–221
  for Rho-square, 208–209
  for Tau, Goodman and Kruskal's, 175–177
Estimation, Chapter 6
  from finite populations, 106–107
  interval, 109–110
  point, 109
  and sample size, 105–110
Eta-square, 236–238
Event, 82, 85. *See also* Outcome
Expected values for Chi-square, 154–155

F-test, 138–139
Fisher's exact test, 161–162
Frequency curve, 25
Frequency distribution, 19–21
  continuous (infinite), 84
  discrete (finite), 84
  rules for construction of, 19
Frequency polygon, 24

Gamma
  discussed, 185–190
  for grouped data, 190–192
  PRE interpretation of, 196–197
  tied ranks and, 190
  significance test for, 202–204
  and Yule's Q, 197
General Social Survey (NORC), 13
Goodman, Leo, 165, 185
Goodman and Kruskal's Tau, 175–179
Gossett, W.S. ("Student"), 119

Histogram, 23
Homoscedasticity, 233
Hypothesis. *See* Null hypothesis
Hypothesis testing, 93–95. *See also* Significance tests

Independence, 147, 150
Inferential statistics, 4
Interaction of variables, 129
Interdecile range, 63
Interquartile range, 64
Interval. *See* Association; Measurement

Interval estimate, 109

Kendall, M.G., 197
Kendall's Tau, 197–199
  significance test for, 202–204
Kruskal's Tau, 175–178

Lambda, 166
  interpretation of, 168–169
  prediction rules for, 167–169
  symmetric, 171–172
Least squares, principle of, 67
Levels of measurement. *See* Measurement
Limits. *See* Boundaries

Marginal values, 153
Matched samples, 125–126
Mean
  and coded values, 47–48
  defined, 39–40
  deviations from, 40–41
  for grouped data, 43–44
  weighted, 51–53
Mean square, 67
  in ANOVA, 142
Measurement, 7–12
  interval level, 11, 12
  nominal level, 8–9, 12
  ordinal level, 9–10, 12
  ratio level, 11, 12
Median
  defined, 36
  for grouped data, 43–44
Modal category, 43
Mode
  defined, 34
  for grouped data, 43
  within category (Lambda), 167
Multiple correlation, 251–255
Mutual association, 170

National Opinion Research Center, 13
Nominal. *See* Association; Measurement
Normal distribution, 71–72
  and binomial probability, 89–90
  and standard deviation, 71–72
Norming variable, 18
Null hypothesis, 93–94

One-tail test, 95
One-way association, 170
Ordinal. *See* Association; Measurement
Outcome, 82, 85. *See also* Event

Parameter, 123
Partial correlation, 247–252
  for Gamma, 251–252
  for r, 247–250
  for Tau, 250–251
Pearson r, Chapter 11
  assumptions for, 232–234
  computation of, 224–230
  as a PRE measure, 218–220
  reversibility of, 235–236
  significance test for, 230–232
  and standard scores, 226–227
Percentage difference, 150–151
Percentile, 39
Phi coefficient, 163–165
Phi-square, 164
Point estimate, 109
Population, 100
PRE. *See* Proportional reduction in error
Probability, 82–85
  basic rules of, 85–87

binomial, 88–89
empirical, 83
event, 82, 85
and hypothesis testing, 93–95
Proportional reduction in error (PRE), 150

Q. *See* Yule's Q
Quartile, 37–39

r. *See* Pearson r
Range, 62
extreme scores, influence of, 62
interdecile, 63
interquartile, 64
Rate, 18
Ratio, 18. *See also* Measurement
Regression line, 221
Rejection, region of. *See* Alpha
Rho. *See* Spearman rank-order correlation coefficient

S (numerator for Gamma), 189
significance test for, 202–204
Samples, types of, 101–103
Sampling distribution, 103–104
Sampling error, 110
Scales. *See* Measurement
Scatterplot, 232–233
Significance tests
for Chi-square, 159
for F, 138–139
for Gamma, 202–204
for r, 231–232
for Rho, 211–212
for S, 202–204
for t, 123, 125, 127
Similar pairs, 186–187
Slope of best-fitting line, 222
Somers's d, 200–201
significance test for, 202–204
Somers, R., 200
Spearman rank-order correlation coefficient (Rho), 206–211
defined, 206–207
Rho-square, 208–209
significance test for, 211–212
tied ranks and, 208
Specification, 244
SPSS, 12
CROSSTABS, 179–181
CORRELATIONS, 238–239
DESCRIPTIVES, 76–77
FREQUENCIES, 26–30
ONEWAY, 143–145
PARTIAL CORR, 257–258
T-TEST, 127–129
Spurious relationship, 243
Standard deviation, 66–69
and normal distribution, 71–73
Standard error, 108–109
of the difference between means, 120, 126
and sample size, 113
Standard score (z-score), 72–74
Student's t. *See* t-test
Sum of squares, 67, 111, 133
Suppression, 245
Symmetric measure, 169

t-test, Chapter 7
degrees of freedom for, 123–124, 127
t for correlated samples, 125–127
t for small samples, 122
Tau. *See* Goodman and Kruskal's Tau; Kendall's Tau
Test factor (control variable), 246
Total sum of squares, ANOVA, 133, 140

True limits, 20–21
Two-tail test, 95
Type I Error, 94–95
Type II Error, 94–95

V. *See* Cramer's V
Variability. *See* Dispersion
Variance, 67–68

Weighted mean, 51–53

Weiss, Robert, 147, 149, 164, 170
Within-groups sum of squares, 133–134

Y-intercept, 222–223
Yates's correction, 161
Yule's Q, 197

z-score (standard score), 72–74

About the Book and Author

This revised and updated edition of *Essential Statistics for Social Research* is designed as the primary textbook for an introductory course in statistics in the social sciences. It can also be used as a supplementary text for courses in research methods. No sophisticated mathematical background on the part of students is assumed.

The first edition of this book was used by more than 10,000 students at colleges and universities in the United States and abroad. This long-awaited revised edition retains the two key features students and their teachers praised most highly in the first edition: clarity of presentation and thorough coverage of essential statistics for the beginning student. The revision brings the material up to date, featuring examples that demonstrate the use of computers to analyze data. The chapters on testing the difference between means and on measuring association between interval-level variables have been considerably expanded, as has the discussion of handling three or more variables. The author leads students beyond a mere understanding of research methods in social science, enabling them to effectively make use of statistical methods of analysis.

Michael A. Malec is associate professor of sociology at Boston College.